AF478429

Studies in Banking and Financial Institutions

Series Editor: **Professor Philip Molyneux**

The Palgrave Macmillan Studies in Banking and Financial Institutions are international in orientation and include studies of banking within particular countries or regions, and studies of particular themes such as Corporate Banking, Risk Management, Mergers and Acquisitions, etc. The books focus on research and practice, and they include up-to-date and innovative studies on contemporary topics in banking that will have global impact and influence.

Titles include:

Yener Altunbaş, Blaise Gadanecz and Alper Kara
SYNDICATED LOANS
A Hybrid of Relationship Lending and Publicly Traded Debt

Yener Altunbaş, Alper Kara and Öslem Olgu
TURKISH BANKING
Banking under Political Instability and Chronic High Inflation

Elena Beccalli
IT AND EUROPEAN BANK PERFORMANCE

Paola Bongini, Stefano Chiarlone and Giovanni Ferri *(editors)*
EMERGING BANKING SYSTEMS

Vittorio Boscia, Alessandro Carretta and Paola Schwizer
COOPERATIVE BANKING: INNOVATIONS AND DEVELOPMENTS

Santiago Carbó, Edward P.M. Gardener and Philip Molyneux
FINANCIAL EXCLUSION

Alessandro Carretta, Franco Fiordelisi and Gianluca Mattarocci *(editors)*
NEW DRIVERS OF PERFORMANCE IN A CHANGING FINANCIAL WORLD

Dimitris N. Chorafas
CAPITALISM WITHOUT CAPITAL

Dimitris N. Chorafas
FINANCIAL BOOM AND GLOOM
The Credit and Banking Crisis of 2007–2009 and Beyond

Violaine Cousin
BANKING IN CHINA

Peter Falush and Robert L. Carter OBE
THE BRITISH INSURANCE INDUSTRY SINCE 1900
The Era of Transformation

Franco Fiordelisi and Philip Molyneux
SHAREHOLDER VALUE IN BANKING

Hans Genberg and Cho-Hoi Hui
THE BANKING CENTRE IN HONG KONG
Competition, Efficiency, Performance and Risk

Carlo Gola and Alessandro Roselli
THE UK BANKING SYSTEM AND ITS REGULATORY AND
SUPERVISORY FRAMEWORK

Elisabetta Gualandri and Valeria Venturelli *(editors)*
BRIDGING THE EQUITY GAP FOR INNOVATIVE SMEs

Kim Hawtrey
AFFORDABLE HOUSING FINANCE

Otto Hieronymi *(editor)*
GLOBALIZATION AND THE REFORM OF THE INTERNATIONAL
BANKING AND MONETARY SYSTEM

Munawar Iqbal and Philip Molyneux
THIRTY YEARS OF ISLAMIC BANKING
History, Performance and Prospects

Sven Janssen
BRITISH AND GERMAN BANKING STRATEGIES

Kimio Kase and Tanguy Jacopin
CEOs AS LEADERS AND STRATEGY DESIGNERS
Explaining the Success of Spanish Banks

M. Mansoor Khan and M. Ishaq Bhatti
DEVELOPMENTS IN ISLAMIC BANKING
The Case of Pakistan

Mario La Torre and Gianfranco A. Vento
MICROFINANCE

Philip Molyneux and Munawar Iqbal
BANKING AND FINANCIAL SYSTEMS IN THE ARAB WORLD

Philip Molyneux and Eleuterio Vallelado *(editors)*
FRONTIERS OF BANKS IN A GLOBAL WORLD

Anastasia Nesvetailova
FRAGILE FINANCE
Debt, Speculation and Crisis in the Age of Global Credit

Dominique Rambure and Alec Nacamuli
PAYMENT SYSTEMS
From the Salt Mines to the Board Room

Catherine Schenk *(editor)*
HONG KONG SAR's MONETARY AND EXCHANGE RATE CHALLENGES
Historical Perspectives

Andrea Schertler
THE VENTURE CAPITAL INDUSTRY IN EUROPE

Alfred Slager
THE INTERNATIONALIZATION OF BANKS
Patterns, Strategies and Performance

Noël K. Tshiani
BUILDING CREDIBLE CENTRAL BANKS
Policy Lessons for Emerging Economies

**Palgrave Macmillan Studies in Banking and Financial Institutions
Series Standing Order ISBN 978-1-4039-4872-4**

You can receive future titles in this series as they are published by placing a standing order. Please contact your bookseller or, in case of difficulty, write to us at the address below with your name and address, the title of the series and the ISBN quoted above.

Customer Services Department, Macmillan Distribution Ltd, Houndmills, Basingstoke, Hampshire RG21 6XS, England

---

Globalization and the Reform of the International Banking and Monetary System

Edited by

Otto Hieronymi
Professor of International Relations,
Webster University, Geneva,
Switzerland

Contents

Illustrations

Acknowledgements

This book is the result of the interest, dedication and support of many individuals, too numerous to be mentioned individually here. It is a collective volume: thanks have to go first and foremost to the authors for their texts and above all for their ideas. A significant amount of the credit goes to Professor Alexandre Vautravers with whom I shared from the start the responsibility for the planning and organizing of the Webster University conference in November 2008. The success of that event was due to the hard work and enthusiasm, as on so many previous occasions, of the Webster Student Organizing Committee. Among its members the following should be noted (without diminishing the merits of those who are not mentioned): Eugene James, Attila Turos, Robert Narvaez, Diana Kuchta, Violla Artani, Gil Lefèvre, Lori Werner, and Sarvenaz Naderzad. Hilary Hofmans, Maureen Gisiger, and Liz Torrente of the Webster University staff also deserve a sincere thank you. Lisa von Fircks and Renée Takken of Palgrave Macmillan have also made this book possible. Their professionalism combined with patience and a cheerful sense of humor is a testimony to the best British publishing tradition. I also appreciate the efficiency of Macmillan Publishing Solutions. Finally I would like to thank Diana Kuchta, Research Assistant and Webster University Graduate Student for her important contribution to the final preparation of the manuscript of this volume.

Otto Hieronymi
Professor of International Relations
Webster University, Geneva
4 April 2009

Notes on Contributors

André Baladi, is a Geneva-based international financial expert and a longstanding corporate governance driven shareholder value advocate. He is Co-Founder, former Co-Chairman, and an active member of the International Corporate Governance Network (ICGN), which assembles investors holding equity assets of US$15 trillion. He was awarded the 2001 ICGN Appreciation Certificate for Outstanding Services and the 2007 ICGN Award for Excellence in Corporate Governance. He is a Member of the Consultative Team of the Intergovernmental Working Group of Experts on International Standards of Accounting and Reporting (ISAR) of UNCTAD in Geneva; of the OECD Consultative Corporate Governance Group in Paris; and of the International Advisory Board of the NYSE Euronext Stock Exchange. He chairs Geneva's International Arbitration Organization, which founded the CARICI Arbitration Court. He is also an Honorary Participant of the Council of Institutional Investors (CII) in Washington DC. After majoring in economics at Geneva's *Graduate Institute of International Studies*, for fifteen years he managed several Nestlé projects in France, Italy, Japan, South East Asia, Switzerland, and the USA. He was then, for five years, associated, as international M&A expert, with the corporate finance group of the consortium set up by Banque Nationale de Paris (BNP), Smith Barney and Société Financière Européenne (founded by Algemene Bank Nederland, Banca Nazionale del Lavoro, Bank of America, Banque Bruxelles Lambert, BNP, Barclays, Dresdner, Sumitomo Bank, and UBS). In 1981, he founded his international financial advisory firm in Geneva. He has also developed an algorithm for enhancing index tracking equity funds with corporate governance inputs.

Norberto Birchler, is Managing Director of the Association Romande des Intermédiaires financiers (ARIF) – Swiss Association of Financial Intermediaries, an organization engaged in combating money-laundering and the financing of terrorism. A specialist of financial and security issues he is also a high-ranking officer of the Swiss Army.

Péter Ákos Bod, is Professor of Economics and Head of Department, Corvinus University (of Economics), Budapest. He was Minister of Industry from 1990 to 1991, President of the Hungarian National Bank from 1991 to 1995 and Director, European Bank for Reconstruction and

Development (London) from 1995 to 1997. His numerous publications on monetary and economic policy issues include a textbook on monetary economics, books and articles on the domestic and international dimension of monetary and economic integration, deregulation and institution building, monetary and exchange rate policy, banking and finance in Central Eastern Europe etc.

Beat Bürgenmeier, has been full professor at the University of Geneva since 1982. Former dean of the Faculty of Economic and Social Sciences, he is currently president of the General Research Fund of his University. His main research interests are in the field of economics, and in particular environmental policies. He is president of the scientific committee of FONDATERRA, a European foundation for sustainable urban planning, member of the federal commission for environmental research and expert in numerous organizations and scientific journals. His numerous publications include the following books: *Economy, Environment and Technology: A Socioeconomic Approach, Analyse et Politique Economiques* (6 editions), *Economie du Développement Durable, (Economics of Sustainable Development)* 3 editions, *Plaidoyer pour une Economie Sociale, Principes Ecologiques et Sociaux du Marché.*

Edmond P. Carton, is currently Vice-Chairman and Member of the board of M.I.F. S.A. Geneva, one of the foremost Swiss based independent multi-family offices, which he joined in January 2008. From 1995 to 2007 he was a Managing Director with Hong Kong Shanghai Banking Corporation (HSBC Private Bank) heading, from Geneva (1995–2005), the global Middle East and North African business while present on the executive committee of HSBC Private Banks Suisse S.A. and on the Board of HSBC Bank Middle East and, from San Francisco, the US West Coast private Banking Division (2005–end 2007). In 1975, he joined the Morgan Guaranty Trust Company of New York and worked with JPM for the next twenty years in Paris, Kuwait, Sao Paulo, New York, London and in Geneva (where from 1990 to 1995 he was Managing Director and Global Head of Middle East Private Banking). He started his banking career in 1973 in Paris with Banque de Paris et des Pays Bas.

Gyula Csurgai, is Professor of Geopolitics and Geo-economics at the Geneva School of Diplomacy, co-founder and Director of the International Centre for Geopolitical Studies in Geneva and Academic Director of the International Studies program of SIT University. He worked as Scientific Collaborator at the Geneva International Peace

Research Institute (GIPRI), and has taught International Relations, Geopolitics and Geo-economics in both undergraduate, master and doctorate programs at several universities. He earned his doctoral degree from the University of Geneva, with a thesis in the field of geopolitics. His publications include: *La nation et ses territoires en Europe centrale Une approche géopolitique, (The Nation and its Territories in Central Europe, A Geopolitical Approach), Les enjeux géopolitiques des ressources naturelles (Geopolitical Stakes of Natural Resources), Republican ideology in Central Europe, Géopolitique de l'Information, (Geopolitics of Information).*

Otto Hieronymi, earned his Doctorate in International Economics and Politics at the Graduate Institute of International Studies in Geneva. He has been Professor of International Relations at Webster University, Geneva since 1995 where he was also Head of the Department of International Relations and of the Program of Migration and Refugee Studies between 1995–2006. Prior to joining Webster, he was a Senior Economist, Responsible for Economic Analysis and Forecasting at Battelle's Geneva Research Centers from 1970 to the end of 1994 and an International Economist with Morgan Guaranty Trust Co. in New York between 1966 and1970. Between 1990 and 1994, while still on the Battelle staff, he was Personal Economic Advisor to the Hungarian Prime Minister Jozsef Antall and Senior International Economic Advisor to Members of the Hungarian Government. He was the Secretary of the Hungarian Bank Reform Commission and a Founding Member of theBoard of Directors, Hungarian Investment and Development Bank. He was also in charge of developing the Antall Government's concept of "loan consolidation" (dealing with the banks' bad debts) and the initial Hungarian program of bank privatization. International monetary and financial issues have been among his principal areas of research and forecasting work since the 1960s. He has published extensively on economic, monetary, political and humanitarian issues. His publications include *Agenda for a New Monetary Reform* (1998), *The Spirit of Geneva in a Globalized World* (Ed.), Oxford University Press, 2007, *The Responsibilities of Business and Governments in the Age of Global Finance* (March 2008), *Hungarian Economic, Financial and Monetary Policies: Proposals for a Coherent Approach*, (January 1990), *Global Challenges, the Atlantic Community and the Outlook for International Order* (Ed.), Emerald, 2004, *International Capital Markets and the Financial Integration of the Transition Countries* (1997), *Wilhelm Röpke: The Relevance of his Teaching Today – Globalization and the Social Market Economy*, (Ed.) Geneva, IUHEI, 2002, *The New Economic Nationalism* (Ed.) Macmillan, 1980, etc.

Daniel Kaeser, earned degrees in economics and law at the University of Lausanne. From 1992 to 1997 he was Permanent Representative of Switzerland to the International Monetary Fund in Washington and an Executive Director of the IMF. From 1977 to 1992 he was Deputy Director of the Swiss Federal Finance Administration in charge of the Treasury and of Economic and Monetary Affairs. Before 1977 he occupied other senior positions in the Ministry of Finance as well as in the Swiss National Bank and the Swiss Permanent Mission to the OECD. His publications include *La Longue Marche vers Bretton Woods (The Long Road Towards Bretton Woods)*, Geneva, 2004.

Sergio Marchi was Canadian Federal Minister, 1993–9 and served as Minister in three portfolios: International Trade; Environment; and Citizenship and Immigration. From 1999 through 2004 he was Canadian Ambassador to the World Trade Organization (WTO), the World Intellectual Property Organization (WIPO), and the Office of the United Nations in Geneva. Between 1984 and 1999 he was a Member of the Canadian Parliament. He was a commissioner on the UN Global Commission on International Migration, established by the UN Secretary General, 2004–06. Currently he is a Senior Business Advisor, Lang Michener LLP, Toronto; President, Canada-China Business Council; and Chairman, Canadian Services Council, Ottawa. He currently is a Senior Fellow, at the International Centre of Trade and Sustainable Development in Geneva, and has recently joined Webster University as an Adjunct Professor.

Carlos Eduardo Pérez del Castillo is Economic Affairs Officer – Trade Policy Review Division (TPRD) with the World Trade Organization in Geneva. Before joining WTO, he worked with the Latin American Economic System (SELA) in Caracas, Venezuela, with the General Directorate on Foreign Trade of the Ministry of Economy and Finance, in Montevideo, Uruguay and with the Administrative Secretariat of the MERCOSUR (SAM).

Michael Sakbani earned his PhD at New York University (NYU). He has been Adjunct Professor of Finance and Economics at Webster University, Geneva since 1981. Before joining UNCTAD in Geneva he was a Senior Economist with the Federal Reserve Bank of New York. At UNCTAD he was responsible for many years for Monetary and Financial Cooperation, and Director of the Division of Cooperation among Developing Countries. One of his principal areas of interest is monetary policy and the international monetary system. His numerous publications in this area include *A Re-Examination of the Architecture of the International Economic System in a Global Setting: Issues and Proposals* (2006), *The Global Economic System: Asymmetries & Inconsistencies* (2005), *The Euro on Schedule: Analysis of its European and International Implications* (1998), *International Monetary Reform: Issues and Proposals* (1985).

Christian Viladent, is an expert and researcher in pharmacology with twenty years of experience in international pharmaceutical and bio-medical companies and a lecturer in management. He has earned a doctorate in pharmacology at University Paris XI, France and advanced degrees in management in the US and Switzerland. His publications include: *Assessment of the Socio Economic Impact of Therapeutic and Non-Therapeutic Interventions Against HIV/AIDS with the Mean of a Generic Policy Model, HIV/AIDS Modeling, Towards a Generic Deterministic Model for Pattern II Countries* (with van Ackere A.), *HIV Tri-Therapies in Botswana, Socio-Economic Consequences*, and *A Deterministic Simulation Model to Assess the HIV/AIDS Interventions* (with van Ackere A.).

Introduction

Otto Hieronymi

This book addresses what is recognized by now as one of the most important issues in the debate on domestic and international order today: the conditions for a successful international monetary and banking reform. The outcome of this debate and of the ensuing reforms will determine the prospects of the world economy for generations to come. Success requires a rollback of monetary nationalism and a return to monetary internationalism, restoring the basic functions and trust within the banking system, and finding a balance between competition and solidarity, in order to assure the political and social acceptance of globalization.

Today, there is a need and an opportunity to move the various political, economic, monetary, social, and environmental debates away from the extremes and draw them back to the center. In response to the crisis, an encouraging awareness of global interdependence and the necessity for closer and more effective international cooperation has grown. There is no politically, socially, and economically valid long-term alternative to the liberal model based on principles of freedom and democracy, economic integration and social progress, and peaceful cooperation and security.

The current crisis has once again proved to be a powerful reminder of how much influence the quality of the international monetary order has in determining the success or failure of political and social systems. Thus, the centerpiece of efforts to recreate conditions, of sustained and sustainable growth, and facilitate social progress throughout the world economy has to be through the return of a stable and equitable rule-based international monetary order.

This will require bold initiatives, as well as innovation, complex negotiations, patience, and determination. History tells us that it may take time until full implementation of reforms will become effective and it is now urgent that the world focuses upon finding common objectives and basic organizing principles for the system. Today there is a great hope for the success of these efforts due to a convergence of interests among all members of the international community. We have the benefit of past (positive and negative) experience with monetary reform at the national, regional and, global level. We also have obtained the technical knowledge, human skills, and resources needed. Therefore, the final conclusion of this book is that chances are very high that these reforms will succeed.

A systemic crisis

There is no doubt that we are currently facing a systemic crisis. Despite the fact that there have been frequent warning signs from many angles, the nature and magnitude of this crisis have come as a surprise and shock to many people in responsible positions. These threat-perceptions and calls for reform had to do with, among others, the growing disconnect between financial flows and the real economy, with the dichotomy between financial globalization and the national or regional orientation of monetary policy, and with the abdication of fiscal and monetary authorities of their prudential responsibilities for both domestic and external stability.

The crisis of the banking and financial systems is also a crisis of "globalization." Over the last decades, globalization – the liberalization and internationalization of trade, investments, and especially of financial flows – has contributed to the sustained growth of the world economy. It has also been a major factor in the expansion and integration into the world economy of a growing number of so-called emerging markets – China and India being the largest and most dynamic examples. As of now, there is no doubt that the financial sector played a leading role in making globalization a success. Without the profound transformation of the financial and monetary sectors, during the last thirty-five years, globalization would not have been possible.

Globalization, however, has also been a source of problems in both developed and in the developing countries (to use a somewhat outdated, but still familiar terminology). And here again, the financial and monetary sectors are generally perceived as aggravating these problems. In fact, for quite some time, it has been recognized that monetary and banking deregulation and liberalization have had not only positive consequences, but also allowed the creation and perpetuation of major disequilibria in the world economy and in some major national economies.

The handwriting was on the wall

Much that could be said about the need for and the nature of monetary reform was defined and published in an "Agenda for a New Monetary Reform", more than ten years ago, and remains valid today, however, under much more dramatic circumstances:

> [T]oday (in 1998) we are in uncharted waters as far as the monetary and financial system is concerned. The current orthodoxy has played a crucial role in bringing about this new world we live in, but (and this is the central thesis of this article) it does not provide a complete and reliable blueprint for an efficient and equitable management of the new monetary and financial order in the long run [. . .] (Thus) once more the time has come for a broad debate on domestic and international monetary order and on the role and the rules governing the functioning of financial markets in the modern market economy. We have to define an agenda and seek a consensus for a new monetary reform that will take into account both the positive and negative lessons learned from more than twenty years of experience with liberalization, deregulation and privatization in the financial sector, with flexible exchange rates and international monetary instability [. . .] In today's world economy there is an especially dangerous contrast between, on the one hand virtually total globalization of financial markets, and the fixation of monetary policy on narrow national objectives on the other hand. The objective of the monetary reform agenda is not to reverse the liberal revolution and the trend towards more freedom throughout the world. Rather it is to consolidate its positive results through a more balanced approach to the division of labor between government institutions and private decision makers, between market winners and losers and domestic and international solidarity [. . .] The need is particularly great to redefine fundamental objectives and the respective roles of government rules and markets and private interests, and to recreate conditions for effective international co-operation in this field.[1]

The need for reform of both the financial and the monetary system

The main theses of this book are as follows:

1. The political and intellectual challenge, in the current situation, is to deal with both the short-term impact of the crisis in the financial and banking system, and simultaneously to prepare and implement a long-term reform of the international monetary and banking system.

2. There is no doubt that "the hand-writing was on the wall" for more than a decade. Contrary to statements of many leading officials, bankers, and academic experts, on both sides of the Atlantic, that the violence and the magnitude of the financial and banking crisis came as a surprise and could not be predicted, for many years, there had been clear warning signs and repeated calls for reform of the international monetary and banking system – explicitly in order to avoid the kind of crisis that has engulfed the world economy in recent months. It has been clear that the achievements of liberalization and globalization were being threatened by prevailing orthodoxy and lack of reforms.

3. Two major dichotomies have made the international economy increasingly vulnerable to the kind of crisis that the world is currently experiencing. The first one is the contrast between, on the one hand, a "rule-based" international trading system with a strong international organization at the center, and, on the other hand, a purely "market-based" international financial system. The second one is while finance has been fully globalized, monetary policy has remained firmly national (or regional in the case of the Euro-zone) without any set of common mechanisms or rules or objectives at the international level.

4. The origins of today's economic and financial crisis are as much intellectual as they are political and institutional. The quality and the scope of the debate will determine the success or failure of innovation at institutional and policy levels. Ultimately, the stakes are so high that failure is not an option – neither for the United States, Europe, Japan, or other OECD countries, nor is it for the rest of the world, including China, India, Brazil, Russia, and the Middle East.

5. It is clear today that overcoming consequences, of the current crisis, requires not only short-term corrective measures aimed essentially at boosting incomes and demand, but also a coherent set of reforms of both the international monetary system and of the international banking and financial system. The reforms are necessary so as not to eliminate or to replace the liberal market economy and to return to a world of protectionism and government planning. The outcome of this (long-delayed) debate will influence the prospects for the world economy for a long time to come.

Main themes and structure

This book is based on the updated and expanded versions of the papers presented at an international conference organized by Webster University in Geneva on November 14, 2008 on *Globalization and the Reform of the International Banking and Monetary System*. The planning of this volume, the definition of the topic and of the program in two parts – global monetary and banking reform in the first part and specific issues and historical examples in the second part – took place well before the actual outbreak of the American and worldwide crisis. The objective was to analyze the complexity and the long-term and systemic nature of what was then an impending crisis. By the time of the November 2008 conference, and even more by the time the revised manuscript was completed during the first quarter of 2009, this approach was fully justified by the nature and the extent of the crisis in the international monetary and banking system and in the world economy as a whole. In the rest of this section some of the key issues raised in the book's thirteen chapters are briefly highlighted in order to illustrate the complexity of the issues – without trying to provide a systematic summary of the arguments of each author.

Chapter 1 deals with the road from "global finance" to the current crisis of globalization. According to the author the current "systemic crisis" is due to the fact that the political, economic, and academic leaders in the major OECD countries have paid no attention in the past decade or so to the warnings that the pendulum of monetary and financial deregulation and marketization had gone too far and was threatening the very foundations of the liberal international economic order. One of the principal dangers was the dichotomy between "global finance," on the one hand, and monetary nationalism and the absence, ever since the early 1970s, of a rule-based international monetary order, on the other hand. There is today a real threat that the pendulum will go too far again, this time in the other direction, i.e., toward too much random and uncoordinated government interventions and regulations. The real challenge today is to overcome the intellectual crisis that led us to the current situation and to find a balanced approach that will preserve the advantages of globalization while correcting its excesses not only in the financial and monetary sector, but also at the more important level of economic and social theory and philosophy.

The principal conclusion of Chapter 2 is that the single most important long-term reform task is the creation of a new rule-based international monetary order. The author argues that what is needed is not a "return to Bretton Woods" or to the gold standard or to any of the other international monetary systems that the world has known during the last hundred years. The challenge is to innovate boldly while drawing the right lessons from the positive and negative experiences in international monetary history, including the last four decades marked by monetary nationalism and recurring monetary disorders. The new system should be rule based and should deal with exchange rates, international reserves as well as correcting major balance-of-payments imbalances and the issue of monetary and fiscal discipline – not only in the developing countries, but also in the leading economies, including the United States. The author proposes the creation of an "extended EMS" by Europe, Japan, and the US as the first stage in the creation of a new universal international monetary order.

In Chapter 3, Michael Sakbani, Professor of Finance, a Former Director of UNCTAD and a former economist with the Federal Reserve Bank of New York, discusses the origins and the unfolding of the crisis and the scale and the unprecedented nature of the rescue efforts. While his main focus is on the United States, he also considers the international dimension of the developments. From what may have looked like a containable crisis of the US "subprime market" became a crisis of the banking sector itself not only in the United States but world-wide. In fact, the initial rescue efforts did not succeed in loosening the fear that seized the markets. Professor Sakbani points out some major differences with previous crises and rescue plans. He points out that the so-called toxic assets are not all worthless and one of the important tasks is to assess the value of these assets while the banks themselves are not bankrupt. He points out that the long-run impact of the rescue operations will weaken the dollar and could contribute to inflationary pressures. The crisis provoked substantial changes in central bank policies: the traditional approach of controlling interest rates and monetary aggregates has been modified through interventions in the balance sheets of the banks and through innovations on both the asset side and the liability side of the central banks' balance sheets. We have probably seen the end of the deregulated global financial model. He also believes that it is time to reform both the IMF and the World Bank.

In Chapter 4, Daniel Kaeser, Former Permanent Representative of Switzerland to the International Monetary Fund, discusses the current and future role of the of the IMF. He points out that, despite the end of the gold-exchange standard and of the par-value system in the 1970s, the Fund has still to promote exchange stability and to prevent competitive exchange depreciations that usually trigger retaliatory measures. He discusses the limitations of the multilateral surveillance carried out by the Fund and the loss of credibility of the IMF as a result of its lop-sided decision-making process. He concludes by saying that if the IMF is to play a more useful role in the future, the distribution of quotas and the decision-making structure will have to be reformed as soon as possible.

Professor Peter Bod, Former President of the Hungarian National Bank, a Former Cabinet Minister in the Antall Government and a Former Director of EBRD, deals in Chapter 5 with the financial and banking crisis from the point of view of Hungary, a "converging country," as a relatively new member of the European Union, but still outside the Euro-group. He starts out describing the sudden shift from optimism and expansion to crisis and gloom in the world of finance. He points out that this time the crisis did not originate on the "periphery" but came from the center of the world economy. The following are some of the key issues addressed in his analysis: the vulnerability of a small, former "transition" economy to major shocks; the way the foreign control of Hungarian banks allowed and even stimulated an excessive indebtedness of Hungarian households in foreign currencies; the way the earlier lack of discipline of the Hungarian government aggravated the crisis; and how a country outside the Euro zone, although a member of the EU, remains more vulnerable than the Euro countries. Finally, the language used by the IMF and the conditionality imposed on Hungary shows the striking contrast between, on the one hand, the fiscal expansion and the efforts to stimulate private consumption preached in the United States, and, on the other hand, the fiscal rigor imposed on a small economy at a time of worsening recession.

Professor Beat Burgenmeier, a Former Dean of the Faculty of Economics and Social Sciences of the University of Geneva, writes in Chapter 6, about the possibility of paradigmatic change from economic growth to sustainable development in the wake of the current systemic crisis. While there has been an increasing awareness of the environmental issue, the central focus remained on promoting economic growth through competitive markets world-wide. This was also the strategy of the principal international economic organizations such as the IMF, the World Bank and the WTO. The recognition of the shortcomings of the "Washington consensus" has led to the call for strategies of sustainable development. In the coming reforms of the international economic organizations, it is important to adopt common environmental standards and to move from a shortsighted "shareholder" mentality to a long-term stakeholder approach.

The global impact on the current and future financial position of households has been one of the most worrisome aspects of the world-wide crisis. André Baladi, a leading international expert on issues of corporate governance and a Co-Founder of the International Corporate Governance Network (ICGN) discusses in Chapter 7 the efforts to introduce better corporate governance standards and thus to improve the protection of savers. There are about 200 national and/or regional corporate governance codes worldwide, but only two major international codes: the OECD and the ICGN Codes. While the OECD represents member states, the ICGN represents investors. Baladi argues that recent history has demonstrated that, when stock market conditions deteriorate, the importance of corporate governance soars as the main guardian of stock market investments. However, corporate governance organizations which aim to uphold corporate governance principles and advocate the adoption of International Financial Standards (IFRS), have failed to reduce the negative impact of the financial perversions which occasionally affect stock markets. The result today is that free-market finance tends to be discredited. While it is not certain that "corporate governance efforts" alone can prevent future major financial crises, it is important that the corporate governance framework should promote transparent and efficient markets, be consistent with the rule of law and clearly articulate the division of responsibilities among different supervisory, regulatory, and enforcement authorities.

Edmond Carton, a senior international banker with thirty-five years of experience (many of which with JP Morgan in the United States and abroad) gives the point of view of the "practicing banker" in Chapter 8. The profound shock felt not only by the author, but also by thousands and thousands of highly skilled bankers and financial experts, comes through clearly in his text. More than an "academic" approach, the analysis of the practitioner shows how far the world of finance had moved away over the years from the basic principles of "sound banking." For the author it is time for a thorough soul-searching by the banking industry itself, at the end of which there should be greater transparency, credibility, reliability and simplicity. There will be a new model of banking, with three essential functions moving back into the center: custody, deposit taking and commercial and consumer lending. How and how fast this will be achieved, the "answer is not around the corner."

The title of Chapter 9 is "Sovereign Wealth Funds: Strategies of Geo-Economic Power Projections". In his detailed analysis, Professor Gyula Csurgai argues that Sovereign Wealth Funds (SWFs) have clear advantages as well as risks both for the investing governments and for the countries where these investments are made. While the objectives of the SWFs are primarily economic and financial, their activities also have important strategic implications. The appropriate answer is not protectionism or discrimination, but a clear definition of rules of behavior to be followed by both sides.

In Chapter 10, Sergio Marchi, former Canadian Cabinet Minister for International Trade, for Environment and for Citizenship and Immigration, and subsequently Canadian Ambassador to the WTO and other Geneva-based international organizations, writes about "The WTO's Doha Development Agenda: An Unclear Roadmap." According to the author, in the current international economic environment it is even more important than before to restart and to successfully conclude the Doha WTO negotiations. He notes that the preceding eight rounds of international trade negotiations since the 1940s have greatly contributed to economic growth and prosperity in the world. Today, more than at any time since the 1930s, the world economy needs a positive impetus from international trade. He concludes by saying that it would be most unfortunate if governments and their negotiators were to be guided by narrow, local political considerations, rather than by their countries' overall long-term interests and allowed the Doha Development Round to fail.

The inclusion of two chapters on international trade and on WTO into the present volume reflects the close links between the international monetary and financial order, on the one hand, and the international trading system, on the other. They are closely interdependent: they represent two essential dimensions of economic globalization. Chapter 11 by Carlos Perez del Castillo deals with the position of the least developed countries (LDCs) within WTO and in the process of trade negotiations and in particular with the so-called integrated framework that allows to optimize the scarce resources of LDCs in trade negotiations and in the development and implementation of their trade policies.

For many years, way beyond the number of its inhabitants or the size of its economy, Switzerland has been rightly considered as a "great power" in international monetary and financial terms. The country earned this position through the quality of its political institutions (one of the oldest democracies in the world), its social cohesion and strong economy, its independence, liberal policies and traditions, its openness on the world, and last but not least, its stable currency, its high savings rate and its strong banking and financial institutions. Yet, UBS, the largest and most ambitious Swiss bank, has become in the current crisis one of the symbols of the excesses of the "age of global finance." More recently, Swiss public opinion, not only in the banking community, was rightly shocked by the attacks levied against the country's tradition of banking confidentiality ("le secret bancaire") in the OECD and at the G20 Summit in London. These accusations (some of them levied by the direct competitors of the Swiss banking industry) had a strong populist undertone and showed little respect for the legal system of one of the most law-abiding democracies in the world. Thus, the readers of the present volume should find interesting Chapter 12 by Norberto Birchler on the important subject of "Swiss Financial Self-Regulation in the Fight against Money Laundering and Terrorist Financing."

It has often been said that financial crises spread like epidemics. Also, one of the recurring themes in the current reform discussion is the need for an international early warning system for the financial sector. Thus, it seems appropriate that the present volume concludes with a chapter by Christian Viladent on "An Epidemologic Approach of Financial Markets" where the author suggests that the approach and experience of the World Health Organization could provide useful ideas for organizing the international efforts to foresee and to prevent the next "financial pandemic."

Note

1. Otto Hieronymi, "Agenda for a New Monetary Reform," in *Futures*, vol. 30, no.8, 1998, pp. 769–81, Pergamon, Elsevier Science Ltd.

1
From "Global Finance" to the Crisis of Globalization

Otto Hieronymi

In Memory of
Professor Emilio Fontela
1938–2007

1.1 The pendulum has gone too far: the nature of the current crisis

The crisis and the debate that is currently underway regarding the future, is not only the crisis of "global finance" but also about globalization. The central question discussed in this book is not only "what will happen" but also about "what should happen" to globlization?

Globalization started out as, and remains, a positive process. Over time, it has contributed and should continue to effect the greater freedom, economic prosperity, rate of technological diffusion, and also provide opportunities of innovation and "upward convergence" in developed and developing nations alike. Reversing this process would not resolve the current crisis. It would deepen and perpetuate it.

It is clear that, by all measures, the "pendulum has gone too far" – and the warning signs were clearly there for quite some time in the field of money and finance.[1]

1.1.1 Globalization and finance

In respect to the three key driving forces of globalization – liberalization, deregulation and privatization – developments have accelerated the furthest within the area of finance.

There is no doubt that without financial and monetary integration throughout the world, neither rich nor poor countries could enjoy the unquestionable benefits associated with an open and integrated world economy. However, over the past twenty years, finance has put its stamp on what is now known as globalization. From being a tool for greater efficiency within the economy, greater security for savers and market-conform access to scarce capital – finance has rapidly become the most dominant influence and reference throughout the world economy.

It was a self-propelling phenomenon: finance became – or seemed to become – the only major activity that could create value out of thin air. In the process, of course, the whole sector, money and finance, underwent a major metamorphosis and along with this, profound changes in economic decisions and leading to new economic structures. Increasingly, all private and public economic decisions – of consumption, creating or closing new companies, of taxation and of public spending fell under the measuring rod of both short-term financial indicators and, in particular, the price of standardized "liquid" assets ("financial products"). This became more and more homogenous over time and easy comparison throughout "markets" and the globe became increasingly distant from the true complexity and diversity of the "real economy."

The principal conclusion of this book is that globalization should not be abolished, but it can be, and it has to be, reformed. However, it will not be an easy task and governments must be willing to take on additional responsibilities and foster a high level of international cooperation in order to strengthen the market economy. This will require both competition and solidarity.

It is essential to ensure that, under the pressure of crisis management and the mantle of long-term reform, the pendulum does not swing back, slowly or rapidly, to the other extreme: depriving the world of the benefits of liberalism and of the free market economy; possibly for generations to come.[2]

1.1.2 Confusion and loss of orientation

There is no doubt that the current crisis is not a "traditional" market crisis or a "regional crisis," but it is a "systemic crisis." Today, we do not know where we are, we do not know how long the downward spiral will continue and, most importantly, we do not seem to know where we should be going in terms of economic and monetary order at both the domestic and the international levels. This utter sense of confusion essentially defines the term "systemic crisis." It is here that we find several commonalities between the current situation and that of the early 1930s.

The most dramatic feature of the current situation is not only a great sense of uncertainty about the duration and severity of the financial crisis and the impact that it has had upon the "real economy"; it is also about the measures that need to be implemented in order to stop the downward spiral of asset destruction and the accelerating trend toward bankruptcies within the banking sector and the economy. There is no consensus among political leaders, economists and other experts, as well as in the business community and in the general public about the desirable features, the objectives, organizing principles, rules, structures and the workings of national economies and of the international economy as a whole.

The situation has been analyzed time and time again – there has been an outpouring of ideas and activism on all levels – but so far, in terms of both action and debate, improvisation has carried the day. The old rules no longer apply, the most successful institutions are now crumbling, and no one knows (and many do not seem to care) what the impact of emergency measures will be (including the fiscal stimuli, the cheap money policies and the de facto nationalizations). To what extent are these measures going to predetermine the shape of the economic, monetary and social order of the future?

1.1.3 The crisis of the dominant doctrines

In the wake of the crisis, one of the most remarkable changes in the banking system and in the world of financial markets is the belated recognition that a new approach is necessary and extensive reforms of the international banking system must occur. There is a sudden and universal consensus that central banks and governments now have a new and increased level of responsibility toward making the financial system work.

This new consensus is all the more impressive because it goes against the conventional wisdom held both among experts and officials as well as market participants – a conventional wisdom that held sway not only in the United States but also in the rest of the world, including Switzerland. There is no question that this dramatic change in thinking was due to not only the magnitude and force of "events," but also the banking and monetary elite – despite the initial "sub-prime" scandal that broke out in the summer of 2007, in the banking system and in world financial markets – was intellectually and technically totally unprepared for a systemic crisis rather than a "familiar real-estate bubble."

1.1.4 The long-term causes of the current crisis

The outbreak, severity and global dimension of the current crisis were caused by the convergence of several factors: policy errors, accidents (e.g., Lehman Brothers), growing imbalances between the financial and real sectors, greed and ultimately the growing instability and fragility of the current economic and social order. Therefore, one of the most important conclusions of this book is that fundamental reforms as well as the current crisis were long overdue.

The principal long-term causes of the current crisis of the financial system and world economy can be summed up under three major headings:

1. The lack of a rule-based international monetary system since the 1970s resulted in the absence of effective external constraints on the policies of major economies, and the gradual elimination of rules and systemic safeguards on the behavior of financial market participants.
2. The glaring contrast between, on the one hand, monetary nationalism (or at best monetary regionalism) embodied within the system of floating exchange rates, and, on the other hand, the rampant globalization of "borderless" finance, in particular that of short-term speculation has become the most widespread concern of all economic and business decision makers and the most "promising" source of profits.
3. The growing gap between the rhetoric of globalization and its effective practice: while the potential positive aspects of competition were undermined through the creation of larger and larger companies in all sectors (and not least in banking and finance) through often predatory M&A policies, facilitated through reckless financing and debt-creation; at the same time, domestic and international solidarity, and the social dimension of the market economy (that has made costs of competition socially and politically acceptable in the post-war period, not only in Europe and Japan, but also in the US), have been undermined or eliminated through "down-sizing," "streamlining," "outsourcing" and systematic rejection of the whole concept of international or domestic "public good" and "public services."

There is no question that, unless these three issues are fully addressed and properly dealt with during the broad reform process that is underway, along with the current phase of "crisis management" and "damage control," the outlook for sustained (and sustainable) long-term growth, stability and equity in the world economy will remain clouded.

The reforms are needed neither to "liquidate globalization," nor to restore the unbridled rule of short-term finance and encourage the continued concentration of market power in fewer and fewer mammoth banks and companies that squeeze out competition while becoming more and more difficult to manage efficiently. No government or business manager is perfect: they both need rules and a fair degree of decision-making autonomy. Finally, the reform process has to address the social dimension of the modern economy that has become increasingly neglected in the name of the alleged requirements of global competition in rich and poor countries alike.

Yet, unless the Ayn Randian "virtue of selfishness" will cease to be mistaken for the organizing principle of our national and international political communities, and a more equitable balance is found between competition and solidarity at national and international levels, the current crisis may turn into a debacle of the market economy itself and of the liberal international political and economic order.

1.1.5   The crisis and the future of globalization

The process of globalization has involved the deepening, broadening and widening of developments that began in the 1940s in the Western market economies, and progressed, with ups and downs and with temporary setbacks, during the following decades. The liberalization of international trade, currency convertibility and exchange rate stability, the fight against inflation, and last but not least, the search for general prosperity and for social progress, were the essential elements of this trend. A balanced approach in the long term between competition and solidarity was the key to the unprecedented period of prosperity and social progress during six decades following the Second World War.

The year 1990 marked the end of the Cold War and the definitive start of globalization. It was from this moment on that the former communist countries were able to choose democracy, market economies and opt for full integration into liberal international economic order. The demise of the authoritarian, state-dominated socialist economic model also accelerated the trend toward open market economies in the so-called developing countries that had begun in the 1980s.

The principal causes of the crisis of globalization are to be found in the growing excesses, not only in the financial markets but also in the very "philosophy" and in the "general practice" of globalization. These excesses include: the spreading and imposition of "market fundamentalism" (the doctrine that the market mechanism could satisfy all individual and societal needs and objectives); the systematic vilification of all government responsibilities (and in particular of creating national and international rules to safeguard the proper functioning of the market economy); the denial of the legitimacy of common goals and community interests, and the glorification of selfishness; and last but not least, the rejection of the concepts of solidarity, social justice and responsibility, at both the national and international level, with the weaker and less successful becoming increasingly marginalized.

While the basis of the market economy is supposed to be fair competition and fair opportunity for large and small companies alike, "globalization" for many became synonymous with the pursuit of bigness, of concentrations of economic and financial power in order to squeeze out competition in national and world markets.[3] The aberrations and the excesses not only created ethical and political problems (and provided ample arguments for the sworn enemies of the market economy), but they also reduced economic efficiency and threatened the stability of the market economy.

The solution, however, is not a return to a world of closed, government-controlled economies. This would not only reduce the living standards of the affluent, but it would also have a lasting negative impact on the future prospects of the poor and the poorest in the world. It would curtail economic freedom and the scope for private initiative and innovation as well as weaken all aspects of freedom. It would not only replace competition through controls and restrictions, but it would also undermine cooperation within and between nations.

1.1.6 Values and interests

The reform of the international banking and monetary system will be a long and complex process. Monetary and banking reform involves both values and interests. It can be successful only if it is part of a broader reaffirmation of the key organizing principles of a global international order based on democracy and respect for freedom and human rights, international economic integration and cooperation, security and progress toward perpetual peace, and finally the search for balance between competition and solidarity at the national and international levels. These principles are not derived from pure idealism: they have been part of our reality during the last sixty years at various times and various places.[4]

1.1.7 Is it only a "bubble?"

In recent weeks and months the term "bubble" has been widely used in both the media and in expert analyses as the cause of the once-in-a-century crisis in the American and world economy. This term, and the enumeration of all the past "bubbles," has included the economic disaster that hit the Japanese economy twenty years ago. It also conveys the idea that "bubbles" are inevitable and largely a punishment for greed.

The idea that large and small financial "bubbles" are an inherent part of the economic system, and that nothing can be done to prevent their recurrence and their bursting resulting in all-round devastating consequences in the market economy, certainly absolves the likes of Alan Greenspan from events after 2007. This is "voo-doo" economics similar to political theories according to which wars among nations are inevitable.

Whatever validity the "bubble theory" had in relation to past crises, it is certainly an incomplete explanation for the nature and the extent of the current one. In fact, over the last two or three decades the global financial system has been turning more and more rapidly into a "global machine of speculation." None of the major international financial crises of the last thirty years – the Asian financial crisis, the Russian financial crisis, the Japanese crisis, or the debt crisis of the 1980s – slowed down this trend.[5]

1.1.8   Systemic crisis or crisis of the system

Developments in early 2009 confirmed the major features of the economic and financial crisis that had been evident at the time when the crisis had broken into the open in the autumn of 2008.

The most important aspect was the systemic nature of the crisis, with financial explosions leading to a credit freeze and to enormous strains on the instruments of monetary policy. All these developments turned the real economy (consumption, investments, trade and employment) on a downward path. This started a vicious downward cycle that was further fueled by the constant barrage of negative news and of pessimistic short-term and long-term forecasts (with recurring references to the Great Depression of the 1930s). This in turn added to the strain of monetary, financial institutions and induced consumers, businesses and banking to greater "prudence," thereby adding to the downward pressure on demand and to the difficulties of the banks and of the lack of response to monetary easing.

1.1.9   Shortcomings of both "all-market" and "anti-globalization" theories

The second feature that should be mentioned is the "short-circuit" at the level of ideas. Not only have markets and market participants (banks and other financial institutions, savers and investors as well companies in the "real economy"), as well as national and international government agencies (governments, including national treasuries and financial supervisory bodies, central banks and organizations like the International

Monetary Fund (IMF), the Bank for International Settlements (BIS) and the Organization for Economic Cooperation and Development (OECD)) been surprised and overwhelmed by what has been deemed as a "once-in-a-century" crisis. Neither the body of economic theory that had been dominant until the outbreak of the crisis (the central tenet of which had been "more market" and "less government" to all economic problems), nor the increasingly virulent "anti-globalization" and "anti-market" doctrines, had a ready answer for how to deal with the crisis and what should be the working model for the national economies and for the world economy, and in particular for the international monetary and banking system.[6]

1.1.10   Improvisation: The hallmark of the policy response

Third, the leaders in both the "government" and the "markets" have been surprised and overwhelmed by the systemic nature, magnitude and swiftness of the crisis. Thus, it remains evident that we (meaning everyone: the officials, the financial and business leaders, the "experts" and the general public) do not know "Where we are," "Where the 'broken system' is taking us," or "where we should be going." For example: "What aspects should we try to preserve and repair?" and "Which ones should we remove from the current economic, financial and monetary order?" Therefore, improvisation is growing and "trial and error," "reversing all gears," "getting rid of all ballast" and "full speed ahead into the unknown" are now the remaining orders of the day. What could be said ten years ago, as an appeal for reflection and debate – that "we are in uncharted waters" – has come back to haunt the world in a dramatic way. After the initial hesitation and lack of coordination, (both in analysis and understanding of the seriousness and extent of the dangers, as in the "case of Lehman Brothers" that may go into the history books as the "Creditanstalt of 2008"), larger and more extreme "rescue plans" have been adopted with a sudden conversion to the belief in the instant efficacy of government actions, and in particular of monetary and fiscal stimuli.

1.1.11   Global downturn – mutual impact: The effect of doom and gloom speeches

Leading policy-makers, just like leading bankers and other market participants, discovered the extent and the gravity of the financial crisis step by step, as events were unfolding. Their efforts to reverse the situation, through fiscal or monetary stimuli, always seemed to be one step, one day, one week behind the unraveling of the system or a few hundred billion dollars or euros short of the amounts needed to avoid a total collapse. This is at least the impression one gets from their public statements – although some may have had serious forebodings they did not go public with their concerns out of fear of provoking the crisis.[7] However, once "the dam broke," these same officials seemed to compete, in speech after speech, to describe the gravity of the situation and the "consequences of inaction" in the most frightening terms. There is no doubt that the unrelenting collective gloom of the American, European, Japanese and other officials (including the internationals) could not but contribute to the pessimism of consumers, investors, and corporate managers and of the bankers who were supposed to provide them with credits. The following quote from a presentation by Chairman Bernanke to the US Congress is a typical illustration of these views:

> The principal cause of the economic slowdown was the collapse of the global credit boom and the ensuing financial crisis, which has affected asset values, credit conditions, and consumer and business confidence around the world ... [The] outlook for economic activity is subject to considerable uncertainty, and I believe that, overall, the downside risks probably outweigh those on the upside. One risk arises from the global nature of the slowdown, which could adversely affect US exports and financial conditions to an even greater degree than currently expected. Another risk derives from the destructive power of the so-called adverse feedback loop, in which weakening economic and financial conditions become mutually reinforcing. To break the adverse feedback loop, it is essential that we continue to complement fiscal stimulus with strong government action to stabilize financial institutions and financial markets.[8]

1.1.12   Policy errors and systemic defects

There seems to be universal agreement that the crisis has been essentially due to laxness, to the lack of prudent management of financial, monetary, fiscal and in general economic affairs. The responsibility for this laxness is widely and globally shared by central banks, financial supervisors, financial institutions, as well as governments and their finance ministers, international organizations and, last but not least, by households. At a more fundamental level, the increasingly complex machinery of global finance that has penetrated more and more aspects of the world economy, and that has been running more and more on "autopilot," ran into serious engine trouble.[9]

If one compares the explanations of the causes and consequences of the 2007–09 crisis with the analyses of, for example, two leading monetary statesmen, Alexandre Lamfalussy and Paul Volcker, of the international monetary crises of the preceding decade, and in particular concerning the Asian financial crisis, the systemic nature of the earlier and of the current crises becomes evident. Neither the current crises, nor the earlier ones were primarily due to policy errors or to the "greed of private bankers," but to defects in the system.

Thus, in a speech in January 2000 on "Globalization and the International Financial System," Paul Volcker emphasized the importance of adequate standards of supervision and the ability to assess risk properly under the more demanding conditions of globalization. Of course, at the time he was speaking about the problems of the "emerging markets":

> The crisis basically reflected institutional and policy shortcoming complicated by the inability or unwillingness of international money managers to assess risk properly. There is emphasis on familiar policy fundamentals – the old story of the importance of responsible budgetary and monetary policies. Beyond that, attention has been focused on institutional reforms, particularly in the financial system. As never before – at least in my memory – questions of adequate bank capital, of banking supervision, of accounting and auditing standards, and of "transparency" have been placed front and center on the policy agenda.[10]

A year earlier he noted the responsibility – for better or worse – of the United States and of Europe and Japan under globalization for the conditions also in the developing countries:

> Paradoxically, an important threat to a satisfactory outcome of the globalization process for the developing world lies right here in the United States, in Europe, and in Japan. We, individually and collectively, provide the economic framework to which others must adapt.[11]

In his incisive analysis on four major crises, *Financial Markets in Emerging Markets. An Essay on Financial Globalisation and Fragility*, Professor Lamfalussy also gave a grave warning for the future:

> The build up of excessive short-term indebtedness and the accompanying asset price bubbles were at the heart of the … crises. The exuberant behavior of lenders and investors from the developed world played a major role in raising leverage and asset prices to levels that eventually became unsustainable … The process of financial

globalization aggravated all four crises and, if left unattended, would be likely to contribute to the eruption of new crises in emerging markets ... [Finally] the jury is still out on the question of whether the process of globalization has made the financial system of the developed world more or less prone to manifestations of financial fragility.[12]

1.1.13   Systemic causes of the current crisis: A summary

At the risk of repeating some of the points raised in my article "Agenda for a New Economic Reform" ten years ago, the following seem to be some of the principal systemic causes of the current crisis:

(1) Growing imbalance between private and public interests.
(2) The dichotomy between the prevailing monetary nationalism and a global financial system.
(3) The abdication of central banks and monetary authorities of their responsibility for external balance and for international monetary stability.
(4) The de facto disconnection between finance and money.
(5) The nature of globalization—everything expressed in short-term asset prices.
(6) The passage from traditional banking to asset trading (securitization).
(7) Excessive speculation and artificial risk taking.
(8) The lack of effective checks and balances (balance of payments).
(9) Illusion that money is just like any other commodity.
(10) Breakdown of the "social contract" between the "winners" and the "losers" in the globalized economy.

1.2   The end of Bretton Woods and the victory of monetary nationalism

An international monetary system is easier to destroy than to rebuild. It was easy enough for a few amateurs in a few hours to wreck the international monetary system in August 1971. Compare that to the protracted negotiations that went into the Bretton Woods Articles of Agreement ... The great significance of the agreement lay in its creation of a multilateral way of managing the international interdependence of exchange rates in a forum in which the interests of the smaller countries could be taken into account.

(Robert Mundell)[13]

Thus, today the single most important, and at the same time most difficult, task is to roll back the monetary nationalism that has prevailed for decades and build a new international monetary order suited for a liberal and highly globalized economy.

1.2.1   Since 1971 the world has come full circle

In the current debate on the financial crisis, there has been a high level of speculation that the "sub-prime bubble" was the leading cause. While it may have been the initial detonator (*la goutte qui a fait déborder la vase*), the real, underlying source was the profound metamorphosis of the domestic and international monetary and financial systems that had begun in the early 1970s. This process, which lasted almost forty years, has led to the gradual elimination of systemic checks and balances, in particular on actors with great market powers. (In fact, the constraints on the weaker ones became even stricter than they had been before the 1970s or the 1980s.)

The progress of global finance, with the creation of homogenous markets and virtually twenty-four hour trading across the globe, was not accompanied by comparable developments at the monetary level. Since the 1970s, the world has seen a multiplicity of attempts to cope with the absence of a common international monetary order. At any given time, the situation can be compared to a kaleidoscope rather than a stable system. There has been free floating, pegged rates, bilateral arrangements, regional multilateral arrangements, unilateral shadowing, currency boards, dollarization, regional systems and even a new common currency, the Euro.[14]

In fact, as noted above, the current crisis has been the most severe and far-reaching crisis in the world financial system and in the world economy as a whole, since the abolition of the gold-exchange standard by President Nixon at Camp David in August 1971.

1.2.2   The debate on the reform of Bretton Woods

The 1960s saw a wide-ranging debate on the reform of the international monetary system. The start of this debate followed only by a few years the effective start of the "full Bretton Woods" system with the establishment of full current account convertibility by the European countries. The end of the "post-war period" (and the end of the European Payments Union) signaled the end of currency discrimination against the US dollar in Europe on balance-of-payments grounds.[15]

Robert Triffin's influential economic and political bestseller entitled *Gold and the Dollar Crisis*, gave a powerful boost to the debate on the adequacy and shortcomings of the Bretton Woods system, the balance-of-payments rules of the IMF, and the constraints it had on the deficit as well as surplus countries.[16] The central theme of Professor Triffin's critiques lay primarily with the use of the dollar as a reserve currency and the issues that it caused for both the US economy and the rest of the world. The need for international liquidity has led to US balance-of-payment deficits, thus resulting in a resource transfer to the world's richest country. Professor Triffin's advocacy for the creation of a new international, jointly managed reserve currency led to the creation of the Special Drawing Rights (SDR), through the first reform of the Articles of Agreement of the IMF.

The central issue of the reform debate was not so much the fixed exchange rate system or international liquidity creation, but the alleged constraints on domestic policy autonomy through the balance of payments: imported inflation and imported recession. The questions were whether (1) external balance-of-payments discipline was a costly obstacle to domestic (expansionary) fiscal and monetary policies and thus to full employment, and whether (2) the inflow of foreign exchange reserves in the surplus countries (and the resulting potential imported inflationary pressures) prevented the virtuous countries from pursuing effective anti-inflationary policies.

In other words, both deficit countries and surplus countries seemed to be seeking greater domestic policy autonomy: the first ones wanted to avoid what had appeared to be excessive restrictions (the UK, France and Italy); the others, mainly Germany but also Holland and Switzerland (although Switzerland was to become a member of the IMF much later, the Swiss authorities "shadowed" the IMF exchange-rate rules from the start).

The fact that the "external discipline imposed by IMF rules" was a convenient scapegoat for the policy discipline that governments in the deficit countries had to pursue, at any rate, was rarely admitted. Nor did the "strong-currency" countries like to admit that their economies benefited, in terms of growth and employment, from their strong export performance and external surpluses. (The rate of inflation and the inflation differentials were of course much smaller than what became the case during the 1970s in the wake of the abandoning of the fixed-exchange rate regime.)

Those who were for flexible and freely floating exchange rates were of a small minority, primarily the followers of Professor Milton Friedman of the University of Chicago.[17]

Friedman ... like [James] Meade, championed flexible exchange rates. Their reasons were very different. Meade, the liberal socialist, saw flexible exchange rates as a device for achieving external balance while freeing policy tools for the implementation of national planning objectives.

Friedman, the libertarian conservative, saw flexible exchange rates as a way of getting rid of exchange and trade controls. Both economists saw flexible exchange rates as a means of altering real wages when money wage rigidities would otherwise cause unemployment.[18]

Once "Bretton Woods collapsed," in fact was destroyed, by the combined effect of the respective monetary nationalism of France and Germany[19] on one hand, and of President Richard Nixon along with his Secretary of the Treasury, the former Democratic Governor of Texas, John Connally, on the other hand, there was an almost immediate intellectual and political "Gleichschaltung" in favor of the "non-system" of a "freely" floating exchange rate among economists, bankers as well as government officials.[20] The failure of their attempts to reverse the situation and to implement reform was ultimately sealed with the Second Amendment that enshrined the system of floating exchange rates in the new Article IV of the IMF.[21]

As Professor Triffin wrote in 1990, monetary nationalism won out over common interests:

> A fundamental reform of the "paper-exchange standard" anchored primarily on an inconvertible and wildly fluctuating dollar, was unanimously endorsed as urgent, fifteen years ago in the June 14, 1974 swan song of Jeremy Morse's "Committee of Twenty" after eleven years of continuous debates at the highest level between ministers of finance, governors of central banks, and their most respected economic advisors. This recommendation was abruptly dismissed at the bilateral Franco-American meeting of Kingston (Jamaica) in January 1976, and in the second amendment of the IMF Articles of Agreement, belatedly put into legal operation on April 1, 1978.[22]

In 1979, Professor Hayek wrote this about the international monetary situation, "Unless we succeed in the reasonably near future to restore monetary stability, the market order is doomed and with it not only our wealth but peace and civilization, with the most frightful effects on the lives of a large part of the World population."[23]

The theoretical argument that flexible exchange rates would help to avoid the systematic over or under valuation of currencies while helping to avoid large imbalances and neutralize the effect of different inflation rates and thus reduce current account deficits and surpluses through a smooth market adjustment, was disproved by actual developments.

In fact, flexible exchange rates have amplified distortions. Paul Volcker is a credible source on this issue:

> The typical academic answer to the systemic question – seems to be floating currencies. And there isn't much doubt that, in the absence of other perceived alternatives, governments in crisis are driven to that approach. But that also seems to be a counsel of despair in terms of a satisfactory policy over time. Nothing in the practical record of the past quarter century lends support to the theorizing that floating exchange rates will also be relatively stable. In the technical terms of economic text books, what it comes down to is whether markets, by sensible international policies, can be dominated by stabilizing speculation – a tendency for market operators themselves to step in against extreme movements for the simple reason that profits can be made. Plainly, more often than not, it is the opposite that has been happening. The perception is that, in the jargon of the market, "the trend is your friend"; the way to make money is to join, even lead, the herd.[24]

According to Professor Mundell:

> The gold exchange standard was a way of putting a check on the dollar money supply. It operated through the convertibility discipline. But when the dollar gold standard broke down, the check to it also broke down and the Federal Reserve System became the world's central bank producing the world's effective reserves. The Federal Reserve System dominates and indirectly runs the financial world economy: all other currency systems have become satellites of the dollar system. This is not an ideal world. I would like to see a world where there is a check on the US financial economy and on the Eurodollar market. I would like to see a global monetary system incorporating discipline reinstated again. I would like to see fixed exchange rates, to control foreign monetary expansion, and a convertibility regime, with some control over the monetary expansion power of the dominant currency, which is still the US dollar. But our new system will have to involve more sharing of control and authority than the previous system.[25]

The so-called gold-exchange standard (the "Bretton Woods system") was an imperfect order, with numerous shortcomings. One of its main objectives was to establish an *international* order, limiting and sanctioning as many temptations and practices of *economic and monetary nationalism* as possible. Therefore, it was a fundamentally *liberal order*. It has often been, appropriately, stated that the IMF bore the marks of the genius of Keynes, tempered by the realism of the US Treasury. While Keynes and Hayek often and systematically differed, in particular over the economic role of governments and of government interventions, they were fundamentally both liberals and defenders of the market economy. Ultimately, both Hayek and Keynes (despite his earlier protectionist temptations) rejected economic nationalism and the system of flexible or floating exchange rates as the very expression of monetary nationalism.[26]

1.2.3   From monetary internationalism to floating exchange rates and monetary nationalism

The return to monetary nationalism was evident. It was the central theme of a conference held in June of 1998 at the Battelle Memorial Institute in Geneva titled, *The New Monetary Nationalism*. (The concept of "economic nationalism" has more or less disappeared from the academic or official debate, while its reality became part of the dominant orthodoxy. The scarce use of the term is attested by recent studies.)[27]

One of the principal objectives of a "rule-based" and "commodity-based" international monetary order is to provide a framework that will help adopt balanced domestic monetary and fiscal policies and avoid excessive swings in the financial markets. These external constraints are aimed at making "discipline" more politically acceptable. Yet, it is this very external discipline that is considered both unnecessary and unacceptable to the opponents of a rule-based international monetary system.

The theoretical argument that flexible exchange rates correct the effect of different inflation rates on the balance of payments, and therefore reduce current account deficits and surplus through a smooth market adjustment, was disproved by concrete developments.

The real advantage seen by the advocates of flexible exchange rates was that they were able to free the national authorities from the "tyranny" of the balance of payments. (This constant desire for more "national autonomy" failed to take into account the fact that the intensification of international economic relations – through trade, technology diffusion and foreign direct investments and the discipline and competition they brought about – proved to be the principal engine of growth in the decades following the Second World War) This was reinforced by the argument that at any rate the current account had little or no role in determining market exchange rates, because these were basically determined by (short-term) financial flows. What has been left out of the argument are the large and growing volumes of short-term cross-border financial flows that resulted from the absence of stable exchange rates, and the fact that these flows increased rather than decreased the instability of exchange rates and financial markets.

1.2.4   Hayek vs. Friedman on relative prices and monetary policy

The principal criticism that should be addressed to flexible or floating exchange rates, has to do with their effect on the uncertainty of relative prices (domestically and internationally) and on investments and asset values. Floating creates and destroys assets that have no connection with conditions in markets for real goods and services and savings and investments. A similar phenomenon occurs with asset-price inflation and asset-price deflation that result from short-term, interest-rate variations and from credit-expansion or contraction. It has been symptomatic for quite some time that the "new orthodoxy" – at the level of both theory and central-bank practice in the United States in particular – was not concerned by exchange-rate instability and systematic overshooting and undershooting, as a result of short-term financial transactions and the classic herd instinct of the stock exchanges, nor by share-price inflation that had nothing to do with the productivity, market position and profitability of the companies listed. This was in sharp contrast with their obsession with the slightest changes in the aggregate consumer price index.[28]

Milton Friedman was the "Godfather" of the flexible-exchange-rate school that has dominated academic and policy thinking since the 1970s, especially in the United States and in Britain, but also the views of many continental economists and policy-makers. Hayek, on the other hand, was opposed to flexible exchange rates since the 1930s and also subsequently remained against them. This difference had to do with their differing opinions on monetary policy and its impact on relative prices in a national economy and in the world economy as a whole. This can be highlighted by a quote from Hayek's important study on *Denationalisation of Money*:

> The problem with the quantity theory of money is that by its 'stress on the effects of changes in the quantity of money on the general level of prices it directs all-too exclusive attention to the harmful effects of inflation on the creditor-debtor relationship, but disregards the even more important and harmful effects of the injections and withdrawals

of amounts of money from circulation on the structure of relative prices and the consequent misallocation of resources and particularly the misdirection of investments which it causes ...' Milton Friedman ... is a dear friend of mine and we agree on almost everything except monetary policy. He thinks in terms of statistics, aggregates and the average price level and does not really see that inflation leads to unemployment because of the distortion of the structure of relative prices.[29]

Ultimately Friedman was and remained a monetary nationalist[30] who was not concerned by international relative prices, whereas Hayek was, and remained, an internationalist.[31]

1.2.5   The consequences

In hindsight, many economists interpreted the "end of Bretton Woods" as inevitable: the system of fixed exchange rates, and in particular the fixed dollar price of gold, is alleged to have imposed an excessive rigidity and excessive constraints on national (in particular US) domestic fiscal and monetary policies. The lifting of this constraint – by ending the promise to convert officially held dollars into gold – was one of the principal sources of the combination of inflation and recession that characterized the world economy during much of the 1970s. "More flexibility" turned into outright instability.

The so-called oil crisis or oil-shocks – that is, the shift from an artificially stable oil price fixed by a consumers' cartel, to a new price fixed by the producers' cartel – was amplified by the decline of the value of the dollar and by the illusion that flexible exchange rates would make balance-of-payments adjustment painless.

The "end of Bretton Woods" was also the beginning of the domestic and international deregulation of banking, a long process that ultimately led to the gradual decline of traditional commercial banking and to the blossoming of "financial engineering," trading in "financial products" and the growing distance between financial institutions, on the one hand, and the actual savers and spenders (including companies and households spending on construction and equipment).

This section will be concluded by quoting a 1993 summary of the consequences and the conditions created by the breakdown of Bretton Woods by Robert Mundell which identifies more aspects of the causes of the current crisis than most of the recent analyses:

The unsound condition of American financial institutions can be traced directly to the instability of the level and structure of real interest rates associated with the breakdown of the anchored fixed exchange rate system. Not only have unanchored flexible exchange rates been responsible for accommodating monetary excesses, but they can also be blamed for the collapse of fiscal discipline. Under the fixed exchange rate system of the past – the gold standard, the gold exchange standard, or the anchored dollar standard – countries have been forced to maintain fiscal discipline. Absence of discipline would result in adverse speculation, reserve losses, and a convertibility crisis.[32]

1.3   The benefits and risks of global finance

1.3.1   The age of global finance

"Global finance" is probably the first truly global phenomenon in history affecting all aspects of the economy simultaneously, in "real time." Thanks to institutional changes and to technology, global finance appears to have eliminated all borders: geographic distance, the dimensions of time and importantly differences between different actors and different types of business and economic decisions and preferences. There is no way that we could have world-wide economic integration – globalization – without global finance.

In fact, the monetary sector and finance and banking have been inextricably linked to globalization. Whereas until the late 1960s and the early 1970s these sectors, money and finance, had been "lagging behind" the liberalization and integration of the Western developed economies through trade, direct investments and the diffusion of technology, in the last forty years the dynamics of cross-border financial links gradually reached and exceeded the extent of integration in the "real economy."[33]

These trends led to two fatal, contrasting illusions: on the one hand that "finance" can be separated from the "real economy," and, on the other hand, that "the real economy" can and should be transformed to follow the requirements of "global finance."

1.3.2   Impending dangers

The major risks implicit in these trends were evident for quite some time. The present writer identified three groups of dangers in early 2008:[34]

(1) excesses (of governments and of the private sector);
(2) errors, accidents, defects of the system (institutions, general vulnerability, irreversible chain of events (domino theory), lack of reserves (lack of redundancy);

(3) political, economic, financial, environmental policies and egoisms, lack of intelligence and willingness to cooperate, egoism and lack of solidarity.

1.3.3   Principal characteristic of "global finance": The shortening time horizon

The most striking feature of global finance is that, for the first time in history, we have a truly planetary system affecting the behavior of economic actors throughout the world economy, in large and small, in rich and developing countries alike. At no point in the recent or distant past was an essential dimension of economic life as tightly and as widely integrated as it has become in finance over the past ten to fifteen years.

Today, there is the perception and the (partial) reality of "real time" transactions twenty-four hours a day around the globe, with the illusion of the abolition of distance.

One of the most important factors is the dramatic shortening of the time-horizon for all economic decisions. There is a virtual abolition of time.[35] Because of the technological developments the material costs of financial transactions have become extremely low (virtually negligible) allowing an enormous flow – back and forth – of financial assets within national markets and across borders.[36]

Everyone knows by now that the "spreading of risks" was supposed to be one of the most important features of the system. This was meant to reduce risk for each market participant to an "acceptable" level. In reality this was one of the most dangerous characteristic, allowing the crises to spread like brush fire. Yet, it was known for quite some time that, under the system, there were not only "true or real" risks and "artificial risks," and more importantly "market risks," but also "systemic risks." The distribution of risks was not equitable and one of the major sources of income in the increasingly bloated financial sector was the creation of "artificial risks."

The other alleged principal contribution of financial globalization was the efficient distribution of scarce capital and the elimination of large disequilibria – balance-of-payments and budgetary – that lead to waste and potential crises. In fact the system allowed and greatly contributed to the development and persistence of disequilibria and has greatly increased the cost of correcting them.

Finally the prices of "financial assets" ("securities") have become the true common standard of the world economy (*l'étalon commun*).

1.3.4   The new "stock-market" mentality

In the financial world, there is a common fallacy that the stock exchange is the perfect model of the market and its habits and rules should be applicable to all economic decisions. This fallacy has been imposed both on experts and the general public as the absolute truth. It was this mentality that created a fundamental misunderstanding about the workings of the market economy.

Thus, the most important and most insidious development has been the passage from a credit-based economy to a stock-market type economy. Short-term "speculation" has become the best-rewarded activity in the modern economy (both for individuals and companies) and large volumes of transactions have become necessary due to the small difference in prices. The volume of transactions in search of gains on margins is particularly enormous when compared to the volume of financing "real" transactions. A very large share of "real" financial transactions is invested in mergers and acquisitions (M&A) and not in financing the creation of new enterprises or expanding existing ones. Much of M&A activity is aimed at squeezing out competition and "buying markets" rather than increasing economies of scale on the supply side.

The principal indicator of economic and business success, or failure, is the price of shares and other "financial assets." These prices and expected gains, as well as losses, on the variation of these prices determine the decisions of companies, savers and other economic actors. However, the fear of a "systemic crisis" guarantees a minimum earning for financial intermediaries that industrial and other companies (their employees) do not enjoy (especially with the outlawing of all government supports as distortion of markets).

Modern financial markets are a particular species of markets. This notion is quite evident and can be seen in their daily functions, "raison d'être" and their ultimate goals. They are markets of intermediaries, markets that are in perpetual motion and markets that are in a continuous search of "liquidity." They are keen on scoops and are marked by a "breaking news mentality" rather than one of in-depth analysis. Price formation is determined by "the impact of news" (often only rumors) with very short-term, instant reactions. It is the crowd effect, follow the leader (sheep rather than bulls or bears) mentality and fundamental structural characteristics, which have not been eliminated by the new financial instruments, that ultimately led to the excessive fluctuations (upward and downward).

The behavior of non-financial corporations has also been profoundly affected.[37] The principal development in this sector has been the shorter and shorter perspective of business decisions. Today, it has become more difficult to develop and implement long-term strategies. There has been a redefinition of profitability, competitive positions and the role of the "financial image" of shared values as the principal indicator of failure or success. Buying and selling companies has become the very heart of corporate strategies. There is a new hierarchy inside corporations. Finance has moved above all other divisions and M&A have become the principal responsibility and preoccupation of CEOs.

1.3.5   Speculation and the principle "wealth is power"

During the last thirty years, speculation has become the most profitable "economic" activity both for "real actors" – households, savers, companies and even governments – and "bankers" and "engineers of financial products." Lack of economic rational in the system, not to mention the "moral" issues, were successfully masked by what seemed to be real profits and the creation of bona fide wealth. The natural tendency of financial markets to "over-shoot" both upward and downward (their traditional "corrective mechanism" according to the textbooks) was supposed to be mitigated by mathematical algorithms. Unfortunately, it was tolerated or even encouraged by the lax monetary and supervisory policies of the leading monetary authorities. This was a system of permanent "fuite en avant". Once the excesses became too difficult to hide or manage, the weakest links in the chain, usually the borrowers, became the victims of the clean up; after which the "perpetum mobile" of creating fake wealth would start again, in a new round, and on an even grander scale.

The cynicism with which anti-competitive behavior and the systematic squeezing out of smaller competitors, through various opaque financial engineering, was tolerated coincided with an increasingly harsh moral attitude toward all the streamlining and downsizing of contemporary "human management" techniques. The idea that "bigger is better" and being second or third in markets that were already highly concentrated, went against all the basic principles of a competitive market economy. The exchange rate and balance of payments were de facto abolished for "rich" countries both in theory and in practice of virtually all-major OECD central banks. For the rest, the devil takes the hindmost.

1.3.6   Predictability and managing risk

There are avoidable and unavoidable risks. One of the principal goals of economic policy and, in particular monetary policy, is to help reduce risk by providing certain measures of predictability of the key aspects of the economic environment, as well as businesses and households. Fighting inflation is an essential result of this objective. A key issue, that has not received a sufficient amount of attention in the dominant theories, is the economic and financial uncertainties and risks resulting from the absence of an international monetary standard.

Future economic or monetary developments are the outcome of a combination of three sets of factors: the nature and function of the system, trends and "events." These events can influence or even break the trends and/or modify or even destroy the system. Some very sophisticated methods of forecasting are based on relatively little theory and purely on information extracted directly from data without going through a theory. The time horizon of decision making is one of the principal issues in economic and monetary analysis and also in forecasting. One of the main problems, in the last thirty years, has been that the short-term horizon of financial markets has gradually penetrated the rest of the economy and has made long-term decision making increasingly difficult.

1.3.7   From risk assessment to risk transfer

"Risk" has become synonymous with "financial-market" risk.[38] The efforts of financial intermediaries in order to minimize risk and maximize profits from "risk-management" on behalf of savers and borrowers was largely responsible for the unimaginably large volume of transactions in "financial assets" and the constant buying and selling in hopes of being ahead of the market and not left behind.[39] The "herd instinct" and legendary "bull" and "bear" overshooting and undershooting have been essential parts of the stock and commodity markets and were traditionally taken into stride by many seasoned market participants, as was the time horizon of these markets, the amount of time it took to place and to execute an order on the stock market. The growing emphasis on "share-holder value," linked to short-term stock-market valuations and the constant search for opportunities to buy and sell companies and parts of companies, with little regard for longer-term business and market logic and synergies, are also part of this phenomenon.

The extension of these principles to the entire range of economic decisions – the central feature of "financial deregulation" and even more of financial globalization – has created new patterns of behavior and wealth creation. The artificial creation of risks and the "spreading" and de facto transfer of risks to other economic agents by financial intermediaries have been among the most striking and dangerous features of the current age of global finance.

One of the most dynamic and profitable business activities became the creation, buying and selling of new "products," derivatives and other complex "investment vehicles" that were more and more distant from any underlying "non-financial" assets or transactions coupled with the financing of M&A.

While the following two quotes refer to "emerging markets," one could replace the term emerging markets with global markets or the United States.

According to François Bourguignon, Chief Economist of the World Bank:

> Structured financial instruments such as credit default swaps allow investors to better manage exposure to credit risks associated with emerging market external debt portfolios ... [In 2006, despite relatively strong growth prospects] downside risks predominate. Persistent global imbalances, elevated [*sic*] current account deficits in some developing countries, and asset price over valuation are potential sources of risks to growth prospects in developing countries ... Regulators in developing countries need to build their capacity to monitor credit default swap transactions and define a clear line of responsibility and necessary expertise to manage the associated risks.[40]

> Credit default swaps – derivatives that provide insurance against defaults – are being applied in new ways in emerging markets. This has potentially important implications for the pricing and supply of debt capital to developing countries, offering investors a new way to gauge credit risk. By transferring banks' credit risk from lending and trading activities to other market participants, credit derivatives have altered, perhaps fundamentally, the traditional approach to credit risk management and the lending business. While the emergence of this market could improve the ability of financial systems to diversify risk across a greater number of market participants, it remains a relatively immature and potentially vulnerable market ... which carries the risk of a single player could have a devastating effect on the market.[41]

1.3.8 Opportunities

Despite the dramatic turnaround in the economy and in people's minds, the list of advantages and opportunities offered by financial globalization has been impressive. It should be the priority of national and international reform efforts to safeguard these advantages and possibly add to them by reducing sources of instability and inequity. The following list, while not complete, contains several weighty items that would help make sure that "global finance" is not abolished, just as "globalization" should not be reversed:

(1) promote the better utilization and remuneration of savings;
(2) facilitate the integration and growth of the world economy;

(3) increase possibilities in catching-up for emerging economies;
(4) integration into international financial markets and access to sources of finance at competitive rates;
(5) setting of a "market discipline" against reckless national policies;
(6) increase freedom of choice for citizens.

1.3.9 Major risks

The list of risks are just as well known as the advantages, many of which materialized with extraordinary swiftness over recent months and should have received a higher degree of attention: (1) increased vulnerability and fragility, (2) artificial wealth creation; (3) asset destruction; (3) transmission of fluctuations and lack of transparency; (4) amplification of disequilibria; (5) over-compensation of the financial sector at the expense of the "real" economy; (6) growing gap between the "strong" and the "weak," between "winners" and "losers" at all levels; (7) excessive capital flows, and last but not least, as mentioned several times (8) the dangerous shortening of the economic horizon.

The elimination of international rules created new risks along with profitable opportunities for those who saw "risk-management," "risk-sharing" and ultimately "risk-transfer" as a new and expanding field of activity. While banking was always about weighing different types of risks – the two most important being the creditworthiness of borrowers and the outlook for the business environment – gradually short-term "risk-management" and "risk-transfer" became divorced from individual borrowers and "real" economic and market conditions.

1.3.10 The principal risks: The weakening of the responsibilities of governments

In light of the sudden upsurge in the belief in government "regulations" and of the governments urge "to regulate" – the term used in virtually all languages now – as also demonstrated at the London Summit of the Group of Twenty – there is a certain danger that the pendulum might swing too far, too fast. Nevertheless, it remains true that the most important source of systemic risks were found in the passivity or outright indifference shown by central banks and governments toward the risks inherent to the evolution of global finance.

Thus it is important to recall the strong and growing emphasis in recent years on the "private," the "markets" and the resulting redefinition of the division of tasks and responsibilities between the public and the private sector. The scope and responsibilities of governments over international (cross-border) transactions that have greatly diminished at a time when the volume and nature of these movements were increasingly out of hand.

Government responsibilities at the national and international levels, in the area of finance and money, have undergone profound changes that have lead to a growing confusion between "money" and "finance." The answers to the following questions have been long overdue:

> What has happened to national and international solidarity? What has happened to international cooperation? What has happened to the central banks' responsibility for currencies? And finally the most vital question: Did governments still see themselves as the protectors of the common good?

Monetary authorities were concentrating on a single variable: the consumer price index, while abdicating all responsibility, and even interest, in other key indicators of disequilibria such as the price of assets and exchange rates. The theoreticians and authorities believed that they could simply delegate the task of providing global monetary and financial stability to increasingly "sophisticated" and increasingly oligopolistic markets and market makers.

If one of the key components of new rescue operations for financial institutions is to tolerate and encourage the creation of new and even larger financial mastodons that would put the old Soviet Gosbank to shame, (one should remember that, despite the ambitions of its masters for world revolution and for domination, the old Gosbank never had the worldwide presence and clout of the modern mega banks), than clearly reform is on the wrong track.

The system of checks and balances was methodically ridiculed and eliminated from economic and monetary theory by putting up a mathematical smokescreen in hopes of frightening away the "non-initiated."[42]

1.3.11 Monetary nationalism vs. global finance: A fatal dichotomy

The single most important issue has been the acceptance of the absence of "checks and balances," at the international level, as a necessary and inevitable element of competitive markets. Because it was assumed that no checks on market behavior were possible or desirable at the international level, the absence of such prudential rules has become more and more accepted as necessary in assuring a "level playing field" and avoiding the weakening of the "competitive position" of international players who might be "constrained" by national rules.

1.3.12 The challenge of reform

Finance has been at the center of the current crisis. Thus, it is normal that most recent comments, actions and reform suggestions have concentrated on this sector. Successful reform of the financial system is not only an urgent task but it is, and will continue to be, a particularly complex and difficult one. These challenges can be summed up in the following points:

1. In the case of banks and the financial sector, saving and reform are closely interlinked. If banks are not rescued, then there will be little to reform. A deepening crisis in this sector would not only have a profound affect on economic activity, but also threaten a further melting of assets of both households and corporations, not only in the United States but also throughout the world.

2. At the same time, however, there is a real danger in having two different sets of measures: a more supportive treatment being applied to banks on one hand, and a harsher set for the "real economy" of workers, households and corporations on the other. The first sector needs to be bailed out while for the second, harsh rules of the market (the labor market, the credit market, the product markets and not the least the international markets) will apply. Otherwise the world might revert back, many in Brussels, London, New York and Washington will argue, to the morass of subsidies, industrial policies, and regional planning, as well the other "socialist" practices that Mr. Reagan and Mrs. Thatcher were thought to have permanently freed the world from. The belief that governments should simply care for the finance sector and not the real sector, is not only politically and ethically questionable, it is also a matter of poor economics. Unless the "real sector" becomes sound again, the economy, including banks, will not be able to heal. There are many ways to provide a reasonable amount of help to the "real economy" without leading toward a socialist system. These include measures other than the previously proposed Keynesian-based massive spending programs in which the long-term economic and social implications are likely to be higher than many want to admit.

3. The third key challenge is directly related to the downsizing and streamlining of the financial sector itself and the reduction in relative weight (not just the salaries of the top speculators) of finance, particularly short-term finance, within the economy as a whole and its various decision-making functions. However, it is not that finance is of little importance; it has assumed excessive importance at the expense of other equally vital decisions by both companies and households.

4. Finally, as the reader may have noticed by now, the underlying theme of this chapter and the following one is that banks (and their clients) cannot work in a vacuum. The international community has now experienced what happens when the world's leading central banks assume that the care for monetary stability can be outsourced to giant short-term traders and speculators such as JP Morgan, UBS, and Goldman Sachs and Company. The top managers of these organizations are highly intelligent and respectable professionals. However, their job was not and should be even less in the future, to substitute their strategic and short-term market decisions for monetary policy and for the existing or non-existent strategy of the central banks. As long as there are no clear signals, to the domestic and international markets, coming from monetary authorities that will allow the banks to plan their strategies for the short and the long term, the reluctance to provide credit will persist. And to assert that the signals from the central banks and their finance ministry partners have been confused and confusing in the last six months, is probably one of the greatest understatements in the current debate. Unless monetary policy and the international monetary situation and rules become clearer and more predictable, the reform and regulation of the financial system will not make significant progress.

1.4   Globalizaton, the information society and the role of forecasting

It would be difficult to understand the origins and the nature of the current crisis without keeping in mind the close links between globalization, the so-called information revolution, the use of information and the role of forecasting, in particular, in the financial sector.

There is no doubt that the crisis, and the resulting loss of orientation, of all the leading organizations and decision makers, ("we do not know where we are, we do not know where we are going, and we do not really know what we should be doing") represents a real-life example on a planetary scale of a "short-circuit," or *une panne* to use the French expression, of the global information society.

The information revolution created the technical and societal conditions for globalization. If "global finance" was the most important and most pervasive economic manifestation of globalization, as it is argued throughout this book, without the information revolution there would be no financial globalization. Also, those who remember the late 1970s and early 1980s know that telecommunications was the first major sector where deregulation, liberalization and the gradual elimination of the absolute monopolies that had been the rule for decades, even in the most competitive market economies, brought about a seismic change, giving a decisive push to both the information revolution and to globalization. In the pressures that gradually built up and led to telecom deregulation, the needs of the banks for new products and services – not only in the US but also worldwide – played a determining role.[43]

1.4.1   The information revolution and the information society

Probably the single most important factor has been the tremendous thrust of information technologies. But, without the profound changes in regulations, without liberalization at the national and international level, technological progress would have been much slower.

The information revolution is in fact a "permanent revolution" that has been going on for decades and is far from slowing down. By now "information," as a concept and a reality, has penetrated all aspects of human activity. As with electricity, it is difficult to imagine any aspect of modern life without "information."

Some of the main characteristics of the information revolution can be summed up in the following points:

1. The first one is extraordinary progress – through hardware, software and services, and increasingly the three bundled into one – in the speed, quality and cost of (a) collecting, (b) processing and analyzing, (c) storing and (d) diffusing information. This process originally was primarily focused on statistical data (and this has remained a privileged dimension), but digitization rapidly made the distinction between numbers and other forms of information obsolete and, from a technical point of view, irrelevant.
2. The original debate about whether the information revolution will be driven primarily by large interconnected systems (a tool and a force of concentration), or by increasingly user friendly individual "terminals," has become rapidly obsolete. The answer was a resounding demonstration that both large systems and increasingly powerful final user devices would play a crucial role. Similarly changes in hardware, software and services represent both competing dimensions and mutually re-enforcing elements of this same process.
3. By and large, the information revolution has been supply-driven, but it has led essentially to a "buyers' market." Also, and this is probably the most important characteristic of the information revolution, instantaneous access to information, and to all the various state-of-the-art tools of processing, storing, transmitting, etc., of information, has become an essential condition of economic, political and social success (or even survival) throughout the world, in rich and poor, in

developed and developing countries alike, and lack of access a major factor of failure.

4. Digitization has been one of the technological wonders that have made this possible. Digitization means the breaking down of all "information" to infinitely small, standardized "building-blocks." Most people are no longer aware of the miracles that are achieved in facilitating and speeding up (and in reducing the costs) of searching for, managing, processing, storing and transmitting these building blocks that the end-user sees and uses as "information." The dependence is on the reliability and on the robustness of the "systems," of the large ones and of the small decentralized ones such as laptops or "mobile phones" that are much more than phones by now. If the hardware or the software breaks down temporarily or for good, those tiny building blocks are gone, temporarily or forever.

5. Thus the information society has created tremendous sources of efficiency but also of great systemic vulnerability. This is not only vulnerability due to "technical vulnerability" – but also, and perhaps primarily because the fairly frequent dichotomy between the technological potential, on the one hand, and of the ability (or willingness) to use the technological possibilities in an effective and safe manner, on the other hand. It should also be added that "information pollution" is a major brake on efficiency. Finally, the passage from "information" to "knowledge" and to useful "know-how" represents important bottlenecks, as has been apparent most recently in the financial and monetary field.

1.4.2 The role of forecasts

All economic and business decisions – in fact all decisions about human action – are about the future: the immediate, short-term as well as the long-term future. What is short term and what is long term depends on the nature of the field and on the nature and implications of the decisions. Thus, all actions, all decisions involve a more or less important task of explicit or implicit forecasting. To help make those decisions, to prepare and choose the best forecasts, "decision makers" have essentially two sources: a more or less complete, structured knowledge and information of the past, and individual or collective judgment and common sense.

It is in the field of economics and finance that the broadest range of quantitative and qualitative forecasting tools has been developed. These tools require detailed and reliable (and primarily statistical) information of the past, a solid knowledge of the system covered by the models, and state-of-the-art skills in statistical analysis and model building. What is less often mentioned, but for the model builders and forecasters goes without saying, is the requirement of relatively stable and homogenous systems as subjects of the models and of the forecasts.

The technique of economic and political forecasting – as it has developed over the last fifty years – is a combination of art and science. While these techniques are rather good in projecting (in fact extrapolating) trends, they are much less reliable, as a tool, when it comes to pinpoint the timing and the extent of major breaks in trends and of turning points. There is also "timidity," excessive caution in the forecasting community. We are reluctant to believe in the occurrence of the truly "unexpected" – be it good or bad.

The forecasting issue, in the context of the subject of this book, can be divided into two distinct but interdependent questions:

(1) The first one is the question about the functioning of the system and forecasting within the system: how could the timing and the extent of the crisis have been forecast on the basis of key indicators and standard theories?
(2) The second forecasting issue was more fundamental and global. It had to do with the general perspective and consequences and the outlook for the system, as a whole.

The magnitude and suddenness of the current crisis is a clear proof of the malfunctioning and breakdown of the various qualitative and quantitative forecasting systems, on which both official and private decision makers rely, in all the advanced and emerging economies. The French saying *gouverner c'est prévoir* – to govern is to foresee – is valid in a complex, rapidly changing world environment.

These defective forecasts have been due to two major categories and errors and shortcomings:

(1) The first one is incomplete, erroneous and rigid theories and analyses of the complex working of the financial system and of its growing fragility; theories on which the forecasting systems and the actual forecasts have been based. The reliance on shorter and shorter time horizons and on extrapolations of massive data flows, without an analysis or explanation of the underlying economic reality, has been one of the key factors in this trend. The use, in national markets and worldwide, of often arbitrarily selected indicators has been part of this phenomenon.

(2) The poor judgment and lack of common sense of the vast majority of decision makers, who have been ignoring the accumulating warning signs, and their stubbornness and refusal to question the dominant orthodoxy, an orthodoxy that has become more and more rigid and doctrinaire over the years. Thus, while the crisis has been a systemic one, in its magnitude and suddenness, it has been largely the consequence of human error and of poor economic and political leadership – in governments and the private sector alike.

1.4.3   Issues and methods in forecasting

The science and the techniques of economic, monetary and financial forecasting have evolved considerably since the Second World War. The quality of forecasts depends on a number of well-known factors. These include: the complexity and stability or instability of the system for which forecasts are prepared; the quality and volume of data for the (past) behavior of the system; the impact of factors that are exogenous to the system; and the general understanding, of the behavior of the system by the forecaster, based on theory, experience, and last but not least, common sense.

All forecasts are based on an implicit or explicit theory and on an explicit or implicit model. The explicit models may be highly abstract mathematical representations of the assumed working of the economy. Most of the economics teaching, in the last thirty to forty years, has been heavily biased toward this method, where the overload of mathematical hieroglyphics is usually not sufficiently compensated by analyses based on the actual workings of the economy.

Econometrics is trying to bridge the gap between the pure logic of mathematical economics and the "messy nature" of most economic phenomena. Most (not quite all) econometrics is based on statistics of "measurable" (quantifiable) aspects of economics phenomena. The more statistics are available, so the theory goes, the information that they will yield will be more reliable not only about the past, but also about the future. The accuracy of econometric analysis and forecasting depends on the "quality of the data," the correctness of the theory, the degree of sophistication of the statistical techniques and last but not least on the judgment of the model builder and of the forecaster. The theory reflected by the equations of an econometric model is most of the time not quite as pure and elegant as those of a purely mathematical representation. Econometric models, however, are better suited to sow doubt and to question the infallibility of theory.

In practice, there are relatively small models, with few variable and equations, that work quite well and reflect the working of the economy.

And there are very large econometric models, often with hundreds of equations, that are a more detailed and accurate representation of complex economic phenomena, that do not necessarily yield better forecasts. Of course, even in very large models there is a hierarchy of variables and equations, and the models (and the forecasts) are often driven essentially by a handful of powerful variables.

All decision makers, and thus all forecasters, like clear and simple answers about the present and about the future. One of the traditional problems, of all forecasters, is the underlying conservatism of forecasters and their reluctance to move away from the trend or even to forecast a break in trend. Thus, forecasters often miss the extent of crises and also often of periods of prosperity.

In general, one should beware of "single-equation" explanations of the working of the economy as a whole, or of the monetary system.

One of the great paradoxes, in the world of economic and business decision making, is the profound need or a veritable urge for aggregation and simplification for clear signals; for few, if possible, for a single indicator. This is not despite, but because of, the extent and the complexity of the systems. This is clearly the role of indicators such as the "GDP" and in particular of key monetary and financial indicators.[44] It is in fact not the "actual GDP" but the "GDP number" that influences decisions and that drives the models of people who use GDP or any other indicator, as an exogenous variable, to drive their forecasts.

Which indicators are being watched and which are considered as irrelevant is one of the most reliable ways to understand the conventional wisdom and the philosophy behind economic and monetary conditions in most countries and in particular in the United States.[45] It is generally assumed that if enough people believe that a given indicator is important, then it will become important.

The de facto lack of interest in the balance of payments, in exchange rates and in the international dimension of monetary policy has been the most direct expression of the tradition of monetary nationalism that has been firmly accepted by academic economists, business practitioners and policy makers in the United States since the 1970s.

1.4.4   Forecasters and decision makers

One of the recurring questions in the development and use of forecasting tools and of forecasts is: What is more important the *theory* or the *numbers*? Of course, all econometric models incorporate theoretical assumptions, and no decision maker, however doctrinaire she or he may be, can ignore quantitative evidence even if it goes against their deepest convictions. Yet, there are different temperaments and also different experiences that shape the decision-making culture in a given organization at a given time, whether it is a central bank, a finance ministry or banks and other financial institutions.

The more sophisticated the tools and the forecasts, the greater the gap or distance between the teams who prepare the tools and prepare the forecasts, and those who actually use the forecasts in their analyses and decisions. This distance or gap is not only one of knowledge and specialization, but also of responsibility and judgment. Decision makers must bear the responsibility for their decisions and cannot simply pass on the responsibility to the model-builders and the forecasters. In fact most decision makers use several sources or sets of forecasts. They often adjust the forecasts according to their own judgment and flair, sometimes on their own, sometimes with the help of the forecasting technicians themselves.

In fact, few are the politicians and business decision makers, such as the late British MP Jeremy Bray, who are both passionate mathematicians and model builders and at the same time equally concerned about the actual economic outcomes. Jeremy Bray, a highly gifted and skilled mathematician and economist, was equally concerned about the quality of British economic policy making under both Labour (the party to which he belonged) and Conservative governments. He was (probably rightly) convinced that if the government had better forecasts, this would improve its decisions. In order to further this goal, he introduced and succeeded in adopting an amendment to the Industry Act of 1975, requiring the Treasury to publish and make publicly available their macro-economic models, and also the adjustments introduced in the process of actually making their forecasts.[46] While this probably did not make Jeremy very popular in Whitehall, it was an important (and probably unique) blow for democracy in economic policy making.

In 1976 the British Government, on the request of the House of Commons, created a Committee on Policy Optimisation under the chairmanship of Professor R. J. Ball the objective of which was:

> To consider the present state of development of optimal control techniques as applied to macro-economic policy. To make recommendations concerning the feasibility and value of applying these techniques within Her Majesty's Treasury.[47]

In the Conclusions and recommendations in its Report submitted two years later, the Committee noted,

As some witnesses have emphasized, there may be times when the key problem is to design new instruments of policy for which there is, invariably, no historic record. At such times models may help one to pose the problem but they cannot suggest novel solutions except to the extent that the model may tell one that, with existing policy instruments, the particular policy objectives one is seeking cannot be achieved. The main task might be to break certain constraints. This is a different kind of policy constraint from that solved by optimal control.[48]

Such a deliberate break with previous policy approaches and instruments was illustrated in the "Consultation Paper" on *Monetary Control* submitted to the House of Commons another two years later in March 1980 by Sir Geoffrey Howe, Chancellor of the Exchequer in the new Conservative Government of Mrs. Thatcher.[49]

Jeremy's long dissertations, in the House of Commons, on how British monetary exchange-rate and fiscal policy could have been more effective if only the Treasury and the Bank of England would have paid more attention to policy optimization with the help of the available models, was usually received with polite indifference, as is the case when a subject requires a minimum of technical understanding.[50]

The case of Alan Greenspan is particularly instructive. The former Chairman of the Federal Reserve was known and prided himself on being a "numbers-cruncher," one who knew how to concentrate on statistics and how to forecast them, and not to be a captive of abstract, rigid theories. Of course, it turned out, as confirmed for readers of his memoirs, that while he may not have considered himself an orthodox monetarist, he held rather rigid, inflexible and often contradictory views on the basic economic and social issues. At this stage, it is still difficult to judge whether the major policy errors for which he was apparently responsible (and on this there is a fairly broad consensus by now) were due to his misreading the numbers (i.e., technical analytical and forecasting errors) or that his underlying theoretical and ideological views prevented him from seeing the consequences of the policies that he implemented and defended.[51]

1.4.5   Time-horizons, different methods and turning points: Short-term, medium-term and long-term forecasts

All economists know that time is an essential component of all economic theories and analyses: the time it takes for different markets to adjust and to find a new equilibrium, for structural changes to be completed, for policy changes to have an impact, for changes in relative prices to have an impact on micro decisions and on major aggregates like consumption, investments, exports and imports.

Also, all professional forecasters – both model builders and model users – know that the structure of econometric models, both in the basic approach and in the individual equations, tend to differ quite significantly according to the purpose of the model: are they to be used to simulate and forecast the behavior of the economy in the short term (including the very short term), the medium term or the long term?

One of the most challenging tasks in model building and in forecasting is the accurate forecasting of turning points. Major turning points are usually the cumulative result of strains and pressures on the trend. Once these pressures reach a certain degree of intensity, there is a sudden change, a break in the trend, a real turning point has been reached. This change in the trend and its impact and extent are not always easy to detect. They are often confused with minor fluctuations in the trend; in some cases it is only much later that the evidence shows that a major turning point had occurred at one point in the past.

This is an important issue for all markets and all aspects of the economy – from individual sectors and products, through stock markets and to economic activity as a whole. The meaning and the time horizon (and time lags) of turning points are not the same for the different categories of markets and different indicators. With official and private decision makers concentrating almost exclusively on short-term markets and on short-term indicators and forecasts, as has been the case increasingly in the world of "global finance," it is not surprising that they missed the cumulative build-up of tensions between the financial markets and the "real economy" of production, savings, investments and consumption in a globalized economy, tensions that led to one of the most impressive "systemic turning points" in recent economic history.[52]

Turning points are the most difficult to predict. The central question today is: can we make this turning point, that according to all indicators is a turning point for the worse, in the long run a turning point for the better?

1.4.6   Forecasting and the financial system

Transparency and predictability of key variables are essential conditions for the proper working of the financial system, for national economies and the world economy as a whole. This is the role of interest rates, exchange rates, price indicators, GDP numbers, unemployment, or balance-of-payments statistics.[53] They are watched and predicted because their future values may lead to policy changes and/or will directly or indirectly influence markets and other important parts of the system. Transparency and predictability are also among the advantages of a "rule-based system" (provided that the rules are correct and not counterproductive) over a purely "automatic" market-based or a purely "policy-based" system.

Mathematics, models and highly sophisticated algorithms have played an important role in the development of the theories behind "global finance" and of the practice of "financial globalization." There have also been widespread and largely justified critiques of the growing distance between the models and statistical tools and analyses, on the one hand, and the reality that they were supposed to reflect and project. There have been a number of reasons for these developments, including some of the excesses to which they have led, some of them positive, others less so. Initially, it was to forecast and to counter primarily foreign exchange risk that hedging became such a major financial activity. Yet the reliability of exchange-rate forecasting models is highly variable – depending on what "equilibrium rate" is at the basis of the exercise.[54]

The question whether the threat of the financial crisis and breakdown of 2007–08 could have been detected, with the help of quantitative forecasting models soon enough to be prevented, will exercise economists, bankers and policy makers for decades to come. An early attempt to come up with an answer was made by a group of economists at the Bank for International Settlements in Basel. Their analysis and results were published in the *BIS Quarterly Review* of March 2009. The authors, Claudio Borio and Mathias Drehman, came to the not too surprising conclusion that "the coexistence of unusually strong increases in credit and asset prices should have provided a fair warning." And then they added (also reflecting common sense): "the analysis confirms the critical role of judgment. And for some this role may be uncomfortably large."[55]

Quantitative indicators play an important role not only in the models of the market participants, but they are also important in the national and international regulatory systems. However, the ratios and the equations developed, with the objective of making banks safer, can just like trading models have major flaws and lead to major negative unintended consequences. Thus, there is a growing consensus that two major aspects of current "safe banking rules," that is, the so-called mark to market pricing of assets and the capital adjustments to credit risk, had a powerful cumulative pro-cyclical effect, both during the boom period and during the downward phase, and have played a major role in the banking crisis and in the credit freeze.

The ultimate forecasting issue, under the current financial system, has been how to integrate the forecasts produced by computer programs and the buying and selling decisions essentially also made by computer programs. These programs also allow instant calculations of risks and earnings and the costs and benefits of buying and selling decisions. Given the speed and volume of transactions, there is no way that all individual transactions should be the result of individual information and individual decisions. Thus, increasingly winning or losing, in the battle for profits, would depend on the sophistication of the forecasting and trading models of the banks. As margins on any given volume of trading would become lower and lower, those that could generate the largest volume would automatically be ahead of the competitors. This would inevitably further the trend of concentration and the squeezing out of smaller competitors. The idea of assuring the economic and social advantages of competition through a large number of banks and other financial institutions has been replaced by the reality of reckless concentration through mergers and pursuit of unbridled growth strategies.

1.4.7   Moral hazard and the prize-winning forecasting team of Lehman Brothers

By now the name Lehman Brothers has assumed the same place in financial mythology, as the perfect proof of the international financial domino theory, as the Austrian Creditanstalt that was allowed to fail in 1931. It was also the biggest forecasting error by the US Secretary of Treasury and the leaders of the Federal Reserve System, in their assessment of the systemic risks of testing the "moral hazard" theory in the case of a major bank in September 2008.

Ethan S. Harris' book, published by Harvard Business Press in 2008, *Ben Bernanke's Fed. The Federal Reserve After Greenspan*[56] is one of the minor cruel paradoxes of the forecasting business. The copyright of Harris' book belonged to Lehman Brothers. In fact, Harris was Managing Director and Chief US Economist of Lehman Brothers and an award-winning economic and financial forecaster in the American financial community, as testified by both *Institutional Investor* and *The Wall Street Journal*. It is worth quoting what Harris had to say about moral hazard: "If investors know the Fed will always be there to bail them out, they may engage in ever more risky investment behavior. This moral hazard can contribute to the next financial bubble." It is also worth quoting Harris' assessment of both Greenspan and his successor Ben Bernanke: "With a combination of luck and skill, Greenspan presided over a remarkably stable and healthy period of the US economy. He was particularly adept in managing financial crises, striking a reasonable balance between bailing out investors and avoiding a recessionary shock. His success, combined with the growing fascination with the stock market and a growing recognition of the importance of the Federal Reserve, made him a pop culture icon. This is a tough legacy for any successor to live up to." And then the assessment in the summer of 2008, only a few weeks before the fateful Lehman decision (Mr. Harris' bank) of the performance of Chairman Bernanke: "The lesson from [the] review of history is that the Fed did no worse than most of the economics profession in anticipating the depth and the impact of the financial crisis."[57]

1.5   The role of theory and systemic change

Ideas have consequences.[58] *Theory Shapes "Reality"*

Time and events have caught up with us. In fact, the current crisis is also an intellectual crisis, a crisis of the economic, monetary and social schools and theories. Whereas it would have been possible a few years ago to start a broad theoretical debate about the necessary corrective measures of the international monetary and financial system that could have led to effective political action by the leading economies in the world to reform the system, today there is little time for theory; action has come once more before reflection, and as so often, many even in the highest places (in government, in the markets and in the most prestigious universities) believe that this is not a problem. As so often *force majeure* and *fait accompli* will pass for innovation and reform.

One of the most frequent questions that we hear today – and one that will be raised even more frequently in the months and years ahead – is whether the current crisis could have been foreseen and prevented, if we had had the appropriate theoretical insights and had adopted the necessary reforms in time. Some of the major actors of the last 30 years, such as Alan Greenspan, argue that the nature and the extent of the crisis caught them totally by surprise: events of this kind happen only once in a century. The surprise was due to the fact that the dominant theories were not providing sufficient warnings about the defects of the system.

One of the most important features of the current crisis in the world economy is the failure of the dominant theories of the recent decades to help foresee and to prevent the crisis of globalization and of the global financial system. In fact, many of the warnings about the future focused on the developing countries, and not on the center of the world financial system, that is, the United States.

Theories, including economic theories, monetary theories and theories of finance, have multiple purposes. First and foremost they aim at explaining the past. However, they also aim at influencing policies and also, importantly, influencing the structures, the institutions and the behavior of economic actors. The more successful a dominant theory, the more it is shaping behavior and institutional structures – and the more the new reality, the future will differ from the reality that led to the development of this theory.

The fact that theory shapes reality, and thus creates its own need for revision, is true not only for economic theory but also for political theory and the theories of international relations. While Kuhn's explanations of the scientific "paradigms" are useful for understanding how we move from one set of theories to a new one through a "scientific revolution," the "reality," that is, the subject matter of the theories does not really change as a result of the new theories (although in some areas science can also change some of its subjects).

Theory plays an important role not only in research and in policy-making, but also in "shaping the world." The most ambitious theories aim not only to improve conditions, but also to bring fundamental changes into a given system. The systemic changes, brought about by the application of such theories, require new theoretical insights that will be different not only from the theories that used to serve for understanding the "old system," but that will also differ to a greater or lesser extent from the initial theories that led to the creation of the new system. To put it simply: the theories that lead to the creation of a new system cannot yet incorporate the experience of the actual working of the system.

This is eminently the case with the various aspects of economic and monetary theories. Theory helps *explain past and current* trends, as well as specific policies and events. It is a tool for *assessing and judging the quality* of specific policies and the system, as a whole, it is indispensable when *designing policies and implementing recommendations,* and ultimately theories (through the policies they inspire) can lead to *systemic change* which then creates a *"new reality" that requires new theoretical insights.*

1.5.1   The battle of ideas and the rise and fall of dominant schools

The role of "schools" around one or a few dominant scholars (or around their legacy) and strong personalities is a familiar phenomenon in economics, political science, and/or international relations. This fact is well known not only by the specialists but also often by a broader public. These schools can achieve a dominant position to the extent that debate about fundamental issues, in a given field, becomes de facto stifled and any questioning of the fundamental features of this conventional wisdom is considered to be unprofessional. Usually it takes a combination of events and of new scholarly insights to shake the hold of the "dominant school." The paradox of this situation is that those whose views had been relegated to the margins of the profession, and had suffered the intolerance of the "dominant school," often will become as arrogant and as intolerant as their predecessor. This process was first brought to the light in the natural sciences in the remarkable study of Thomas Kuhn on *The Structure of Scientific Revolutions.*[59] Kuhn's analysis fits perfectly well the shifts from neo-classical economics to Keynesianism and then to liberalism and onto monetarism and the domination by the Chicago School of Economics.

On the efforts to shape opinion and policies, in the long run, through research and debate (as distinguished from political organizations or political lobbying), three examples, relevant for the current situation and debate, are discussed later in this section: the Mont Pélerin Society,[60] the Institute of Economic Affairs (IEA)[61] and the Sziràk Seminars (later the Robert Triffin – Sziràk Foundation).[62]

The attached box (Box 1.1) illustrates the sequence of ideas and theories and how a given reality can influence policies, which in turn can change reality, which then calls for changes in theory.

1.5.2   Runaway finance

The questions of the respective role of markets and governments, of monetary and financial factors vs. the "real economy," national autonomy vs. open economies and worldwide integration, and finally competition vs. social equity and solidarity, were at the heart of theoretical and policy debate throughout the last hundred years.

For quite some time, there has been concern about the inherent and growing volatility and fragility of the international monetary and financial system and the economic and social distortions and disequilibria that it has created in a globalized world. There were voices – largely ignored by experts and policy-makers – who have been warning of an impending systemic crisis that could lead to a major backlash that would reverse and even destroy the positive features and achievements of the market economy and of a liberal international economic and political order.

Box 1.1   The role of theory.

To explain – to assess – to guide – to improve – to change

Reality – System (a)

↓

Values – Ideas – Observation – Analysis (a)

↓

Theory (b)

↓

Policy (b)

↓

Reality – System (b)

↓

Ideas (c)

↓

Theory (c)

↓

Policy (c)

↓

Reality – System (c)

etc.

What was the role of the dominant theories in these runaway developments and in the ensuing current global financial and economic changes? The question is whether the central tenet of the dominant theory, according to which all markets, and in particularly financial markets (and especially foreign-exchange markets), are automatically "self-correcting" and tend to reach equilibrium without rules and policy interventions, was correct or not.

The verdict of George Soros, one of the most successful speculators of modern times, is that they are not. Also a prolific writer, in his book on the current crisis, he clearly advocates a "new paradigm for financial markets":

> This is the first time since the Great Depression that the international financial system has come close to a genuine meltdown. That is the crucial difference between this financial crisis and previous ones ... The prevailing paradigm cannot explain what is happening ... The case for abandoning the prevailing paradigm is even stronger: The belief that markets tend towards equilibrium is directly responsible for the current turmoil; it encouraged the regulators to abandon their responsibility and rely on the market mechanism to correct its own excesses. The idea that prices, although they may take random walks, tend to the mean served as the guiding principle for the synthetic financial instruments and investment practices that are currently unraveling.[63]

1.5.3 We were in uncharted waters

"We are in uncharted waters" in international monetary and financial relations – the current theories do not provide adequate guidance for understanding and for dealing with the uncertainties and instability engendered by the simultaneous elimination of common international monetary rules, and the deregulation of the financial and banking sectors that followed in the wake of the breakdown of the Bretton Woods system.

These warnings concerning the need for a new, open debate on how to reduce imbalances and inequities and tensions and crises engendered by the absence of a common monetary order, were often repeated ever since the 1970s.[64] The current situation provides proof that these calls went largely unheeded by policy-makers and market participants, academic experts as well as other opinion leaders.

The principal shortcoming, at the theoretical level, has been the absence of an adequate theoretical framework dealing with global finance, as it has developed since the 1970s. When Alexandre Lamfalussy wrote in 1987 that we are in "uncharted waters," he was referring to the fact that the international financial and monetary system had changed so profoundly since the early 1970s that none of the standard theories could provide a reliable and complete explanation of the working of the system. At the time of Lamfalussy's article, there was no reliable navigational guide, for neither governments and central banks, nor savers, investors, corporations and financial intermediaries. The principal conclusion, of the present volume, is that the situation has not improved during the last twenty years. In fact, the extent of the current crisis is proof that it has further deteriorated.

How did we get here?

Today, when as a result of the crisis of globalization and of global finance, there is once more great uncertainty about the appropriate division of tasks between markets and governments, and the basic organizing principles of the liberal economic and social model are subject to doubts, "we are again in uncharted waters." While current theories and the events of the past are, once more, only imperfect guides for mapping out the future, it is useful to remember the general interaction between theories, on the one hand, and systemic change, on the other hand. These interactions will be briefly illustrated in this section with examples of a number of debates and schools of thought around liberalism, the market economy and the role of the state, and around the desirable features of the international monetary system. They have been also directly relevant to the evolution of globalization and its current crisis.

1.5.4   The great battle of ideas of the twentieth century: Totalitarian regimes vs. free democratic societies and the market economy

The twentieth century witnessed the recurring clash of two age-long European political and intellectual traditions: the ideas and forces of the authoritarian and oppressive tradition, on the one hand, and the liberal and democratic ideas and systems.[65] The most extreme manifestations of the first tradition were the totalitarian ideologies of Communism, on the Left, and of National Socialism and Fascism, on the Right, and the oppressive and aggressive regimes that were built around their organizing principles. The core challenge of the last hundred years has been how to resist the temptations of this first tradition and its outright attacks against the ideas and regimes based on this second, the liberal and democratic tradition. The emergence after the Second World War of a strong community of free, democratic and prosperous nations, with permanent peace among its members – the Western world – has been an extraordinary vindication of the strength and superiority of liberal ideas and of the liberal tradition. Ultimately, it was the success of this domestic and international order based on freedom and cooperation that led to the peaceful end of the Cold War and to the victory of liberal ideas over Communist ideology.

1.5.5   The post-war challenge for economic theory: The issue of the economic role of the state

The principal post-war challenge to theory and policies was the return to the market economy without repeating the errors and neglects of classical laissez-faire capitalism that had been responsible for the economic and societal crises of the first half of the twentieth century, including the rise of collectivist ideologies.

The central question in the economic theory and policy debate throughout the twentieth century was: what should be the economic role of the state, what should be the division of responsibilities between the state and the private sector. The communist ideology called for total control – ownership, planning and all the important decisions – by the state, under the supervision of the Communist party. Yet it was not only the communists who believed that the state had to play a preponderant role in the economy, including the nationalization of key sectors (including the major banks). Those Socialists and Social Democrats who held these views were often strongly opposed to the Communists on political grounds. The Keynesians, in turn, argued that governments had to assume a major role in "managing" the economy, especially through expansionary fiscal and monetary policies, to counter the allegedly structural tendency of the capitalist economy toward unemployment, excess savings and insufficient demand.

During and after the war there was a broad consensus that in order to avoid recessions and high unemployment, it was important to maintain close government controls that had been part of the "war economy" for years, during the hostilities both in the Axis dominated countries and on the side of the victorious Allies. It was especially strongly argued that Germany's war-torn economy could not afford a significant easing of the myriad of restrictions, prohibitions and controls on economic decisions by households or companies. The Allied victory was to bring democracy and freedom – but not an immediate restoration of the free market economy.

1.5.6   Economic and currency reform, the Marshall Plan and the German "economic miracle"

The rapid reconstruction and the spectacular growth of the German economy, following the liberalization of markets in 1948 by the Minister of Economy Ludwig Erhard, simultaneously with the currency reform and the creation of the Deutsch Mark, proved as baseless the arguments that without controls there would be no recovery. The danger that a liberalized German economy would constantly be on the verge of collapse never materialized.[66] The contribution of the Marshall Plan to the recovery of Germany and of the entire Western European economy was threefold. It provided an important resource transfer (which in Germany helped in particular finance investments in both industry and infrastructure. Through the mechanism of the Organization for European Economic Cooperation (OEEC) and European Payments Union (EPU), it jump-started the trade and payments liberalization among the Western European countries,[67] an essential condition for a return to normalcy. And finally, the massive expression of solidarity gave a psychological boost to all the actors in the economy – wage earners, companies, entrepreneurs, and households.

1.5.7   The theory and practice of the "social market economy"

Even after the Marshall Plan, the reconstruction of Europe, and the reduction of exchange controls and quantitative restrictions got well underway and began to show impressive results, important differences remained, at the level of both theory and policies, on the question of the role and the weight of the state in the economy. Britain remained the principal stronghold of the Keynesians and of the supporters of the welfare state, whereas Germany was recognized as the leader in demonstrating the superiority of the market economy over government planning and intervention.

The theoretical basis of the German model, however, was new. It did not mean a return to the classic pre-1939 or pre-1914 laissez-faire philosophy and practice. It was not simply the restoration of "classical capitalism." It was meant to be and in many respects it was the successful "third way."

The model of the so-called social market economy represented a new and original approach between, on the one hand, the Keynesian theories and policies of economic planning, and, on the other hand, the pre-war versions of nineteenth century liberalism of "laissez-faire." The model of the "social-market economy" originated in Germany (under the strong influence of the Swiss experience) and may be considered as one of the most successful political, economic and social models in history.

The model of the "social market economy" was a "radically centrist one." Its essence was defined in the objective: "as much market as possible, and as much State as necessary."

Röpke's writings had great influence in the development of the concept and the implementation of the policies of the "social market economy," which was at the basis of the post-war economic, monetary and social reconstruction of Germany – a process that came to be known as the "German economic miracle."

For Wilhelm Röpke, the principal lesson of the crises of the twentieth century was that neither economic collectivism, (the attempt of complete control by the state of all economic processes), nor the extreme version of nineteenth century laissez-faire liberalism, provided an acceptable theoretical basis for the modern economy and a free political order. It was these two extremes that had been responsible for the economic, political and social crises of the 1930s that culminated in the Second World War. In order to reconstruct a more stable and also more prosperous market economy, it was necessary to recognize that the state has important responsibilities to not only monetary and financial stability but also to avoid excessive economic and market power. These lessons were succinctly summed up: "as much market as possible, as much state as necessary."

1.5.8   Keynesianism and its critics

John Maynard Keynes was without doubt the most inspired and most articulate advocate of international economic and monetary reform. He played a crucial role, during the Second World War, in the efforts to create the common rules and international institutions that would reconcile the three principal dimensions of international economic relations: currencies and the balance of payments, long-term capital movements and trade, the IMF, the International Bank for Reconstruction and Development (IBRD) and General Agreement on Tariffs and Trade (GATT) representing the principal pillars of the new post-war international economic order.[68] His legacy, at the level of ideas and at institutional level continue to influence the terms of the debate up to the current moment – whether one is "Keynesian" or "anti-Keynesian."

While the market economy, linked to representative democracy, was the common basic model, there was constant debate within each country and between the "right" and the "left" about the role of the state in the economy – about planning, price and wage controls, the level of taxation compatible with a market economy, as well as about the respective power of unions and of employers. So-called "Keynesian" economics held sway both at the policy level and among academic economists in many countries for many years – especially the United States and Britain. One of the major preoccupations of Keynesians (as well as of the Socialists) was the alleged limits on domestic policy autonomy (to pursue full-employment policies) resulting from "external balance-of-payments discipline." Deficit countries saw the external account as a constraint on growth; surplus countries saw it as a source of inflationary pressures. The concern with "imported inflation" was a major domestic and international political issue in particular in the Federal Republic of Germany, but also in Switzerland and some of the other continental European economies.

There is no question that in the 1950s and the 1960s, the Kenyesians became more and more intolerant both at the methodological level and in their policy analyses and recommendations. Most of "Keynesians" forgot in fact that the greatest strength of Keynes had been intellectual innovation and his constant search for new solutions to new problems. Thus, there was a justified sense of frustration among non-Keynesian economists, in Europe as well as in the United States. Liberals (in the traditional European sense of the term) did not fail to vent their resentment and in particular their criticism of the (real or alleged) belief of Keynesians in the governments' power of fiscal and monetary policy management and their conviction that the problem of economic fluctuations had been solved for good.

1.5.9   The end of an epoch

The passage, in Britain and in the United States, from the domination of the Keynesian school to the monetarism of the Chicago school in the wake of the breakup of the Bretton Woods System is a well-known story.

The crisis of 1971–3, that is, the destruction of the gold-exchange standard, and the ensuing inflation cum recession, led to the revolutionary triumph of the most extreme form of monetarism, represented by Milton Friedman. Friedman's ideas on international monetary economics – essentially monetary nationalism[69] – became overnight the dominant doctrine in universities, in central banks and in banks and other financial institutions. While even in the United States, strict monetarism à la Friedman was never fully implemented in domestic monetary policy, the hold of his doctrine, of the superiority of floating exchange, continues to hold sway in the United States and at least also in Britain.

A major systemic crisis is usually also the crisis of a dominant doctrine. The vacuum that arises as a result of the crisis (or even the collapse) of a system and of the dominant doctrine allows various schools of thought – that have been waiting in the wings – to move in as the savior to supply the ideas and solutions necessary for reform and systemic reconstruction.[70]

1.5.10   Preparing for the liberal counter-revolution: The Mont-Pélerin Society and the Institute of Economic Affairs

In the post-war period, political and especially economic liberalism were on the defensive even in the Western democracies. Extensive and active interventions and controls of economic decisions and processes (prices, investments, credits, imports, etc.) by governments were seen as necessary and justified by the nature of the modern economy. It was widely argued that without such interventions the problems of unemployment, reconstruction and modernization, widespread shortages, etc. could not be dealt with. This line of thinking had multiple origins: the experience of the controls under the war economy, Marxist-socialist ideology, the memory of the debacle of laissez-faire economics in the 1930s, as well as, the increasingly dominant "Keynesian full-employment economics."

In order to combat these trends and to revive the liberal tradition, the Mont Pélerin Society and the IEA were founded and brought together a large group of scholars from Europe and overseas, primarily North America. Each in its own way made an important contribution to the success of the "liberal revolution."

Yet, while many people, even among non-economists, have heard of Milton Friedman and of University of Chicago economics not only in the United States but throughout the world, much fewer have heard (even in the UK) of Anthony Fisher and of the Institute of Economic Affairs, and certainly even fewer (even among economists) are familiar with the story of the Mont Pélerin Society.[71]

In the context of the impact of ideas and of debate on economic and monetary policies and reforms, it is useful to recall the evolution of these two important initiatives, their initial impact and final outcomes. They are both relevant for a better understanding not only of the intellectual battles of past decades, but also how the evolution, and even the metamorphosis of important and legitimate ideas, initiatives and objectives, have ultimately contributed to the current crisis of the liberal and free-market model.

Friedrich Hayek, a leading theoretical economist, but also the author of the very influential *The Road to Serfdom*, and subsequently recipient of the Nobel Prize in Economics, played an important role in the founding of both the Mont Pélerin Society in 1947 in Switzerland and of the IEA in London in 1955.

The Mont Pélerin Society brought together, in regular annual meetings, liberal economists, philosophers from the various European countries and from the United States. (Many of the American participants were former refugees from Europe.)

Beside Hayek, the most active in the founding of the Mont Pélerin Society, was Professor Wilhelm Röpke, a German refugee at the Graduate Institute of International Studies in Geneva, who was one of the best known and most influential liberal critiques, from the 1930s through the 1960s, of collectivist ideologies and totalitarian regimes of the Right and of the Left, not only in Germany and Switzerland but throughout Europe. It should be mentioned here that from the 1940s through to the 1970s, liberal ideas and liberal policies were part of the mainstream in continental Europe (with the exception of the Scandinavian countries), whereas they were a minority view in the United States and UK. Wilhelm Röpke played a major role in the development of the ideas at the basis of the "social market economy" and of the "neo-liberalism" of the time (not to be confused with the current version of "neoliberalism") that were incorporated into Ludwig Erhard's economic policies and were a major factor in the so-called German economic miracle.

While both liberals and personal friends, Hayek and Röpke differed on the economic role of the state and in their view of the need to reinterpret the classic nineteenth century liberalism. Röpke argued that the classic laissez-faire liberalism bore an important responsibility for the economic and social disasters of the twentieth century and that there was a need for a "third way" between socialism and nineteenth century Manchester school laissez-faire. Private concentrations of economic power were as dangerous, according to Röpke, as government economic planning and control. There is an important division of tasks between the state and private sector. And finally markets and competition are important for an efficient and prosperous economy, but they are not the ultimate source of values in society.

Both Hayek and Röpke believed in the importance of monetary stability and they were both committed internationalists. However, Hayek was much less critical of the classic liberal model and saw less dangers to freedom from markets and private initiative, whereas he rejected the concept of social justice and was much more skeptical of the role of governments even in case of "market failure."

The tensions within the Mont Pélerin Society reflected the differences between the representatives of the continental "social market" views, of which Röpke was the most famous and influential exponent, and those of the more hard-line ultra-liberal doctrine, of which Luwig von Mises, and increasingly Milton Friedman, were the most prominent exponents.

In the case of the IEA, the hard-line liberals had a more dominant role from the start. The pronounced differences, at the level of liberal theory and policies, combined with personal intrigues within and between the Mont Pélerin Society and the IEA, undermined the health of Röpke and were probably a major cause of his untimely death in early 1966.

The Institute of Economic Affairs was more centered on sponsoring research and publications than the Mont Pélerin Society and, especially in the beginning, it was primarily focused on British problems. Its objective was to promote the idea of liberalism and the market economy as an alternative to the dominant theories and policies involving extensive government interventions in the British economy, through high quality, well-researched, well-argued scholarly publications. Over a period of 20 years, the IEA managed to establish the radical liberal view as a credible theoretical and policy alternative of the dominant Keynesian and government interventionist schools.

The economic and monetary crises of the 1970s, and in particular the failure of fiscal stimulus and of government interventions in production and investment decisions, the price and wage controls and the inflation and rise in unemployment, provided the terrain for a major "shift in paradigm." The analyses and policy recommendations contained in a long series of IEA publications were ready to be tested. In fact, the IEA and its US sister organizations (in the founding of which Anthony Fisher also played an important role) provided a substantial portion of the theoretical and policy basis of the "Thatcher revolution" in the UK and of the "Reagan revolution" in the US.

1.5.11 Social market economy vs. ultra-liberalism

While largely recognized as responsible for the post-war "German economic miracle," over the years the principles of the social market economy, in one form or another, became the common policy framework for most of the continental European economies – without being necessarily under this label. In Germany, from the 1970s onwards, the Social Democrats, who were initially strongly opposed to this model and to Ludwig Erhard's policies, accepted the basic principles of the social market economy. In fact, under German influence the development and the strengthening of a "competitive social market economy" became one of the basic objectives of the European Union, as defined in the text of the European Constitution and of the Treaty of Lisbon.[72]

Yet, ultimately the social market economy lost out against the much more radical British and American neo-liberals. The current crisis is the culmination of that lost battle. In fact, even the German (and the Swiss) academic community had abandoned the theories of the "social market economy" in favor of the much more elegant and clear-cut – but also more extreme – theses of the dominant Anglo-American approach to economics.

One of the major paradoxes of economic history and of economic thought on which economists and economic policy makers in the United States and in Britain, from the right and from the left, agreed upon was their inability and their unwillingness to understand what the social market economy stood for.[73]

There is no doubt that the turn to more liberal and more market-oriented theories and policies was welcome and highly overdue in general and in particular in the United Kingdom and the United States.

However, it was clear already at the time, and it has become increasingly clear over the last thirty years, that it was highly unfortunate that the most radical version of the liberal doctrine – Friedman, von Mises, Hayek prevailed – rather than the more balanced ideas of Erhard and Röpke. From one extreme, constant growth of government interventions, the world rapidly went to another extreme, that is, "market fundamentalism" where all government is evil and markets and private companies, can do no wrong. This became increasingly evident, as the original reasoning and the often legitimate and nuanced arguments as well as conclusions, were gradually replaced by doctrinaire statements. The "Young Turks" of monetarism and of the market economy became just as arrogant and intolerant of dissent as the "Keynesians" had become – after Keynes was no longer there – in the 1940s and 1950s.

1.5.12 The debate on the international monetary system and the end of Bretton Woods

A number of issues have been at the heart of the debate in the twentieth century on international as well as domestic monetary order. A key issue is the role of (commodity) reserves and automatism vs. discretionary management, convertibility into gold or other currencies for some or all transactions, stable (fixed) or freely floating exchange rates. The central, recurring questions have been: What should be the role of "market automatisms" and what should be the scope of "policy"? What are the legitimate interests of the individual states in the monetary field and what are the common interests and the common rules to be respected by the members of the international community in the monetary field? And ultimately, which standard, which monetary order is compatible with international economic integration and which is the equivalent in the monetary area of protectionism in the field of trade?[74] Regionalism vs. universalism was and remains an important dimension of this issue.[75]

The 1960s saw a widespread debate on the reform of the international monetary system. The start of this debate followed only shortly the effective beginning of the "full Bretton Woods System" for the

European countries with the establishment of overall current account convertibility at the end of 1958. The end of the "post-war period" (and the end of the European Payments Union) signaled the end of currency discrimination against the US dollar in Europe on balance-of-payments grounds.[76] Robert Triffin's economic and political bestseller on *Gold and the Dollar Crisis* gave a powerful new boost to the debate that never really ceased, about the adequacy and shortcomings of the Bretton Woods system and the constraints for deficit countries and for surplus countries of the balance-of-payments rules of the IMF.[77]

The central themes of Professor Triffin's attacks on the Bretton Woods system and of his proposal for fundamental reform can be summed up in the following points: the international liquidity problem; the inequity of the use of the dollar as a reserve currency and the problems resulting for the US balance of payments; the insufficient supply of gold; the replacement of the dollar by a new commonly managed reserve (which became the Special Drawing Rights (SDRs) with the First Reform of the IMF at the end of the 1960s).

The following brief comments and quotes may be added to the discussion in section 1.2. of this chapter, which deals with "The End of Bretton Woods and the Victory of Monetary Nationalism."

In the 1950s and 1960s the debate about the reform of the international monetary system, as noted above, dealt with two sets of closely related issues. The first one had to do with the main "technical" aspects and characteristics of the international monetary system: the exchange-rate mechanism, international reserves and balance-of-payments adjustment process, and the role of capital international capital movements. The second group of questions had to do more with the broader and more fundamental political questions and preferences, such as the objectives and basic organizing principles of national and international economic and monetary order. Those who were for maintaining a system of stable exchange rates were also the ones who were ready to accept "external discipline" as a welcome aspect of an integrated, liberal world economy. Those who were for floating exchange rates rejected external discipline in the name of the goal of absolute national monetary and economic sovereignty.

In the early 1950s Milton Friedman argued, in an article that twenty years later became, and remains today, the *locus classicus* for all the advocates of floating exchange rate:

> The sooner a system of flexible exchange rates is established, the sooner unrestricted multilateral trade will become a real possibility.

> *And it will become one without in any way interfering with the pursuit by each nation of domestic stability according to its own lights.*[78]

At the "technical level," of course, Friedman's forecast turned out to be utterly wrong. As was noted by the present writer in the early 1980s:

> It is undeniable that without the relative stability provided by the system of fixed exchange rates and the gold-exchange standard the degree of international economic integration achieved by the early 1970s would have been inconceivable. The economic history of the 1950s and 1960s shows that fixed exchange rates were a *condition sine qua non* for the progress of trade liberalization … The post-war international monetary system … for over twenty years had come under unrelenting criticism from right and left. Liberal critics had insisted that … the balance-of-payments discipline was not strict enough; others, more inspired by the Keynesian fear of imported deflation … argued that the gold-exchange standard put an excessive constraint on domestic policy autonomy. *The system of fixed exchange rates was a key part of this external discipline itself.*[79]

As for the "political part," the second sentence of the paragraph quoted above revealed Friedman as the veritable *Trojan horse* of monetary (and hence also of economic) nationalism.

This was echoed thirty years later by Rudiger Dornbusch in an article in the *Brookings Papers*:

> There is no reason to believe that countries today are more prepared to live by an international rule than they were in the 1920s and 1930s. The one important difference is that now we believe we know how to achieve stability, and it is certainly not by going along with the rest of the world, whatever may be happening there.[80]

Prominent academic economists have been insisting ever since not only on the alleged "technical" advantages of floating exchange rates, but also on the alleged "political" desirability of isolating American policy-making from "outside influences." Thus, they are as responsible as the political leaders, for transforming the United States from the principal architect and defender, into the principal obstacle to a stable and liberal international monetary order.

1.5.13 Continuing the search for a rule-based monetary system: The Szìràk Conferences and the Robert Triffin-Szìràk Foundation

> An international monetary system is easier to destroy than to rebuild. It was easy enough for a few amateurs in a few hours to wreck the international monetary system in August 1971(See full quote above)[81]

The Szìràk Conferences and the Robert Triffin-Szìràk Foundation attracted a very wide range of well-known and highly competent academic scholars and other experts. The quality of the papers and of the discussions was remarkable. Nevertheless, Szìràk was less known and has had less direct influence so far than the much better known Mont Pélerin Society and IEA. Nevertheless, the focus of Szìràk on international monetary order and monetary internationalism, makes the debates and the outcomes relevant in the current situation and for the new, unfolding debate on the objectives and the process of international monetary reform in the years ahead.

The first Szìràk conference on international monetary issues was held in 1986. This meeting of a group of international monetary experts, and the following series of conferences held at fairly regular intervals until about 1998, and the publications that were based on the papers and the debates were essentially the result of the ideas, the dedication and hard work of Miklos Szabo-Pelsöczy, an American economist of Hungarian origin.

In terms of ideas and objectives Szabo-Pelsöczy was directly inspired by Professor Robert Triffin, one of the great monetary statesmen of the twentieth century, who until his death actively participated in the meeting and in the "Szìràk process." Szabo-Pelsöczy had known Professor Triffin from Yale. Some of us, like the present writer, knew Triffin from the Graduate Institute in Geneva, where he had also lectured during several summers.

In organizational terms, and as a concept of organizing a debate on international monetary order outside the recognized academic venues of dominant orthodoxy, Szabo-Pelsöczy's original inspiration came from the three-day conference on *The New Economic Nationalism* organized by the present writer in 1978 at the Battelle Memorial Institute in Geneva, Switzerland.[82]

While not all of the Szìràk participants, were 100 percent "Triffinites" on all issues, the example of Robert Triffin, his deep concern for international monetary order, his capacity both to innovate and to adjust his proposals to circumstances, his mastering of the technique and of all the political complexities of international monetary order, were an inspiration for all of us in the younger generation.

Triffin was both an intellectual fighter and a diplomat. In a long and exceptionally productive professional career he never lost sight of the ultimate goal: a stable and equitable international monetary order. He made decisive contributions to some of the key international monetary reform projects of our time: the European Payments Union (EPU), the first reform of the Articles of Agreement of the IMF (the introduction of the SDRs), the European Monetary System (EMS), and ultimately also to the concept of the European Monetary Union. He did not live to see his ultimate goal realized: the creation of a stable, equitable and universal international monetary order.

At the Sziràk conferences there was a wide range of views among the participants on the various aspects of the monetary system and of monetary reform. There was, however, a consensus on the need for global monetary reform, not only because of the smaller economies, but also in the long-term interests of the United States. For many of us, the end of the Cold War, the peaceful victory of the liberal Western model of domestic and international order, was seen as a historic opportunity for a "grand design" also in the international monetary field. However, such a grand design was developed only at the regional, Western European level. Szabo-Pelsöczy and the present writer were not the only ones who believed that this was a major missed opportunity – a "sin of omission" not only by the United States, but also by the Western Europeans and Japan.[83]

Ultimately, the Sziràk conferences lost their momentum – and when the foundation moved to Belgium, the country of origin of Robert Triffin, its dedication to the goal of international monetary reform was lost in the maze of traditional academic politics. Yet, there is no doubt that today and in the months and years ahead, the spirit of the debates and some of the ideas developed at Sziràk could be valuable for the efforts to reform the international monetary system.

1.6   International order and the "western community"

1.6.1   Nationalism vs. internationalism

Since 2007, the economic and monetary role of states and their governments has been rediscovered with a vengeance. This, however, should not lead to more, rather than less, nationalism. In fact, nationalism has played a significant role in the malfunctioning of the monetary and banking system as well as the outbreak of the crisis. Nationalism, rather than internationalism, has been the source of most of the suffering, destruction, violence, and oppression in the 20th century. It was also one of the major contributors to the economic crises that the world has witnessed in the last hundred years. Today, there is an urgent need for a truly international spirit and approach to creating a stable and efficient international monetary and financial system. It should be based upon the principle of subsidiarity rather than the concepts of centralization and uniformization. Internationalism means that where there is international activity, there is also a need for common legislation and basic rules of behavior. It is not simply meant for the rule of the biggest and strongest.

Internationalism is not possible without pluralism and diversity. In a truly international order, the rights and interests of small and large countries are equally respected. But there is no true international order without common basic values and mechanisms for reconciling real or apparent conflicts of interests. Internationalism does not mean the end of national sovereignty. However, it does put firm limits on the external and internal abuse of sovereignty by governments or private groups.

From the second half of the 1940s until 1990 there have been three "international orders" or "international sub-orders" in the world: (1) the "Western community" of free societies, democracies and market economies (2) the communist countries, and (3) the so-called Third World.

The basic organizing principles of the "Western community" (where, of course, Western was not meant in geographic terms) were simple and straightforward: (1) in political terms, democracy and the respect for freedom and human rights; (2) in economic terms, competition and social solidarity, as well as, international economic integration regionally and worldwide; and (3) in terms of security, perpetual peace among the members of the community (war has become "unimaginable" between even countries that had gone to war countless times in the past), with common deterrence and defense against military or ideological threats from the left or the right. It was a community built upon common interests and values. Respect for the rights of the weaker and smaller nations was an essential feature of this community. There was never a better time to be a small country in the Western community than during the post-war decades.

1.6.2   Democracy, freedom and the market economy

It was the strength, the cohesion and the extraordinary record of economic prosperity and social progress, of this open-ended community, that led to the peaceful end of the Cold War. This was during a time when most people in the East and West had given up hope that they would see the fall of Communism and its ideological values within their life time.

This was an extraordinary historical moment and a unique opportunity to extend the basic organizing principles of the "Western community" to the rest of the world: those of freedom and democracy, of peace and cooperation, market economies, and the integration of solidarity at the national and international level.

Much has been achieved over the last twenty years, but the current crisis is the result of several factors: the difficulties of "transition" from dictatorship to democracy, countless "internal wars" that led to untold violence and suffering on four continents, and the rise of new forms of ideological and religious extremism. A significant portion of the failure to create a truly new universal international order belongs to the members of the Western community themselves: to the European, to the Japanese and of course also to the Americans. Conceit, jealousy, egotism, and the lack of historical perspective kept them from being able to transmit the essence of their unique experience in building the most successful community of free peoples in the history of mankind – to transmit this experience to those who desperately wanted to "catch up" but at the same time also wanted to "remain themselves." This concept was key to the success of the Western community but this was a lesson they could not transmit to the countless countries suffering from overly strong or weak governments, from poverty, inequality and endemic violence. The substitute, the "ersatz" that we gave them was "globalization." Globalization was important, but it was only half of the story. The other half, the complex political skills and patience needed in free national and international communities, we failed to transmit. Not only did we fail to transmit it to the many new and/or failed states, but we also began to forget to incorporate it into our relations with each other in the "enlarged Western community."[84]

The foundations of the Western community are extremely solid. But even such a strong and resilient community cannot afford to be taken for granted without a clear understanding of its importance by political leaders, the public or the academic community. The hubris that we are currently experiencing might not have occurred if our political parties, businessmen, economics professors and historians had had a better understanding of what it took in terms of innovation, dedication, cooperation and sheer staying power to build the Western community of free societies.

This means that the key to overcoming the crisis of the world economy must be to find a similar combination of unity, diversity, bold innovations, prudence, clear values and organizing principles that had helped to save the world from the nightmare of unfree ideologies, as well as the aggressive, oppressive and inefficient political and economic regimes; twice within the twentieth century.

Democracy and the market economy should be the models to which people aspire in order to make sure that the principles of liberal free societies will not be, once more, on the defensive in our countries and in the rest of the world. This is not only in order to save our own peace and living standards; it is in the best interest of the entire international community.

According to the present author, as it will be argued in the next chapter, a crucial test case for our ability to rise to this challenge will be whether we are able to build a new international monetary order.

Notes

1. "The period since the 1970s has witnessed an unprecedented pace of change in both domestic and international monetary order. One of the most striking developments has been the globalization of financial markets, and the simultaneous loss of power of domestic and international official institutions. Parallel with the globalization of financial flows, there have been attempts at regionalization, and efforts to impose uniform (deregu-lated) rules on financial institutions operating in what are today still very different economic environments. Many of the features of this new world are positive and should be recognized as such. Nevertheless, politicians and the general public are increasingly concerned about the domestic and international monetary system and about the reforms that continue to aim at increasing the weight of the markets and reducing the responsibilities of national and international monetary authorities. Increasingly it is felt that the *pendulum may have swung too far* and that once more the time has come for a fundamental rethinking of our assumptions about the role of money in the economy and about the appropriate monetary and financial policies and institutions in the 'good society'—at the national level and in the world at large. The need is particularly great to redefine fundamental objectives and the respective roles of government rules and markets and private interests, and to recreate conditions for effective international co-operation in this field." Otto Hieronymi (1998), "Agenda for a New Monetary Reform," in *Futures*, vol. 30, no.8, pp. 769–81, Pergamon, Elsevier Science Ltd.
2. "The article (1998) does not offer set solutions for all these issues. Its conclu-sion is, however, that without such a debate and a consensus on a balanced new approach, there is a real threat of a backlash, the threat of losing the advantages of liberalization and globalization and of a return to increased monetary and economic nationalism and to excessive government inter-vention and control" (Otto Hieronymi (1998), "Agenda for a New Monetary Reform").

3. The contrast between theory and reality was already obvious, as the number of major auditing firms was dangerously shrinking as a result first of mergers and subsequently through fraud and mismanagement at one of the remaining majors. The situation was similar in the banking sector, as can be illustrated by the example of JP Morgan Chase. JP Morgan Chase was already a huge bank by any standards at the start of the financial crisis, with the assets and liabilities representing roughly the equivalent of ten percent of the US GDP. Yet, as a result of the crisis and of the government orchestrated rescue operations, its balance sheet increased by another 25 percent and exceeded for the first time $2 trillion. It should be also mentioned that JP Morgan has been one of the great innovators in the field securitization and a dominant force in the derivative market. Thus, according to the office of the US Controller of the Currency, at the end of the 3rd Quarter of 2008, the "notional amounts of derivative contracts held for trading" by JP Morgan Chase amounted to more than 50 percent (close to $80 trillion) of the total held by US banks. The total amount of "derivative notionals" in the US increased from less than $5 trillion in 1990 to close to $170 trillion by mid-2008. Virtually this entire amount represented "dealer notionals," with so-called end-user notionals never reaching 2 percent of the total. Office of the Comptroller of the Currency (2008), *Quarterly Report on Bank Trading and Derivative Activities*, third quarter 2008, OCC, Washington, DC, 2008. It is worth indicating the order of magnitude of the world total of derivative trading and the factors that are considered relevant for its evolution. According to the BIS, in the 4th quarter of 2008, total turnover on "international derivative exchanges based on notional amounts decreased to $408 trillion from $543 trillion in the previous quarter. The decline in trading activity reflects a confirmation of significantly reduced risk appetite, expectations of stable low interest rates in major markets and lower hedge fund activity." Bank for International Settlements, (March 2009), *BIS Quarterly Review*, BIS, Basel, March 2009, p. 27.

4. Otto Hieronymi, "Political Order and Universal Values in the 21st Century," in *Humanitarian Values for the 21st Century, Proceedings of the 7th Annual Humanitarian Conference of Webster University*, Refugee Survey Quarterly, vol. 21, no. 3, pp. 126–34, UNHCR, Oxford University Press, 2002; Otto Hieronymi, "The Spirit of Geneva and Globalization," in Otto Hieronymi and Kathleen Intag (Editors): *The Spirit of Geneva in a Globalized World*, Refugee Survey Quarterly, Oxford University Press, vol. 26, no. 4, 2007, pp. 274–305.

5. The late Professor Kindleberger, a prominent student of a broad range of the past financial crises, did not believe in the inevitability of financial crises. Cf. Charles P. Kindleberger and Robert Z. Aliber, *Manias, Panics and Crashes. A History of Financial Crises*, fifth edition, Palgrave Macmillan, London, 2005. Cf. also Alexandre Lamfalussy, *Financial Markets in Emerging Markets. An Essay on Financial Globalisation and Fragility*, Yale University Press, New Haven and London, 2000.

6. By now there is a vast literature on the advantages and shortcomings of globalization. In recent years the debate had become more and more virulent between the two extremes: unconditional defenders of the current version of globalization and those who reject the market economy and all liberal ideas on ideological grounds. Probably the best-known and most serious critique of globalization is Professor Joseph Stiglitz. As a high-ranking member

of the national and international policy establishment in the first half of the 1990s (in the Clinton Administration and in the World Bank), he was a relative latecomer to the issue of "international economic and monetary reform." He made up for this with the intelligence, clarity and productivity of a world-class Nobel-prize winning economist. Cf. for example: Joseph Stiglitz, *Globalization and its Discontents*, Penguin Books, London, 2002; also Jagdish Bhagwati, *The Wind of the Hundred Days, How Washington Mismanaged Globalization*, The MIT Press, Cambridge, Mass., 2002 and Jagdish Bhagwati, *In Defense of Globalization*, A Council on Foreign Relations Book, Oxford University Press, 2004. Professor Bhagwati, while an ardent defender of globalization from the point of view of both the developed and the developing economies, rightly (according to the present writer) sees the lack of social dimension as the Achilles heel of globalization and a major cause of a potential protectionist backlash. Cf. also Martin Wolf, *Why Globalization Works. The Case for the Global Market Economy*, Yale University Press, New Haven and London, 2004 and Martin Wolf, *Fixing Global Finance*, The Johns Hopkins University Press, Baltimore, 2008.

7. This may have been the case of the President of the Swiss National Bank who in a long interview in November 2008 revealed that the Swiss National Bank began to work on contingency plans to come to the rescue of UBS already in the fall of 2007. Roth, Jean-Pierre, "Wir Schweizer sind ein Volk von Uhrenmachern," Interview, *Neue Zürcher Zeitung*, Zürich, 1–2 November, 2008.

8. Ben S. Bernanke, "Presentation of the *Semiannual Monetary Policy Report* to the Congress," before the Committee on Banking, Housing and Urban Affairs, U.S. Senate, Washington, DC, February 24, 2009.

9. Alan Greenspan compared the position of central bankers today to that of a "U.S. Airforce B-2 pilot who (does not) know, or *need (not) to know*, the millions of automatic split-second computer-based adjustments that keep his aircraft in the air." Alan Greenspan, *The Age of Turbulence. Adventures in a New World*, The Penguin Press, New York, 2007, p. 490. Greenspan did not elaborate on *what happens to the plane* in case of engine trouble and after the pilot has ejected.

10. Paul Volcker, "Globalization and the International Financial System," A speech at a dinner honoring the 72nd birthday of His Majesty King Bhumibol Adulyadej, Bangkok, Thailand, January 27, 2000.

11. Paul Volcker, "The Implication of Globalism is Globalism," The Joseph I. Lubin Memorial, Stern School of Business, New York, April 20, 1999.

12. Alexandre Lamfalussy, *Financial Markets in Emerging Markets. An Essay on Financial Globalisation and Fragility*, Yale University Press, New Haven and London, 2000, p. 172.

13. Robert A. Mundell, "Optimum Currency Areas," Extended version of a luncheon speech presented at a *Conference on Optimum Currency Areas*, Tel- Aviv University, December 5, 1997.

14. For a listing of the major exchange regimes cf. quoted in Shalendra D. Sharma, *The Asian Financial Crisis. Crisis, Reform and Recovery*, Manchester University Press, Manchester, 2003, p. 324.

15. Cf. Otto Hieronymi, *Economic Discrimination against the United States in Western Europe, 1945–1958, Dollar Shortage and the Rise of Regionalism*, Librairie Droz, Geneva, 1973.

16. Robert Triffin, *Gold and the Dollar Crisis,* revised edition, Yale University Press, New Haven, Conn., 1961.
17. Cf. Otto Hieronymi (Editor), *The New Economic Nationalism,* Macmillan, London, 1980.
18. Robert A. Mundell, "Optimum Currency Areas."
19. A major representative of German monetary nationalism was SPD Minster of Economy Karl Schiller who is reputed to have coined the term "aussenwirtschaftliche Abschirmung" – keeping out external economic influences – and who claimed to be a disciple of the Social Market Economy, despite his evident lack of faith in European and international economic convergence and integration. In fact, the "official" or "self-proclaimed" guardians of the tradition of German "neo-liberalism" – whether they were Socialists or Conservatives or leading lights of the Bundesbank like the late Otmar Emminger – showed a large dose of disdain for the "weaker, less virtuous economies" (the list included not only Italy, France and Britain, but also the United States) that were congenitally unable to keep their house in order and that were likely to infect the more stable, more virtuous "strong currency countries." Fortunately, two outstanding chancellors – Helmut Schmidt and Helmut Kohl – had the courage to go against the current and against the monetary nationalism of the Bundesbank and of the German academic establishment, realizing that without exchange-rate stability within Europe in the long run the future was going to be bleak for economic and political integration in Europe.
20. A typical example of this phenomenon was Rimmer de Vries, Chief International Economist of Morgan Guaranty Trust at 23 Wall Street, who for many years was probably the best known and most influential international bank economist in the US. Rimmer de Vries, the creator and editor of Morgan's highly successful and respected monthly publication *World Financial Markets,* who had never wrote anything in favor of floating before August 1971, never used this forum to raise questions about the long-term consequences of the effective end of international monetary cooperation and of the post-war international monetary system. As in every other bank publication, there was not much in *WFM* that went against the views of Morgan's top management. Yet, in those days the management of Morgan Guaranty was sufficiently convinced of the importance of *ideas,* if Rimmer (given his strong personality and the respect he enjoyed within and outside the bank) had had serious qualms about floating, the issue would have found its way into the pages of *World Financial Markets.* Cf. also Rimmer de Vries, "The International Approach Towards the US Balance-of-Payments Problem," in Otto Hieronymi (Ed.) *The New Economic Nationalism,* pp. 62–79.
21. International Monetary Fund, "Article IV of the Fund's Articles of Agreement: An Overview of the Legal Framework," prepared by the Legal Department in consultation with the Policy Development and Review Department, June 28, 2006.
22. Robert Triffin, "Foreword," in Miklos Szabo-Pelsöczy (Editor), *The Future of the Global Economic and Monetary Systems,* (2nd Sziràk Conference, 1988), Budapest, 1990, p. 29.
23. Quoted in Nicolas Krul, "The Enduring Voice of Hayek," manuscript, London, 1995, p. 10.

24. Paul Volcker, "Globalization and the World of Finance," *The 2001 Hutchinson Lecture*, University of Delaware, April 30, 2001.
25. Robert Mundell, "Monetary Nationalism and Floating Exchange Rates," in Otto Hieronymi (Editor), *The New Economic Nationalism*, Macmillan, London, 1980, p. 40.
26. One of the principal studies on the nature of monetary nationalism – and on its incompatibility with a liberal international economic order – is still Hayek's classic 1937 statement: Friedrich A. Hayek, *Monetary Nationalism and International Stability*, Augustus M. Kelley, Reprints of Economic Classics, New York, 1937, 1964. In the vast literature that has developed on the *oeuvre* of Hayek since the 1970s this seminal work is very rarely mentioned and for obvious reasons. A rare exception is the study by a remarkable historian of political and economic theory: Alan Ebenstein, *Friedrich Hayek, A Biography*, The University of Chicago Press, Chicago, 2003. On Hayek and the rejection of monetary nationalism see also: Otto Hieronymi, "In Search of a New Economics for the 1980s: The Need for a Return to Fixed Exchange Rates," *Annals of International Studies*, Institut Universitaire de Haute Etudes Internationales, vol. 12, Geneva, 1982, pp. 107–26; Otto Hieronymi (Editor), *The New Economic Nationalism*, Macmillan, London, 1980.
27. Cf. HELLEINER, Eric and PICKEL, Andreas: *Economic Nationalism in a Globalizing World*, Cornell University Press, Ithaca, 2005.
28. Otto Hieronymi, "Agenda for a New Economic Reform."
29. Friedrich Hayek, *Denationalisation of Money*, Institute of Economic Affairs, London, 1990, p. 80, quoted in Alan Ebenstein, *Friedrich Hayek, A Biography*, The University of Chicago Press, Chicago, 2003, p. 278.
30. On Friedman's monetary nationalism cf. Otto Hieronymi, "In Search of a New Economics for the 1980s."
31. Friedrich A. Hayek, *Monetary Nationalism and International Stability*.
32. Robert Mundell, "Panel Session II: Implications for International Monetary Reform," in Michael Bordo D. and Barry Eichengreen (Editors), *A Retrospective on the Bretton Woods System. Lessons for International Monetary Reform*, A National Bureau of Economic Research Project Report, University of Chicago Press, 1993, p. 609.
33. Among those whose theories have been receiving renewed attention in recent months is Hyman P. Minsky and in particular his writings about the inherent instability of financial markets. It is interesting to note that in his extensive discussions about the various aspects of financial instability – of its nature, sources and consequences – Minsky pays very little attention to the international dimension of the issue and in particular to the role, positive or negative, of international order or of its absence on financial markets. Cf. Hyman P. Minsky, *Can "It" Happen Again? Essays On Instability and Finance*, M. E. Sharpe Inc., Armonk, N.Y., 1982; Hyman P. Minsky, *Stabilizing An Unstable Economy*, McGraw Hill, 1986, 2008; and Hyman P. Minsky, *John Maynard Keynes*, McGraw Hill, New York, 2008 (first edition 1975). Minsky was a participant in the 2nd Sziràk Conference held in 1988, where he did address international financial issues and the exchange-rate regime. Cf. Hyman Minsky, "Money Manager Capitalism, Fiscal Independence and International Monetary Reconstruction," in Miklós Szabó-Pelsőczy (Editor), *The Future of the Global Economic and Monetary Systems*, (2nd Sziràk Conference, 1988),

Budapest, 1990, Institute for World Economics of the Hungarian Academy of Sciences, pp. 209–18.

34. Otto Hieronymi, "Les responsabilités des gouvernements et les enterprises à l'époque de la finance globale," unpublished manuscript presented at Modena Office of Confindustria, 14 March 2008.

35. For a similar view cf. Tommaso Padoa-Schioppa, *La Veduta Corta. Conversazione con Beda Romano sul Grande Crollo della Finanza*, Il Mulion, Bologna, 2009.

36. The objective of the so-called Tobin tax – first proposed by the famous Nobel-Prize winning economist James Tobin – was twofold: to create an international source of income for the benefit of the developing economies by levying a small tax on cross-border financial transaction, and at the same time reducing the volume of these astronomically large short-term flows.

37. Diversification into financial activities has become a common strategy for large industrial companies

38. On the various categories of financial risks, including "artificial risks," cf. Otto Hieronymi, "Agenda for a New Economic Reform"; and Paul H. Dembinski, *Finance Servante Ou Finance Trompeuse?* Parole et Silence, Desclée de Brouwer, 2008, pp. 81–8.

39. One of the dangerous paradoxes for economic and financial stability is the contrast between, on the one hand, the claim of contemporary financial theorists that information is the key factor in managing economic risk and financial innovation and financial engineering help households, savers, companies and banks obtain the necessary information for the functioning of "efficient markets", and, on the other hand, the virtual impossibility for the average economic decision-makers to penetrate the thicker and thicker wall of mathematical wizardry that protect the insiders, "those few who know and understand" both theory and market practice, and those who have access neither to the models nor to the "information" fed into the models. A typical example of a combination of rather simplistic (and questionable) assumptions and conclusions about both "finance" and the economy at large with an overdose of abstract mathematical presentation is the following successful book: Jean-Pierre Danthine and John B. Donaldson, *Intermediate Financial Theory*, 2nd edition, Elsevier Academic Press, Amsterdam, 2005.

40. World Bank, *Global Development Finance. The Development Potential of Surging Capital Flows*, World Bank, Washington, DC. 2006, pp. xi–xii.

41. World Bank, *Global Development Finance. The Development Potential of Surging Capital Flows*, p. 6.

42. The fact that many sophisticated political and business leaders cannot "read" the "basic" texts and "professional articles" on finance and money says a lot about the economic professions intellectual limitations in communicating with economic actors. In one of his numerous books on finance and economics, George Soros wrote (tongue-in-cheek) that he was "not very good in mathematics."

43. The banking and finance sector has been one of the most eager customers of these new technologies. In fact, the information revolution has greatly helped this sector to catch up with manufacturing in terms of productivity and modern management techniques and has allowed this sector to achieve a veritable leap-frogging in many respects. In all businesses, and in fact in all areas of modern society and the modern economy, the information

revolution has led to: greater flexibility, greater freedom, and simultaneously (although this may sound paradoxical) to both greater decentralization and greater powers of concentration and centralization. Having said all this, it is a dangerous fallacy to believe that banking and finance are just like any other business. This is, in fact, one of the most questionable features of the current monetary philosophy. It is a fundamental error to believe that the objectives and the framework of domestic and international order can or should be determined primarily by technology. The goal is not to slow down or reverse technological progress. Modern information and telecommunications technologies are a tool that can and should to be mastered, in order to create the appropriate regulatory framework of monetary order, at the national and the international level. Understanding this issue has to be one of the principal items on the agenda of monetary reform.

Otto Hieronymi, "Agenda for
a New Monetary Reform"

44. "(The) Fed has really only one tool – changing the funds rate," in Ethan S. Harris, *Ben Bernanke's Fed. The Federal Reserve After Greenspan*, Harvard Business Press, Boston, Mass., 2008, p. 12.
45. It was reported, at the time, that former German Chancellor Helmut Schmidt was stunned when, in a conversation in late 1989, Mr. Gorbachov had no information on and showed no interest in the evolution of the money supply in the Soviet Union.
46. Cf. *Hansard, Commons Sitting, Dr. Jeremy Bray, 6.41 PM*, House of Commons Daily Debates, 2 December 1993.
47. Committee on Policy Optimisation (Chairman Professor R. J. Ball): *Report Presented by the Financial Secretary to the Treasury by Command of Her Majesty March 1978*, Her Majesty's Stationery Office, London, 1978, Cmnd 7148, p. v. See also Jeremy Bray, "The Making of Economic Policy," *The Times*, London, April 19, 1978.
48. Ibid., p. 104.
49. *Monetary Control, A Consultation Paper by HM Treasury and the Bank of England, March 1980*, Her Majesty's Stationery Office, London, 1978, Cmnd 7858.
50. George Cooper, in his recent book on the origin of financial crises, suggests that central banks should be provided with models that would incorporate the principles of control system engineering first developed by James Clerk Maxwell in 1868. George Cooper, *The Origin of Financial Crises. Central Banks, Credit Bubbles and the Efficient Market Fallacy*, Vintage Books, New York, 2008, pp. 133–40. It may be mentioned in this context that Jeremy Bray, while briefly associated with Battelle, tried as early as 1972–3 to develop and market a series of on-line short-term forecasting models for the major European economies, incorporating the principles of controls theory. However, we had to find out at Battelle Geneva that while there was a market for the *Prospect* program's forecasts in Europe (with and without models), the market was not ready yet for the application of control theory. The situation may be different by now.
51. Fleckstein and Sheehan in their "indictment" of Greenspan put the emphasis on Greenspan's allegedly dismal record, as a professional forecaster,

    going back to the early 1970s and then moving forward to the end of the "Greenspan Era" in 2007. Cf. William A. Fleckenstein with Frederick Sheehan, *Greenspan's Bubbles. The Age of Ignorance at the Federal Reserve*, McGraw Hill, New York, 2008.

52. On systemic turning points cf. Otto Hieronymi, "A Turning Point for the Better or the Worse? The Current Outlook for International Order," *Foresight, Journal of Future Studies and Strategic Thinking and Policy*, vol. 6, no. 4, pp. 204–07, Emerald Group Publishing Ltd, 2004.

53. Of course, there are times when there is a need to reverse a trend and to "break expectations" through deliberate and even drastic policy measures. A classic case was the sharp monetary tightening introduced by the Fed in 1979 under its new Chairman Paul Volcker. One may wonder to what extent the decision in September 2008, by the Fed and by the US Treasury, to let Lehman Brothers go under was inspired by a similar logic: "Let us shock the markets into discipline and let us show that playing on 'moral hazard' is not rewarded." Whatever the motivations of the Lehman decision, it is clear that it reflected one of the gravest economic and financial forecasting errors of this generation.

54. Cf. Ashby Mccown, Patricia Pollard, and John Weeks, *Equilibrium Exchange Rate Models and Misalignments*, Occasional Paper NO.7, US Department of the Treasury, Office of International Affairs, Washington, DC., 2007.

55. Bank for International Settlements, *BIS Quarterly Review*, BIS, Basel, March 2009, p. 44.

56. Ethan S. Harris, *Ben Bernanke's Fed. The Federal Reserve After Greenspan.*

57. Ethan S. Harris, *Ben Bernanke's Fed. The Federal Reserve After Greenspan*, pp. 70–1 and p. 184.

58. Borrowed from a famous American political philosopher: Richard M. Weaver, *Ideas Have Consequences*, The University of Chicago Press, Chicago, 1948.

59. Thomas S. Kuhn, *The Structure of Scientific Revolutions*, The University of Chicago Press, Chicago, third edition, 1962, 1996.

60. An excellent recent study provides a fascinating, detailed history of the Mont Pélerin Society: Philip Plickert, *Wandlungen des Neoliberalismus. Eine Studie zu Entwicklung und Ausstrahlung der "Mont Pélerin" Society*, Marktwirtschaftliche Reformpolitik, Schriftenreihe der Aktiengemeinschaft Soziale Marktwirtschaft, Lucius & Lucius, Stuttgart, 2008. If Plickert's has one shortcoming it is that he overemphasized the "personality" issues, and underestimates the importance of the difference at the level of values and conclusions, between, on the one hand Wilhelm Röpke and his disciples, and, on the other hand, the more extreme "Manchester type" mainly American (especially Friedman) and English liberals and the Institute of Economic Affairs.

61. On the "intellectual path" leading to the Thatcherian revolution cf. Richard Cockett, *Thinking the Unthinkable, Think-Tanks and the Economic Counter-Revolution, 1931–1983*, Harper Collins, London, 1995. Beside a thorough discussion of the history and role of the Institute of Economic Affairs, Cockett also discusses the role of the Mont Pélerin Society. Both Cockett and Plickert provide fascinating about both theories and personalities. Fridrich Hayek played an important (intellectual) role in the creation of both the Mont Pélerin Society and the IEA. One of the most interesting and most influential personalities in this story was Anthony Fisher, without whom the IEA would not have developed and thrived, and probably the history

of Britain and of the world might have taken a somewhat different course. Fisher was a successful businessman, courteous and direct, not snobbish or pretentious in the least, but driven by an important cause: liberalism and the market economy. While scholars like Friedman and Hayek remain household names years after they dies, relatively few people knew of Anthony Fisher, and even fewer of the work he accomplished, even during his life time.

62. The initiator, the organizer, and the driving spirit was Miklos Szabo-Pelsöczy, an American economist of Hungarian origin. The following are the principal Sziràk publications: Miklós Szabó-Pelsőczy (Editor): *Fifty Years After Bretton Woods*, (Sixth Conference of the Robert Triffin-Sziràk Foundation, Brussels 1994), Averbury, Aldershot, 1996; Miklós Szabó-Pelsőczy (Editor), *The Global Monetary System After the Fall of the Soviet Empire*, (In Memoriam Robert Triffin – 1911–1993, Sixth Conference of the Robert Triffin-Sziràk Foundation, Sziràk, 1993), Averbury, Aldershot, 1995; Miklós Szabó-Pelsőczy (Editor), *The Future of the Global Economic and Monetary Systems*, (2nd Sziràk Conference, 1988), Budapest, 1990, Institute for World Economics of the Hungarian Academy of Sciences; Miklós Szabó-Pelsőczy and Gusztáv Báger (Editors), *Global Monetary and Economic Convergence. On the Occasion of the Fiftieth Anniversary of the Marshall Plan*, Ashgate, Aldershot, 1998; Miklós Szabó-Pelsőczy (Editor), *The Future of the Global Economic and Monetary System With Particular Emphasis on Eastern European Developments* (Foreword by Otto Hieronymi) Robert Triffin-Szirak Foundation, Budapest, 1993.

63. George Soros, *The New Paradigm for Financial Markets. The Credit Crisis of 2008 and What It Means*, Public Affairs, Perseus Group, New York, 2008, pp. 100 and 102.

64. Cf. Robert A. Mundell and Jacques J. Polak (Editors), *The New International Monetary System*, Columbia University Press, New York, 1977; Otto Hieronymi (Editor), *The New Economic Nationalism*, Macmillan, London, 1980; Otto Hieronymi, "In Search of a New Economics for the 1980s"; Alexandre Lamfalussy, *Financial Markets in Emerging Markets. An Essay on Financial Globalisation and Fragility*, Yale University Press, New Haven and London, 2000; Paul Volcker and Toyoo Gyothen, *Changing Fortunes: The World's Money and the Threat to American Leadership*, Times Books, New York, 1992.

65. Cf. Otto Hieronymi, "Political Order and Universal Values in the 21st Century," in *Humanitarian Values for the 21st Century, Proceedings of the 7th Annual Humanitarian Conference of Webster University*, Refugee Survey Quarterly, vol. 21, no. 3, pp. 126–34, UNHCR, Oxford University Press, 2002.

66. Cf. Wilhelm Röpke (1953), "Deutschland – Massengrab falscher Voraussagen," reproduced in Wilhelm Röpke, *Gegen die Brandung*, Eugen Rentsch Verlag, Zürich, 1959, pp. 206–18.

67. On the Marshall Plan OEEC and EPU cf. Otto Hieronymi: *Economic Discrimination Against the United States in Western Europe, 1945–1958. Dollar Shortage and the Rise of Regionalism*, Librarie Droz, Genève, 1973.

68. Cf. Keynes' famous speech in the debate on the International Monetary Fund in the House of Lords on May 23, 1944, in Seymour E. Harris (Editor), *The New Economics, Keynes' Influence on Theory and Public Policy*, Augustus M. Kelley, Reprints of Economic Classics, New York, 1965 (First Edition 1947), pp. 369–79. See also: Richard Gardner, *Sterling-Dollar Diplomacy, Anglo-American Collaboration in the Reconstruction of Multilateral Trade*, Clarendon

Press, Oxford, 1956 and Robert Skidelsky, *John Maynard Keynes, Volume 3: Fighting for Britain, 1937–1946*, Macmillan, London, 2000.

69. On Milton Friedman and monetary nationalism cf. Otto Hieronymi, "In Search of a New Economics for the 1980s: The Need for a Return to Fixed Exchange Rates."

70. Thomas Kuhn's famous theory of "scientific revolutions," developed for the evolution of "hard sciences" fits perfectly well the case of economics, politics and international relations. Thomas S. Kuhn, *The Structure of Scientific Revolutions.*

71. Otto Hieronymi, "Wilhelm Röpke, the Social Market Economy and Today's Domestic and International Order," in Otto Hieronymi, Chiara Jasson, and Alexandra Roversi (Editors), *Colloque Wilhelm Röpke (1899–1966), The Relevance of His Teaching Today: Globalization and the Social Market Economy*, HEI-Webster University, Cahiers HEI, Geneva, 2002; Richard Cockett, *Thinking the Unthinkable, Think-Tanks and the Economic Counter-Revolution, 1931–1983*, Harper Collins, London, 1995; Philip Plickert, *Wandlungen des Neoliberalismus. Eine Studie zu Entwicklung und Ausstrahlung der "Mont Pélerin" Society*, Marktwirtschaftliche Reformpolitik, Schriftenreihe der Aktiengemeinschaft Soziale Marktwirtschaft, Lucius & Lucius, Stuttgart, 2008.

72. Cf. On the original analysis of the need to confront the dual danger of "collectivism" and of extreme "Manchester type liberalism," that have been jointly responsible for the political, social crises of the interwar period, see the famous trilogy of Wilhelm Röpke, one of the principal contributors to the development of the successful post-war German and European model: Wilhelm Röpke, *The Social Crisis of Our Time, Civitas Humana* and *International Order*, first published in German in 1942, 1944 and 1945 respectively, all by Eugen Rentsch Verlag, Zürich. See also *Mass und Mitte*, (1950) also published by Eugen Rentsch. See also Wilhelm Röpke, *International Economic Disintegration*, William Hodge, London, 1942.

73. The confusion that still prevails about what the "social market economy" stands for was also partly due to the fact that there never was a single text or textbook that would have defined (especially not using mathematical logic) what the model was about. Moreover, with a few notable exceptions, there was little effort either by Germans or the Swiss to try to explain and to spread beyond the borders of their countries the principles and the working of this model. Theo Waigel, at the time German Federal Minister of Finance in April 1994 told the author of the present article point blank: "The social market economy is not an export article."

74. Robert Mundell, "Monetary Nationalism and Floating Exchange Rates," in Otto Hieronymi (Editor), *The New Economic Nationalism*, Macmillan, London, 1980, pp. 34–50 and Robert A. Mundell and Jacques J. Polak (Editors), *The New International Monetary System*, Columbia University Press, New York, 1977.

75. On the impact of the post-war balance-of-payments debate and of the theories of a so-called permanent dollar shortage on the shift toward regionalism and on the origins of European integration cf. Otto Hieronymi, *Economic Discrimination Against the United States in Western Europe, 1945–1958. Dollar Shortage and the Rise of Regionalism*, Librarie Droz, Genève, 1973.

76. Cf. Otto Hieronymi, *Economic Discrimination Against the United States in Western Europe*.
77. One of the best sources for appreciating the wealth of analyses and arguments in this debate are the famous Princeton Essays in International Finance, published by the International Finance Section of Princeton University.
78. Quoted in Otto Hieronymi, "In Search of a New Economics for the 1980s: The Need for a Return to Fixed Exchange Rates," in Otto Hieronymi, *International Order – A View From Geneva, Annals of International Studies*, Institut Universitaire de Hautes Etudes Internationales, vol. 12, Geneva, 1982, p. 114.
79. Ibid., pp. 114–15.
80. Quoted in. Ibid., p. 118.
81. Robert A. Mundell, "Optimum Currency Areas."
82. Otto Hieronymi (Editor): *The New Economic Nationalism*.
83. Otto Hieronymi, "The Case for an 'Extended EMS': A New International Monetary Order to be Built by Europe, Japan and the United States," in Miklos Szabo-Pelsöczy (Editor), *The Global Monetary System After the Fall of the Soviet Empire*, (In Memoriam Robert Triffin – 1911–1993, Sixth Conference of the Robert Triffin-Sziràk Foundation, Sziràk, 1993), Averbury, Aldershot, 1995, pp. 57 67
84. Cf. Otto Hieronymi and Daniela Bensky, "The Outlook for the Post-War Western Model of International Order and the Prospects for Perpetual Peace," *Paper presented at 8th International CISS Millennium Conference*, Paris, June 13–15, 2008.

2

An Agenda for the Reform of the International Monetary System

Otto Hieronymi

2.1   From crisis management to long-term reform

It is clear that beyond the level of crisis management that largely prevailed in late 2008 and in the early months of 2009, there is also a need for more systematic and balanced long-term reforms. The growing awareness of the need for longer-term reforms was reflected in the debate that led up to the London Summit of the Group of 20 (G20), in the "Global Plan for Recovery and Reform" adopted by the 20 participants on April 2, 2009 and in the several more detailed texts also adopted by the G20. A first reading of these texts confirms the strong desire to create an atmosphere of positive change, of broad national actions and of international cooperation.[1]

The London Summit, both the common text and declarations made by individual leaders, including those of President Obama, President Sarkozy and Prime Minister Gordon Brown, confirm two major impressions that have been gained over the months since the full outbreak of the crisis last year. The first one is that the leaders and their advisers are carefully avoiding some major issues, such as monetary reform as distinguished from financial regulation, and how far the major players are willing to cut down on their own nationalism. The second one is that the "experts" do not seem to fully admit, and the political leaders do not realize, the complexity and duration of what will be a protracted reform process.

The objective of the present chapter is not to try to provide a blueprint for the final outcome of this reform process, but to indicate some of the key issues and objectives and conditions of success.

There are four interdependent sets of challenges and tasks in the reform process. They all require political leadership and close international cooperation (and less nationalism), trust and agreement on basic objectives and organizing principles.

1. The first one is dealing with the impact of the crisis, including the measures that have been adopted, in the wake of the crisis, as part of national and international crisis management.
2. The second one is the creation of a new rule-based international monetary order that will allow a permanent break with monetary nationalism. This is the most important and probably the most difficult challenge.
3. The third one is the re-dimensioning of the banking and financial system.
4. The fourth is reforming the current model of globalization and strengthening the liberal and democratic international order through a better balance between national and international interests and also between competition and solidarity within and between states.

Designing and implementing reforms will require clear ideas and determined leadership. There is room, but only limited room, for trial and error. There is no space, however, for "turf wars," or for intellectual or bureaucratic speculative infighting. There is a need for modesty and a sense of community and cooperation from organizations (such as the leading Treasuries and central banks, the leading universities and think tanks and professional associations and, last and not least, bodies such as the International Monetary Fund (IMF), World Bank or the European Central Bank (ECB)) that individually and collectively have been in a state of denial about the fragility of the world's financial and monetary system.

As a result, today a new balance has to be found between "the real economy," "the monetary dimension" and "finance." Profound reforms must be made at both the level of "ideas" and at the level of "rules," of structures and modes of behavior, while there is a need for a soft lending in the bloated network of speculative flows, contracts and hedging operations.

While the goal of these reforms is ambitious, the process will have to be informed by a sense of urgency: there is not much room for error and there is no acceptable alternative to success.

The reform has multiple dimensions:

- Short-, medium- and long-term tasks
- Reforms at the global and at the national and regional levels
- Reforms at the level of governments, central banks and of banks and financial institutions

What must kept in mind, by all, is that in defining and creating international order the definition of the objectives and of the organizing principles comes before political decisions and technical solutions. This is as true for international monetary order as it is for the political or security dimensions of international order.[2]

2.2 The objectives and scope of creating a new international monetary order

The following are the principal objectives of an international monetary system: (a) help integrate free economies; (b) help avoid distortions in international competitive positions; (c) provide "external discipline" and help protect against massive monetary and economic policy abuses by small and large countries; (d) prevent the exploitation of the weaker by the more powerful (beggar-my-neighbor policies); (e) last but not least: provide "politically acceptable" external constraints on fiscal or monetary excesses (inflation or deflation).

The crisis of 2007–09 has been the latest, and so far the most sudden and extensive, in the series of monetary and financial crises that followed the end of the rule-based international monetary order of the 1970s. The need for more systematic cooperation has been evident to many for a long time[3] but it was also denied by important decision makers despite the mounting evidence.[4]

The central thesis of the present book is that if recurring crises are to be avoided, and the world economy is to return to a path of sustained and sustainable growth, the ultimate goal of systemic improvements has to be the fundamental reform of the international monetary system; what is needed is a clear break with monetary nationalism and a return to monetary internationalism.[5]

The reform of the banking system and stricter supervision of financial markets alone, however important and urgent they are, will not solve the fundamental problems that initially led to the current crisis. Unless dealt with, they will continue to threaten the achievements of globalization and the liberal international economic order.

The key elements of the objectives, organizing principles and architecture of the international monetary order of the future can be summed up in the following points:

1. The system should be rule based, rather than linked to gold or any other commodity, and on cooperation between governments and central banks.

2. It should be based on non-discrimination and open competitive market economies. Its organizing principles should also include "solidarity" and "equity."

3. Its central objective should be to provide a framework and a mechanism for an integrated world economy, where trade and capital movements contribute to general economic prosperity.

4. The system should allow room to reconcile its central objective, i.e., international monetary stability, with a certain degree of flexibility in order to be able to cope with structural changes in the world economy.

5. There has to be a clear division of tasks and responsibilities between central banks and governments and banks and other market actors. Central banks and governments have to be responsible for monetary policy and stability, including currency stability. These functions must not be delegated to the private sector.

6. The design and the function of the system have to address the following major functions and issues:

   a. The overall balance-of-payments issues, including the transfer of resources and the prevention and correction of "global imbalances."

   b. The exchange-rate issue. Governments and central banks have to be responsible for external price stability as they are responsible for fighting inflation at home and they cannot "outsource" the issue of exchange rates to futures markets. The "surveillance approach" is clearly insufficient.

   c. The issue of capital movements.

   d. The question of international reserves and international liquidity.

   e. Fiscal and monetary discipline and the balance between freedom and constraint on national policies.

   f. The role of the central banks.

7. The system has to be designed and function as a "federal" or multi-layered system with different degrees of "monetary independence" or "monetary integration" for different countries or groups of countries, such as, for e.g., the European Monetary Union (EMU). Global rules, as well as the rules for the different degrees of integration into the system, will have to be clearly defined from the outset. There is no question that this will be not only the most important, but also the most challenging part of the reform process.

8. There is a need for fundamental reform of the IMF, if it is to play a major role again. Its scope has to be broadened, to include the

international monetary order as a whole, and should not be limited to dealing only with "emerging" or "developing" countries or only play the role of "international crisis manager." Should a major reform of the IMF Articles of Agreement prove to be politically impossible, there is the need to create a new institution.

9. The role and responsibilities of the Bank for International Settlements (BIS) will have to be expanded. It could become the effective center for monetary and currency coordination and also assume operational functions within the system. Its links with the IMF (or the new institution to be created) will also need to be clearly defined.

10. Finally, the new international monetary order will have to be based on the principle of political cooperation of democratic societies and the reconciliation of the interests of large and small countries alike.

2.3   Elements of a new international monetary system

In this section, some of the key issues will be briefly discussed in general terms, without technical details. In the following two sections, the reform of the IMF and the combination of the "regional" and "universal" approach will be discussed.

2.3.1   The issue of the balance of payments: Limiting global imbalances

One of the key objectives of a rule-based international monetary order has to be to limit the development of major imbalances between national economies – in the interests of both deficit and surplus countries – without recourse to restrictions on trade and on capital movements.

The balance of payments of national economies used to be one of the most widely discussed issues among professional economists and in the world of political debates. The balance of payments is the accounting system that allows one to assess net movements of goods and services (tangible resources and the ownership and title of assets – liquid financial reserves or less liquid direct investments). As an accounting balance, the balance of payments is in equilibrium by definition.

The economic and policy debate centered around three interconnected issues:

1. What are the principal factors responsible for the deficits or surplus in the so-called current account and what is their impact on the general well being of the population? Is it lax public policies, is it too much private spending, or is it a loss of competitiveness? Are the factors responsible

mainly domestic or external? Is it due to the short-term economic situation or is it more structural or even systemic? Is it better to have a surplus or a deficit? Are deficit countries "weak"? Are surplus countries "strong"?
2. What is the role of exchange rates? What is the role of financial transactions that, in accounting terms, are the balancing item to the current account? Are exchange rates important in the disequilibrium or not? Are they or should they be the global price indicators between a given country's goods and services and the rest of the economy?
3. Are "balance-of-payments" disequilibria an essential issue or an unimportant one, not only for national economic, policy-making but also for the international economy as a whole? Are they an obstacle for the development of an integrated, open economy?

From 1945 onwards, for a quarter of a century, these issues were at the center of the economic policy debate for the major developed economics not only in Europe, but also in the United States.

During this period, the dominant answer to these questions was: Yes, the current account is very important; exchange rates ought to be as stable as possible because they are a key anchor in monetary stability as a whole; and finally, the current account balances were eminently a common issue. There was both national responsibility in dealing with them and an international solidarity to help ease the "adjustment process," and common rules to be followed in avoiding major imbalances that were assumed to threaten international trade and international economic integration.

As a result of the so-called gold-exchange standard, the rules applied to the United States were different from those applied to other economies. Some economists emphasized the greater constraints, others a greater degree of freedom (even an obligation) to run current-account deficits.

2.3.2 "Restoring" the balance of payments

One of the consequences of the absence of the rule-based system since the 1970s was the "abolishing of the current account" for the powerful developed countries, whereas for the weaker countries the balance-of-payments constraints became even greater. Alexandre Lamfalussy wrote more than twenty years ago:

> Sometime in the 1970s it became fashionable among an active and influential section of academic economists to dismiss the traditional concern of policymakers with the current account of the balance of payments. Whatever respect I may have for the ability of market forces

to correct even large and sticky imbalances, I am still unconvinced by the counterargument. The economics profession has not been able to provide us with even a remotely satisfactory understanding of how exchange rates are determined. Since we are navigating in truly unknown waters, only future experience will tell us whether the current financial revolution, which combines innovation and domestic deregulation with international financial integration, increases or reduces the fragility of the financial system, or to be more precise, whether it heightens or lessens the risk that a local financial crisis may be rapidly transmitted to the world.[6]

The ability of the major economies, and in particular of the United States, to disregard imbalances between domestic savings and investments in the absence of balance-of-payments discipline, was described by Alan Greenspan:

Implicit in the movement of savings across national borders to fund investment has been the significant increase in the dispersion of national current account balances. In recent years, the negative tail of the distribution of current account balances has been, of course, dominated by the U.S. deficit. The decline in home bias, as economists call the parochial tendency to invest domestic savings at home, has clearly enlarged the capacity of the United States to fund deficits. Arguably, however, it has been economic characteristics special to the United States that have permitted our current account deficit to be driven ever higher, in an environment of greater international capital mobility [...]. All told, home mortgage debt, driven largely by equity extraction, has grown much more rapidly in the past five years than during the previous five years. Surveys suggest that approximately half of equity extraction shows up in additional household expenditures, reducing savings commensurately and thereby presumably contributing to the current account deficit.[7]

The consequences resulting from the lack of concern for balance of payments in the current situation were eloquently summed up by Alan Greenspan's successor, Bert Bernanke:

The world is suffering through the worst financial crisis since the 1930s, a crisis that has precipitated a sharp downturn in the global economy. Its fundamental causes remain in dispute. In my view, however, it is impossible to understand this crisis without reference to the global imbalances in trade and capital flows that began in the latter half of the 1990s. In the simplest terms, these imbalances reflected a chronic lack of saving relative to investment in the United States and some other industrial countries, combined with an extraordinary increase in saving relative to investment in many emerging market nations [...]. The global imbalances were the joint responsibility of the United States and our trading partners, and although the topic was a perennial one at international conferences, we collectively did not do enough to reduce those imbalances. However, the responsibility to use the resulting capital inflows effectively fell primarily on the receiving countries, particularly the United States. The details of the story are complex, but, broadly speaking, the risk-management systems of the private sector and government oversight of the financial sector in the United States and some other industrial countries failed to ensure that the inrush of capital was prudently invested, a failure that has led to a powerful reversal in investor sentiment and a seizing up of credit markets. In certain respects, our experience parallels that of some emerging-market countries in the 1990s, whose financial sectors and regulatory regimes likewise proved inadequate for efficiently investing large inflows of saving from abroad. When those failures became evident, investors lost confidence and crises ensued. A clear and highly consequential difference, however, is that the crises of the 1990s were regional, whereas the current crisis has become global.[8]

While everyone agrees that these imbalances are a major problem, there has been no political will, at least so far, to reintroduce rules that would help to prevent and correct such developments, not only in the case of developing countries (where IMF conditionality has been a dreaded weapon), but also for the powerful economies. Simple "consultations" lead nowhere.[9]

2.3.3   Monetary policy and exchange rates

The most important element in any sound monetary system is that monetary policy be predictable. In a firmly fixed exchange-rate system, the key component is that there is little if any expectation of a change in the exchange rate because the monetary policy of the country is automatically geared to making that exchange rate an equilibrium rate.

No one claims that floating rates have fulfilled the claims made by their proponents. At most their defenders can assert that it is difficult to replace them with a "better system." Yet, it is on the subject of exchange rates that the orthodoxy of the last 35 years has become the most deeply entrenched, both on the Left and on the Right. There was no reference to negotiating a new exchange-rate regime at the G20 Summit in London, and this seems to be of little concern to the authors of the "Stiglitz Report" (including Stiglitz himself) prepared for the General Assembly of the United Nations.

The views of Bert Bernanke, expressed in a speech five years ago at a Cato Institute Conference, do not seem to have changed as a result of what has happened in recent months "on his watch":

> For the economically advanced nations that use the world's three key currencies – the euro, the yen, and the dollar – I believe that the benefits of independent monetary policies and capital mobility greatly exceed whatever costs may result from a regime of floating exchange rates. My view is widely – though not universally – shared among economists and policymakers. In particular, what was once viewed as the principal objection to floating exchange rates, that their adoption would leave the system bereft of a nominal anchor, has proven to be unfounded.[10]

Yet, without a rule-based exchange-rate system it is difficult to imagine the restoration of the balance-of-payments discipline and the reduction in the scope and volume of international currency speculation and erratic currency fluctuations. It is not enough to "regulate"; it is more important to reduce or eliminate the market incentive for speculation.

The only reservation that one can formulate about this quote, from Robert Mundell, is that the importance of rules for the "superpower" has, by now, been fully demonstrated:

> I have long believed that the interdependence of exchange rates and balances of payments in the world economy could best be managed multilaterally. It is true that the rest of the world needs an international monetary system much more than the United States. In the absence of an international monetary system, the superpower dominates and bilateral bashing replaces multilateral rules. Although superpower pre-eminence will be apparent even in an international monetary system, there is at least a set of rules that apply equally and a multilateral framework for resolving disputes.[11]

It has been argued that one of the principal causes of the systemic crisis was the reduced role of central banks. This narrowing of the role of central banks was partly due to the criticism of central bank policy from Milton Friedman in general and during the Great Depression in particular,[12] and of the general "single variable" approach to policy objectives favored by the various monetarist clans.

The fixation of most central banks (including the ECB) on a narrowly defined inflation target (de facto the consumer price index), while ignoring fluctuations in other prices such as exchange rates and financial asset prices, has been one of the major shortcomings of central bank policy in the last thirty years. The de facto prohibition imposed on the ECB to show concern about the general economic situation, apart from inflation, in the member countries is only the most extreme example of this theoretical and practical fallacy.

At the same time, there has been a growing divorce between money and monetary policy and finance and financial markets. By gradually reducing the role of banks, both as collectors of savings and as providers of credit, in favor of new actors and new instruments and practices ("financial engineering"), the regulatory and prudential role of the central banks has been seriously undermined. This development, i.e., the triumph of the "market approach" over the "banking approach" was welcomed as a source of greater efficiency (in the allocation of savings one has to assume) even by cautious and experienced financial experts.

2.3.4   The issue of international capital movements

Among the multiple causes of the current crisis, the increasing disconnection between general economic rationality, on one hand, and the direction and the vertiginous volume of speculative capital movements, on the other hand, comes very close to the top of the list, if not the very top.

Yet, if a useful function is perverted, if traffic, because of the lack of road signs, of speed limits and other rules to prevent reckless driving, leads to murderous accidents and traffic jams, the answer is not to abolish the function or to ban the traffic. The instability and the inequities generated by the vast amount of speculative capital transactions almost killed international finance and jeopardized the future of the liberal, integrated and open world economic order. This is not a reason to return to exchange controls (and even less of outright prohibitions) on international capital movements, but it is clear that the issue of capital movements has to be at the heart of the debate on international monetary and banking reform.

All cross-border payments, the objective of which is not to pay for trade in goods and services, falls under the accounting definition of "international capital movements." In the theory of international economic relations, international capital movements have a similar rational and positive explanation to imports and exports. By allowing the movement of capital, from countries where capital (i.e., savings) is abundant to countries where it is more scarce, capital movements, like trade, contribute to a better allocation of production factors and thus increase the overall welfare of the world, compared to a situation that lacks capital mobility. Traditional accounting distinctions between "long-term" and "short-term" movements do not subtract much from this general thesis.

This theoretical conclusion remains valid in today's world notwithstanding the veritable caricature that the practice of global finance has made of it. To imagine a world economy where there is no movement of private capital is just as scary as imagining a world where there is no international trade or international diffusion of technology.

It has been argued that the larger a currency area, the greater its benefits will be, and in a truly globalized world the optimum currency area is the world, regardless of the number of regions of which it is composed.[13] Inter-regional adjustment of the current account to capital flows occurs without dramatic problems between regions of the same monetary area so one must ask: Why should it be any different between countries under firmly fixed exchange rates?

2.3.5 International liquidity and international reserves: The role of SDRs

Over the last hundred years, the world has known a series of international monetary systems: some of them more structured and disciplined and others more chaotic. One of the common characteristics, however, was the coexistence under all the systems of several international reserve vehicles: gold, dollars, pound sterling, and more recently Deutsch Marks, Swiss Francs, Yen, Euro and the Special Drawing Rights (SDRs). During this period of calm and turbulence, the supply of international reserves was to a very large extent a function of a combination of national and international policies. The question of "sufficient supply of international liquidity" cannot be answered independently of the question of demand for international reserves.

The international monetary order of the future – with or without the fundamental reforms suggested here – will continue in all likelihood to be a system of multiple reserve vehicles. What will change, as in the past, is the relative weight of the individual vehicles and the conditions of supply. The dollar will remain an important reserve currency, but it is to be hoped that its relative weight will diminish in the interests of both the American economy and the rest of the world. At the same time, the SDRs should come to play a more important role as both a safe and flexible reserve vehicle. Should this be achieved, it could reduce greatly the demand for currency hedging as well as the overall demand for international liquidity.

2.4   From regional to universal international monetary order: A proposal for an "Extended EMS"

The present writer's principal suggestion for reform of the international monetary system is that it should be based on the general approach of the European Monetary System (EMS). It is the general approach that is important: the technical details would be different because the EMS had not only advantages, but also shortcomings, and also because the "Extended EMS" would include not only the United States, the Euro area and Japan, but potentially the entire world economy. It can be argued that some of the problems encountered by the EMS in the early 1990s could be overcome because of the greater scope and presence of all the major currencies in the "Extended EMS."

The idea is not new. It was first defined in the 1990s.[14] In fact, in the 1990s there was a great – missed – opportunity to create simultaneously the EMU and the "Extended EMS." At same time, however, neither economists nor political leaders were ready for such a bold initiative.

2.4.1   The 1990s and the missed opportunity for international monetary reform

At the time of the Maastricht Treaty and launching of the process leading up to the EMU, the ECB and the Euro, it was clear that there was a need to match this regional system of monetary stability with a worldwide return to a rule-based international monetary order. This could have taken the form of an "Extended EMS."[15] The initiators and three pillars of this system could have been the United States, the EU and Japan.

Such a system would have allowed a return, not only to more stable exchange rates but also to greater "common discipline" for the leading economies, without the rigidity and asymmetry between the United States and the rest of the world that characterized the gold-exchange standard. The idea remained, however, alien to political leaders, bankers and the dominant academic circles, not only in the United States, but also in Europe and Japan.

In fact, there was no willingness to benefit from the positive lessons of the 1960s – that progress at the regional level boosts liberalization at the global level. It was one of the greatest missed opportunities of the Western world.

It would have been in the interest of both the EMU and of the United States and Japan.

The creation of a regional monetary union, a common central bank, and a common currency was the European response, both to the centrifugal monetary forces among the Western European countries and to the monetary and currency instability emanating from the lack of a rule-based universal international monetary order.

The first and most important objective was to eliminate the temptation for independent and contrasting national monetary policies in an integrated economy. The currency speculation among continental countries was not the primary cause of these differences, but they made it more difficult to pursue convergent policies.

The second objective of the EMU, and of the Euro, was to avoid a disruptive effect on monetary relations between member countries resulting from the monetary and currency vagaries that characterize the system of floating exchange rates. There is no question that maintaining monetary stability among a group of "like-minded countries" in a world of floating was more difficult without a common currency than it would have been in a more stable international monetary and currency environment. When there is peace and stability, you do not need a monetary fortress, but in turbulent monetary times a fortress may be the most logical common defense.

The strength and the weakness of the EMU and of the euro is that the project (one of the boldest in the history of political and institutional innovation) was conceived and realized as a fortress or as an island – an essentially inward-looking system.

Neither the initial Delors Report nor the subsequent founding documents addressed the issue of the global international monetary order. The contribution of the EMU to international monetary stability was keeping the rate of inflation low within the Euro zone. This was the task of the ECB and they did not worry about currency fluctuations on the outside. The ECB has no mandate and no right to try and pursue an exchange rate target for the Euro. Any concern regarding the exchange rate would have interfered with its precious domestic inflation target. The EMU, the ECB and the Euro were full participants in the wonderful world of floating exchange rates, just like the Fed and the dollar and the Bank of England with the pound, after the end of the EMS.

In this world it is the domestic rate of inflation that separates the saints from the sinners. If exchange rate instability with the outside world creates some pain, too bad; it is the necessary price for virtue. This belief is the basis of the Bundesbank doctrine from the 1970s. In order to make the project politically acceptable in Germany, the architects of the EMU had to swallow it lock, stock and barrel. This preliminary condition was even more important than the fiscal clauses within the Stability Pact, as these seemed to be an afterthought. Without the exchange rate doctrine and the indifference to the rest of the international monetary scene, even the skills of the master persuasion artist Helmut Kohl could not have overcome the German reluctance to embark on this project.[16]

This doctrine together with the profound hostility of American experts, and the leading lights of the Clinton administration in particular, to any discussion about a rule-based international monetary system involving the United States, as mentioned above, led to a major missed opportunity in the 1990s.

2.4.2 Monetary order from regionalism to universalism: The postwar experience

Monetary regionalism was first introduced under the impact of the so-called dollar shortage.

When the international community began planning the post-war economic order, one of the key issues up for debate was: where do regional institutions and arrangements fit into the future international order? The United States was strongly committed to the principle of universalism and non-discrimination. Britain insisted on room for regional exceptions. On the whole the American universalist point of view prevailed both at the IMF and the General Agreement on Tariffs and Trade (GATT), although there was accommodation within the agreement for the Commonwealth, the sterling area, customs unions and free trade areas in general.[17]

Although non-discrimination became a commonly accepted rule after the 1940s, it was still slow to be implemented both at the trade level (in particular in the elimination of quantitative restrictions) and in currency convertibility. In fact, systematic discrimination against imports from America and other dollar countries was not only accepted but was also actively organized with the support and encouragement of the United States in Western Europe from 1948 onwards. This discrimination reflected the prevailing perception of the nature and consequences of the so-called dollar shortage. It was a condition of the Marshall Plan: regional cooperation in trade and payments – through the Organization for European Economic Cooperation (OEEC) and the European Payments Union (EPU) – was meant to reduce European dependence on imports from the Unite States and on American aid.[18]

The success of the European Recovery Program (ERP), as well as OEEC and EPU, coupled with lingering fears of a "permanent dollar shortage," contributed to the initial impulses of European integration. It was only in 1958, with the devaluation and reform of the French franc, that European countries finally ended temporary payments and trade (QRs) discrimination against the United States. They accomplished this by adopting full current account convertibility for their currencies. Thus, Bretton Woods finally became operational.

By then, however, at least at the trade level, a much more ambitious project of permanent regional trade liberalization was implemented. It was a project that received not only the full support of the Truman and Eisenhower Administrations, but also that of every single American Administration thereafter. It was the creation of the European Economic Community (EEC), and shortly after the European Free Trade Association (EFTA), that gave the original impulse to the incoming Kennedy Administration and inspired them to submit the Trade Expansion Act to Congress. This Act was the basis of GATT's "Kennedy Round" between 1962–7.

There is a general consensus that the Kennedy Round created the basis for the multilateral and global trade liberalization of market economies: it cut the edge of discrimination against third countries that was implicit in the European Common market and the European Free Trade Area. It also brought Japan in as a full respected partner of the world trading system.[19] Equally,[20] there is no doubt that without European integration the success of the Kennedy Round would have been more limited. In fact ever since the 1960s, regional and universal trade liberalization has been a mutually reinforcing process.

A similar opportunity for the regional or European model to have a positive impact on the universal or global level arose in the 1990s, but this time in the monetary system.

The breakdown of the Bretton Woods system and its liquidation were due to a number of factors, prominent among these were the tensions and misunderstandings between the United States and its European allies. However, as equally important were the economic and monetary divergences and policy dissensions between the so-called strong-currency countries and the so-called weak-currency countries in Europe. The first group accused the latter of "exporting inflation," while the second accused the former of "exporting recession and unemployment."

The end of the gold-exchange standard and the floating of the US dollar led to a worldwide crisis: inflation combined with recession. The floating of European currencies aggravated the gap between "inflationary" and "non-inflationary" countries. In practice it made it more and more difficult for the first group to return to the path of virtue and price stability, whereas it made it easier, at least in the short term, for the second to uphold the virtue of stable prices and wages. Currency instability threatened to wreck the whole experience of European integration.

In the 1970s, it became clear that both the regional and the worldwide crises were mutually re-enforcing each other. However, the American political, economic and intellectual leadership remained oblivious to the costs of the international monetary and financial disorders for the American and world economies. The long-term economic impact of this situation on the European economies became politically unacceptable at least for the leading continental countries.[21] This was especially true for the leaders of Germany and France, the two leading pillars in the process of European integration.

The EMS, a far from perfect instrument, was a tool to achieve both a political and economic goal: greater currency stability among the European countries and a greater monetary convergence among the members of the EMS.[22] Again, it is clear that without the EMS, there would have been no Single European Act, no "internal market" and no "European Union," as we know it today. For better or worse, as in 1948–58, the Europeans once again chose a regional way to avoid the consequences of a global crisis.

However, the "regional" solution was not enough, neither for Europe, nor for the world economy. This was a lesson generated over twenty years ago. It was not enough under the EMS and it is not enough under the EMU or the Euro either.

One of the major shortcomings of the 1989 Delors Report and subsequently of the EMU Treaty, the ECB and the Euro was that the external dimension, i.e., the exchange rate of common European currency was absent from the Delors Report and the subsequent documents.

2.4.3 Regional and global monetary order: The multiple levels of political communities

Globalization has been accompanied by "regionalization." This is quite pronounced in the area of trade and the approach of the World Trade Organization (WTO) regarding the key principle of non-discrimination. It has not been an obstacle to the proliferation of bilateral agreements, often disguised as "WTO-compatible free-trade areas."

Global – International Community (Global Rules – Extended EMS)
Regional (1) e.g., OECD countries (Extended EMS)
Regional (2) e.g., European Union (Euro)
National (State)
Intermediate, Regional (Cantons, etc.)
Local Municipal

Figure 2.1 Levels or scope of political communities and binding and non-binding rules and legislation.

A similar situation prevails in the monetary and financial areas within the EU and the Euro as the most important and most successful example of a regional solution.

One of the important features of the current international order is co-existence of different levels of "political communities," decision-making, legislation rules and customs. The relevant level differs according to issues and varies also in time. The phenomenon is familiar in federal states where there is a distinction or division of responsibilities and political power or sovereignty according to issues or subjects. This distinction exists for both public law and for customs and private conventions as well as rules of good practice.

One of the principal manifestations of globalization has been the changing scope of the national regulation of various economic activities, both within national borders and internationally, the increasingly complex and constantly evolving state of rules and regulations in the economic and financial area on all levels. There is a very wide range of distinct or common overlapping state of affairs, from completely "deregulated" issues and areas to highly "regulated" or "re-regulated" activities (see Figure 2.1).

2.4.4 A compromise solution for a "rule-based" system

The world economy needs a multi-layered, flexible but "rule-based" banking and monetary system: common "rules of the game" are needed, not arbitrary and unpredictable government interventions. What is needed is a combination of bold initiatives and institution building with willingness for compromise where it is needed.

Most of those who speak about a new "Bretton Woods" do not really know what they are talking about and have not studied the complex road from the original idea to the "revolutionary compromise" that came out of this long process, where the conference itself was only one stage in the creation of a new rule-based monetary order. The process began with clear initial objectives and concepts with distinct preferences and interests between the two principal sides: the United States and Britain. They compromised on a solution. In the light of the issues at stake even the watered-down compromise was a great achievement. Because of the novelty of the idea, implementation was slow and neither the IMF nor the International Bank for Reconstruction and Development (IBRD) were sufficiently big and robust enough to play a significant role in the rough waters of the initial postwar period. It was the ERP (the Marshall Plan) and the institutions it created that allowed progress toward the goal of a universal order and it was only then that the IMF became truly operational.

The post-war planning for a liberal international monetary order had two facets: the issue of money and finance (balance of payments, convertibility, exchange rate stability, international reserves and long-term capital), and of trade liberalization and non-discrimination. The two systems – IMF and IBRD on the one hand and GATT on the other hand – were distinct but also linked through the issue of the balance of payments and current account convertibility.

Today, in the WTO we have a strong rule-based system for trade, which is in great contrast to the banking and monetary system in place. The WTO experience, in contrast to GATT, seems to be overly rigid and the whole system is undermined not only by the failure of the Doha round, but perhaps even more so by the creeping bilateralism and the systematic erosion of the principle of non-discrimination. This has accelerated since the establishment of the WTO and does not seem to be slowing down.

Yet, the WTO does not provide a valid reason for rejecting a rule-based international economic order, just as the list of shortcomings and breakdown of the IMF did nothing to prove that international monetary order was not functioning or worthy of its name. WTO does, however, demonstrate that we need both rules and a strong sense of willingness to cooperate. We must apply these rules for both common and particular interests, and the objective of the rules must be to make market competition a source of general prosperity and upward convergence, not a source that widens economic and social gaps within and between nations.

2.4.5 From design to implementation

All major reform processes consist of three successive stages:

(1) The recognition of the need to change, innovate and develop new concepts and direction within people's minds (the level of ideas);
(2) negotiation and decisions on new rules and institutions; and

(3) the change in perception and expectations as well as in behavior from households, companies and government agencies to bring about change in economic performance and economic structures – for better or worse, depending on the nature and quality of the reforms.

Previous crises and reform attempts cannot provide an applicable blueprint of how to deal with the current situation. In fact, the reform process has already begun, but progress is limited and there is still great uncertainty at stage one – the level of ideas – and this obviously hampers any real progress at stages two and three.

There is a long list of international monetary, banking and financial crises and attempts at implementing reforms (preceding or following them) that can provide both positive and negative lessons to be heeded in the current situation. This is without, however, providing a direct blueprint either for national or international authorities or for market participants. This list includes: (1) The late nineteenth century and early twentieth century crises that led to the creation of proper central banks, (2) The post-World War 1 Genoa conference and the creation of the gold-exchange standard, (3) The great German inflation of the 1920s, (4) The issue of German reparations in the 1920s, (5) The Creditanstalt crisis, going off gold and the spreading of exchange controls in the 1930s, (6) The creation of the IMF, the illusion of the so-called dollar shortage, the Marshall Plan and the emergence of economic regionalism, (7) The German monetary reform, (8) The reform debate of the 1960s (SDR), (9) The collapse of the fixed exchange-rate system, (10) The crisis in Europe and the move to EMS and to the EMU, the Euro, etc., (11) One should also remember the "monetarist shock therapies" in Yugoslavia and in Argentina as some of the failed attempts at reform that resulted in devastating consequences.

It takes exceptional political leadership for successful reform in any major area. However, it also takes time and is often accompanied by powerful intellectual and political tensions and divisions. Whatever the merits of the Roosevelt presidency, the 1930s did not provide the most encouraging example of a "crisis" followed by "reform." Two key points should be mentioned here: (1) The difficulty, as well as the inability, to slow down and stop the downward spiral once the magnitude of the crisis was recognized; and (2) The utter failure in bringing an effective remedy to the damage incurred by the international system. In fact it was the international crisis (including the cumulative international impact of the national crises) that led to the worldwide depression and that gave the world the Second World War.

The magnitude of reform with which the international community is currently being challenged can only be compared to that of the period from 1943 to 1950. This was a period when virtually all of the principal foundations, of the exceptional (unprecedented) prosperity and stability for the next sixty years, were laid in the Western world. This period was also one of trial and error and of considerable oppositions and divergences.

The key questions surrounding the reform debate currently underway (as in most major reform debates) include: What is the role of damage control and building a new order or system? What are the respective merits of improvisation and of careful detailed planning? What needs to be repaired and what should be replaced?

The principal lessons we can gather from previous experience with monetary and financial reform is that not all reforms are successful and not all reforms will go in the right direction. This, however, is certainly no argument for avoiding reform and trying to continue with business as usual. When there is a seriously damaged and virtually rudderless system, the option of "no reform" does not exist.

2.4.6   The long-term interests in monetary order: Europe, Japan, and the United States

The current crisis should have finally convinced everyone that the absence of a global and stable international monetary system was not in the interest of the United States. Those on the Left and on the Right argued for years that this erratic, unstable and crisis-prone system served the interests of the American economy. Even though they were wrong from the start, their views dominated the academic and the public debate on policy-making because they shared a common consensus.

Of course, there were those concerned, who hoped to see the return of a more stable system. Many looked quite wistfully at the success of the Europeans who had overcome political and material obstacles on the way to a monetary union. (Despite the views of the skeptics in Europe, Britain and America who, up to the last minute, firmly believed that it would never happen.)[23]

The academic and political weight of arguments, by individuals in favor of a more stable global system, was further diminished by the fact that the majority of them (and the best-known and most prestigious ones) shared a questionable conclusion that stemmed from the 1970s. This was the belief that large economies, and in particular the largest of them the United States, can easily disregard the absence of external constraints that had existed, for example under the Bretton Woods regime, while small open economies cannot.[24] Small countries learn early on that they are responsible for their stability and prosperity, whatever the outside conditions.[25]

Yet, due to its large size, the US economy had to rely heavily on the external guideposts that help to curb the temptation for monetary, fiscal and financial excesses and imbalances. When these imbalances occur due to the absence of imposed "constraints," the domestic and external consequences are much more disruptive in larger economies then in smaller ones.[26] The fragility of the US financial sector and the gradual deterioration of the philosophy and instruments of public action – especially monetary policy and financial supervision – could not have occurred without the perceived absence of external constraints. Finally, the paradox of the enormous expansion of American indebtedness to what is still a Communist regime (the relative size of this debt has been further increased by the massive destruction of assets owned by American households) certainly does not suggest that the global imbalances made possible by the current system were in the long-term interest of the United States.

Also, the warnings represented by the succession of the international financial crises of the 1980s and 1990s were "easy" to ignore because they were considered to be "regional crises," those of Mexico, Latin America, Russia, and Asia. "It may have happened to them, but never to us" type of attitude was adopted. We chided, we helped them or even forced them to declare open bankruptcy, but then we also conveniently forgot that the root causes of the crises were systemic and not regional, and that they hit with equal force both "virtuous" (in macro-economic terms) and inflation-prone countries. What finally anesthetized both economists and bankers, as well as the broader public, in the United States to the pain caused by these "regional crises" was the fact that there was no equal sharing of costs between borrowers and lenders: in order to "save the international financial system" time and time again the borrowers were made to absorb the bulk of the financial and economic burden.

Therefore, there is no question that the "floating dollar standard" did considerable harm to the American economy: it did not serve the nation's best interests.

How to get out of this quagmire, politically and technically? Propose, negotiate and implement what, for the lack of a better word, can be called an "extended EMS." This is a more flexible but still rule-based system that would include the dollar, the euro and the yen, and whichever currency and country would be willing and interested to accept and respect the rules of the system.

The creation of such a system would provide very important, immediate and long-term advantages for the United States. It would benefit the banking, financial sector, the real economy and monetary and fiscal policy-making. Despite the rules and obligations under the new system, the Federal Reserve would have a much better grasp and control over the money supply and domestic and external credit. There is no question that it would also be in the best interests of the members of the Euro-zone, greatly facilitating the task of the ECB and their management. Japan has suffered enough from the existing non-system to welcome the creation of the extended EMS. It is also obvious that such an initiative would bring a high level of benefits to the rest of the world economy, both in the "emerging countries" and the rest of the world.

2.5   The reform of the IMF and of the BIS

The IMF occupies a large amount of space in the debate about the necessary reforms. Yet, some of the fundamental shortcomings from which the IMF has suffered in recent years, and even decades, are not being addressed by most of the reform proposals, in particular those coming out of the G 20 process.[27]

These missing elements can be illustrated by two important examples: (1) there is no call for a new reform of Article IV of the Second Amendment (the one that basically made the IMF irrelevant for the international monetary system), and (2) linked to this issue, there is an explicit or implicit acceptance of the idea that the IMF exists to "take care of the developing countries" and has no business to be involved with the big and powerful.

All of the proposals for an "increased role" of the IMF go in this direction: crisis management and lending to the "poor." These are valid objectives, but not very ambitious ones. If there is no broadening in the scope of IMF reform, then it would be better to create a new institution that would work with the IMF, but would not be weighed down by these constraints.

The same goes for the BIS. The BIS is a very important and worthwhile institution whose recent record, however, like that of its member central banks, has been at best mixed.[28] In the light of recent developments, as the crisis gained full momentum, one can agree that neither the national rules and financial supervision in the leading financial centers, nor the common ("Basel") rules were adequate and there is a need for fundamental reforms both at the national and at the international levels.[29]

Beyond the "regulatory function," the BIS ought to play a more active role in coordinating monetary policy, not only in crisis situations, but also under "normal circumstances."

2.5.1 Emerging markets or developed markets: Where did the risks originate?

Ever since the 1960s, it was clear that the international monetary order was, first and foremost, the responsibility of highly developed countries and not just an issue for developing nations ("emerging markets"). The crises of the 1970s, 1980s and 1990s were just as closely linked to the dollar and to the international banking system as they were to the emerging markets.

Yet, since the 1970s, the IMF has played no role at the global level and, in particular, has had no influence whatsoever on the policies of the leading OECD countries. De facto, since 1973 the IMF became an instrument for lending to and watching over "developing" or later so-called transition economies that might be in need of traditional balance-of-payments assistance, and countries that could not cope with their more or less short-term international liquidity problems through recourse to the private international financial markets.[30] With regard to these countries, the IMF exercised due severity ("conditionality") to make sure that they followed the kind of fiscal and monetary rigor that the IMF had no longer any business to expect from the major players such as the United States. The feeble attempts at "multilateral surveillance" and the discussions about "global imbalances" did not lead anywhere.

While the IMF recommended a whole range of exchange-rate regimes for its various clients from developing countries, no real ideas or suggestions have come out of the IMF for decades about the possibilities of a return to a global monetary system.

In the debate over the role and forecasting errors of the IMF, in particular in connection with the Asian financial crisis, many saw their future role as a "crisis manager" and "true international lender" as a last resort. Others focused upon "emerging markets," developing countries, and on the temptation to over-borrow knowing that in case of trouble the IMF would bail them out (the "moral hazard" issue). In this context, many suggested the outright abolition of the IMF. Thus George Schultz, William Simon (both former Secretaries of Treasury) and Walter Wriston (former Head of Citicorp) argued in 1998 that "the IMF's promise of massive intervention has spurred global meltdown of financial markets [...] the IMF is ineffective, unnecessary and obsolete and it should be abolished."[31]

Can the IMF and the BIS rise to the challenge? To read the G20 proposal, one gets the impression that these two organizations are not being offered the opportunity to do so.

2.6 The conditions of success

2.6.1 From passivity and indifference to activism on all fronts

The guardians of the world economy fell asleep on their watch. From leading central banks and ministries of finance, to international organizations such as the IMF and the BIS, to the richest and most powerful banks on earth such as JP Morgan, Citicorp, UBS or Goldman Sachs, or to the members of the most elite groups of monetary and financial experts in the world, such as the "Group of 30" or the Stability Forum, the individuals with the most-up-to-date information and the most experience at high levels, were not able nor willing to read the warning signs that had been evident for quite some time. They did not raise their voices although, given their high profile and visibility, they might have been listened to. They did not call for reforms to prevent disaster: instead they bided their time; individually and collectively, they let the opportunity pass.

Yet, once catastrophe struck, some of the most prominent names on Wall Street, New York City, Zurich and elsewhere began to tremble and many of them ultimately collapsed. This occurred at a time when the specter of a worldwide credit freeze was, or seemed to be, just around the corner, and massive calls for help started to come from the most unexpected quarters – passivity and lack of concern gave way to an unprecedented activism not only in the United States but all over the world.

All began to sound their alarm bells: central banks and governments – led by the United States in the waning days of an arch-conservative and "market-fundamentalist" administration – pulled out all the stops; they began pushing all their buttons, and tried feverishly to compete in shouting louder than the others that "we are fighting the crisis." As I write this text, the bells are still ringing, and the horns are still blowing.

Given the nature and the dimensions of the crisis, crisis management requires action at both national and international level. It is normal that action at national level should encounter fewer obstacles than at the international level. In most countries there has been a general consensus across political party lines about the gravity of the situation and the necessity to act, and to act rapidly, in a determined and massive manner. Also, considering that decision makers in governments and central banks are just like everybody else in a situation that they claim to have never encountered before, and for which virtually all the organizations they head admitted they had no contingency plans. There has been relatively little political division or even substantive debate over the essential question:

> How can we define, adopt and implement, in the shortest possible time, effective measures that will essentially fulfill two key requirements: stop the downward spiral and help restart the growth process, as well as make sure that the emergency measures adopted will not have even worse long-term consequences on economic activity, the institutional framework and the economic, monetary and social order in general.

The most remarkable common denominator was the speed and unprecedented acceleration of monetary, fiscal, and regulatory decision-making. There was no time to reflect upon or to debate. Improvisation was from the start and, so far, remains the necessary order of the day.

Rapid action was and remains important. But virtually all the measures have been reactive rather than anticipatory. Monetary, fiscal and regulatory authorities are all navigating by sight. All of the models – the highly sophisticated econometric models and the more traditional ones have broken down. The system, in particular the credit system, does not seem to respond to any of the traditional or even the less orthodox stimuli: virtually zero interest rates, the most generous liquidity creation ever, the lending to government, the shoring up of balance sheets, etc.

The dominant doctrine of recent years (not without justification) assumed that there was a significant limit on the governments' and central banks' ability to fine-tune and macro-manage complex and large economies with any combination of fiscal, monetary and regulatory measures. These limitations are even greater in the case of open economies. This was one of the central issues, during the postwar period until the end of the 1960s, between the Keynesians and socialists and their liberal opponents. It was during this time that the crisis of the 1970s tipped the balance in favor of the liberal skeptics. First and foremost it was a crisis of economic and monetary policies coupled with recession and high levels of inflation and unemployment.

In recent weeks and months, however, there has been a sudden leap in faith not only in the virtue of government interventions – despite the enormous responsibility of the governments through sins of omission and sins of commission for the crises in the markets – but also in the effectiveness of quantitative macro-economic management. This has been, at least on the surface, one of the most radical breaks in the doctrine and practice prevailing since the 1970s and 1980s.

Short-termism (the factor that was one of the principal causes of the collapse) prevails. We are expecting instant results – not investing enough energy into thinking about long-term reform of monetary cooperation. There is no real understanding of the nature of the future international architecture. International financial uncertainty continues, because no one thinks about the future role of monetary policy and of the central banks – nationally and internationally. Liquidity is important but as long as the uncertainty remains about the long term, credit will remain tight – the banks will adopt a position of "wait and see."

2.6.2   Discordant voices

The world has now seen the consequences of American unilateralism and of the inward-looking policies of Europe.[32]

Yet, the loudest voices come once more from America, from Joseph Stiglitz to Bernanke, from the former to the new Secretary of the Treasury, and all of the commentators and experts outside the official circles. While not denying the major intellectual and material responsibility of the United States, the private sector and government combined, for what has happened in recent months to the very foundations of the market economy, most Americans refuse to listen to ideas or proposals that are not stamped "Made in the USA."

They are victims of the belief that only Americans know how to solve the problems of the world economy and it is enough to pay lip service to international cooperation. This reflects the same kind of intellectual provincialism and nationalism that got us into trouble in the first place. What is remarkable is how little interest there seems to be, both within the Obama Administration and among leading experts and advisers, in what the Europeans and Japanese have to say about the crisis and how the United States should try to work with its two oldest allies to save the international liberal economic order.

The problem is compounded by the passivity of the Europeans and the Japanese. The Europeans have the most extraordinary record of international institution building throughout the past fifty years (admittedly with the encouragement of the United States). They have also managed to create – through long trial and error – a regional solution to monetary stability among sovereign states with considerable differences in their approaches and record of managing their financial affairs. But they have not come up with a single major institutional initiative to help reform the global international monetary order. This lack of initiative and lack of ideas includes the successive heads of the IMF – who have all been Europeans (and most of them French).

What has been even more startling is the passivity and lack of imagination of the Japanese. With the most dynamic economy that the world has seen in a long time, its next-door neighbor China has also declared itself a rival for Japan's position as the second largest economy of the world. One would think that Japanese officials, Japanese economists, Japanese banks and companies would be calling for strengthening of their institutional ties not only with the United States but also with the other democracies.[33]

2.6.3 Solidarity: National, regional and global

Without solidarity, there cannot be globalization. This was true ten years ago. It was true twenty years ago at the end of the Cold War – and it has become dramatically apparent in the last twelve months. Unless the importance of solidarity is well-understood, by both the "stronger" and "weaker" groups at domestic and international levels, the chances for adopting coherent long-term reforms will be considerably reduced.

Solidarity is an essential component of a competitive market economy and of a democratic political order based on the balance between public and private interests.[34] The forms, conditions, accountability, as well as the institutional and legal framework of solidarity, are a central topic of the political debate in all free, modern societies, under both conservative and social democratic governments. The manner in which the challenge of solidarity is handled in a given society is a telltale indicator of the quality of its political and social order and the efficiency of its economy. The common fundamental error of both the extreme left and the modern day market fundamentalists is the belief that the competitive market economy is Hobbes's "state of nature," while solidarity is Marx's and Lenin's egalitarian socialist economy.

Solidarity does not make the market economy socially and politically acceptable only within a national community; it also plays an important role at the international level. It was the concept of solidarity with the weaker members of the Western community that has allowed the liberalization of trade and payments and the growing integration (and competition) of national economies, and the unprecedented prosperity and social progress in Europe and in the broader Western community – thus giving the impetus to the process of globalization.

Defining and applying the concept of solidarity in the numerous contexts relevant to the proper working of the political and social order is a complex task for political leadership and for the "technical experts" who have to translate the political decisions into workable institutions, rules and policies. This is all the more difficult under current circumstances, not only because of the current crisis – when the "stronger" and "weaker" have undergone great changes – but also because both the short-term measures and the long-term reforms have to make up for numerous shortcomings accumulated over several decades. The difficulties are compounded by the need to remain vigilant and to ensure that the application of solidarity does not lead, once more, to the other extreme. This would seriously undermine domestic and international cooperation and threaten the market economy and the open international liberal order.

2.6.4 Globalization, democracy and the market economy: The key to successful monetary and banking reform

At present, the world is going through the most important and difficult test of what we have all come to call "globalization." This is a test not only of resilience and flexibility, but also of the system's ability to withstand shocks and crises at the economic, monetary and financial levels. It is a test of its capacity for reform – what in German would be called its "Reformfähigkeit." Survival – until the next crisis – is not enough.

The monetary, finance and banking sectors have been inextricably linked to globalization. Until the late 1960s and the early 1970s, these sectors, money and finance, had been "lagging behind" the liberalization and integration of the Western developed economies through trade, direct investments and the diffusion of technology. In the last forty years, the dynamics of cross-border financial links gradually reached and exceeded the extent of integration in the "real economy."

There is no doubt that the reform of the international banking and monetary system will have major implications for the economic and social model at both the national and international level. The issue is not one of Right or Left; it is the rediscovery of one of the essential ingredients of the successful market economy during postwar decades: the ability to reconcile competition with solidarity. It was in fact this solidarity with the weakest members of the community, the conscious policies to avoid marginalization of the weaker members of the national or international community that made the model of a competitive market economy socially and politically acceptable. It was this ingredient that allowed a period of unprecedented economic growth together with a high level of social progress in all advanced Western economies. The break with this tradition – at the level of values and ideas as well as the policy level – in some countries and some sectors was more gradual, and in others more abrupt. The accumulated benefits – in terms of both concrete policies and social values – were so important and evident that they could not be wiped out overnight, despite the vicious and unjustified attacks on the very concept of the "social market economy" (to cite the term commonly used in Continental Europe).

The conclusion has to be that, in the long run, the reform of the international banking and monetary system will succeed. We have no other choice. This is due not only to the fact that the system is very important and that its reform is long overdue, but also because there is a worldwide convergence of interest in the success of reform. All these factors are important, and yet would not be sufficient to discard a "worst case scenario."

This conclusion, which may sound overly optimistic, is based on the strength of the model of responsible and free societies. The balance had clearly gone too far at the national and the international levels, in the markets and in governments, among political leaders and in the general public – in the "real world" and in the minds of people.

It is time for a new upsurge, not only to repair and correct, but also to innovate and consolidate. The strength of democracy and of the market economy is not to be free of errors and crises. It is the process of trial and error; it is its capacity to correct errors, to overcome their consequences and to offer new beginnings. The true sense of the opportunity of globalization that emerged as a result of the end of the Cold War (with the bloodless victory of the ideals of freedom, peace, democracy and economic prosperity) is, for the first time in over two hundred years, a free society. This model combines competition and solidarity, private initiative and public responsibility, intensive debate and common goals and purposes, diversity and a sense of belonging simultaneous to both small and large communities and has the chance to become a truly universal model, without domination, and without the misuse of power.

Notes

1. "We have today therefore pledged to do whatever is necessary to

   - restore confidence, growth, and jobs;
   - repair the financial system to restore lending;
   - strengthen financial regulation to rebuild trust;
   - fund and reform our international financial institutions to overcome this crisis and prevent future ones;
   - promote global trade and investment and reject protectionism, to underpin prosperity; and
   - build an inclusive, green. and sustainable recovery.

By acting together to fulfill these pledges we will bring the world economy out of recession and prevent a crisis like this from recurring in the future." Group of 20 (April 2, 2009) *The Global Plan for Recovery and Reform*, London, April 2, 2009; Cf. also: Group of 20 (April 2, 2009) *Declaration on Delivering Resources Through the International Financial Institutions*, London, April 2, 2009; Group of 20 (April 2, 2009) *Declaration on Strengthening the Financial System*, London, April 2, 2009; Group of 20, Working Group 2 (WG2) (April 2, 2009) *G20 Working Group on Reinforcing International Cooperation and Promoting Integrity in Financial Markets*, London, April 2, 2009; United Nations General Assembly, Commission of Experts on Reforms of the International Monetary and Financial System (March 19, 2009) *Recommendations*, United Nations, New York, March 19, 2009.

2. Otto Hieronymi and Catherine Currat, "The Complexity and the Organizing Principles of International Order," *Foresight, Journal of Future Studies and Strategic Thinking and Policy*, vol. 6, no. 4, pp. 198–203, Emerald Group Publishing Ltd, 2004.

3. "Finally, governments, central banks, and regulatory agencies will have to meet the greatest of all challenges: setting up a well-structured and efficient cooperative framework at the global level. The process of globalization throws up problems of worldwide dimensions, which cannot be handled on an ad hoc basis. Even if all preventive measures by national authorities work, their sum total may turn out to be dismally inadequate for reducing the risk of systemic crisis. And there is a genuine risk that in the case of a major crisis, national policy reactions will tend to diverge rather than converge. Establishing a cooperative framework should therefore be the major assignment for all those who are given the task of designing a new financial architecture." Alexandre Lamfalussy, *Financial Markets in Emerging Markets. An Essay on Financial Globalization and Fragility*, Yale University Press, New Haven and London, 2000, p. 175.

4. Alan Greenspan, a life-long disciple of Ayn Rand and of her philosophy, represents one of the most extreme examples of an ardent advocate of free markets and globalization. However, he shows a lack of concern for the international dimension of US financial developments. For someone who has always been an ardent fiscal conservative, it is surprising, to say the least, how unconcerned he has been about the American balance of payments and about the impact of American budget deficits on the dependence of the US economy on short-term capital imports. His faith in the natural tendency of markets for self-regulation remained unshaken even after he left the Federal Reserve. The "complexity of markets" became an added argument for the absence of rules in the domestic and the international financial system:

> Only belatedly did many of my colleagues and I, come to realize that the power to regulate administratively was fading. Since the markets have become too complex for effective human intervention the most promising anti-crisis policies are those that maintain maximum market flexibility – freedom of action for key market participants such as hedge funds, private equity funds, and investment banks ... The purpose of hedge funds and others is to make money, but their actions extirpate inefficiencies and imbalances, and thereby reduce the waste of scarce savings ... Regulation,

by its nature, inhibits freedom of market action, and that freedom to act expeditiously is what rebalances markets. Undermine this freedom and the whole market-balancing process is put at risk ... (There) are currently a number of feared financial imbalances that are likely to be resolved with far less impact on US economic activity than is generally supposed ... (The) unwinding of our current account deficit is not likely to have a major impact on economic activity and employment.

> Alan Greenspan, *The Age of Turbulence. Adventures in a New World*, The Penguin Press, New York, 2007, pp. 489–90

5. The last chapter in Paul Volcker's and Toyoo Gyothen's joint book on international monetary issues bears the title "A New World Order or a New Nationalism". It is clear that both Volcker and his Japanese friend and co-author were for a "new (stable and open) world order" where both the Unite States and Japan (and Europe) would have had to play a constructive role. But neither author felt it appropriate to go beyond the call for "cooperation," "leadership" and "responsible policies". Their ideas fell far short of outlining any suggestions for a new rule-based international monetary order and how to make it politically acceptable for the Japanese and for the Americans. Paul Volcker and Toyoo Gyothen, *Changing Fortunes: The World's Money and the Threat to American Leadership*, Times Books, New York, 1992.
6. Alexandre Lamfalussy, "Current-Account Imbalances in the Industrial World: Why They Matter," in Peter B. Kenen (Editor), *International Monetary Cooperation: Essays in Honor of Henry C. Wallich*, Essays in International Finance, no. 169, December 1987, International Finance Section, Princeton University, Princeton, NJ, pp. 31 and 36–7.
7. Alan Greenspan, "Remarks on the *Current Account*," at Advancing Enterprise 2005 Conference, London, February 4, 2005, Federal Reserve Board.
8. Ben S. Bernanke, "Financial Reform to Address Systemic Risk," Speech at The Council on Foreign Relations, Washington, DC, March 10, 2009, Federal Reserve Board.
9. Tommaso Padoa-Schioppa, *La Veduta Corta. Conversazione con Beda Romano sul Grande Crollo della Finanza*, Il Mulino, Bologna, 2009; International Monetary Fund, "Staff Report on the Multilateral Consultation on Global Imbalances with China, the Euro Area, Japan, Saudi Arabia, and the United States," Prepared by a Staff Team from PDR, RES and WHD, June 29, 2007.
10. Ben S. Bernanke, "Remarks," at the *Cato Institute 22nd Annual Monetary Conference*, Washington, DC, October 14, 2004.
11. Robert A. Mundell, "Optimum Currency Areas," Extended version of a luncheon speech presented at a *Conference on Optimum Currency Areas*, Tel-Aviv University, December 5, 1997.
12. Milton Friedman and Anna Jacobson Schwartz, *A Monetary History of the United States, 1967–1960*, (A Study by the National Bureau of Economic Research), New York, Princeton University Press, Princeton, 1963.
13. Robert A. Mundell, "Optimum Currency Areas."
14. Cf. Otto Hieronymi, "The Case for an 'Extended EMS': A New International Monetary Order to be Built by Europe, Japan and the United States," in Miklos Szabo-Pelsöczy (Editor), *The Global Monetary System After the Fall of the Soviet Empire*, (In Memoriam Robert Triffin – 1911–1993, Sixth Conference

of the Robert Triffin-Sziràk Foundation, Sziràk, 1993), Averbury, Aldershot, 1995, pp. 57–67. An earlier version of this article was published by Nikkei in Japanese, but never as far as I know in their English language publications.

15. Ibid.

16. The current crisis has revived the old German fears of being infected by the "viruses of the weak-currency countries" within the Euro zone. This time it is not France and Italy but the new members in Eastern Europe. Cf. Wilhelm Hankel, Wilhelm Noelling, Karl Albrecht Schactschneider, and Joachim Starbatty, "Die Europäische Währungsunion vor einer Zerreissprobe. Kritik an der Rolle der Schwachwährungsländer im Euro-Einzugsgebiet," *Neue Zürcher Zeitung*, February 14–15, 2009, Zürich. Incidentally Wilhem Nölling, the former head of the Hamburg Landeszentralbank (Bundesbank) was a founder member of an anti-EMU group that had sued the Kohl government in front of the German Constitutional Court that the euro was incompatible with the German constitution. They lost their case.

17. Cf. Robert Skidelsky, *John Maynard Keynes*, Fighting for Britain, 1937–1946, vol. 3, Macmillan, London, 2000 and Richard Gardner, *Sterling-Dollar Diplomacy, Anglo-American Collaboration in the Reconstruction of Multilateral Trade*, Clarendon Press, Oxford, 1956.

18. Cf. Otto Hieronymi, *Economic Discrimination Against the United States in Western Europe, 1945–1958. Dollar Shortage and the Rise of Regionalism*, Librarie Droz, Genève, 1973.

19. For a similar conclusion: "In the case of the creation of the EEC, American exporters lobbied their government to react to the potentially discriminatory effect of the PTA (Preferential Trade Arrangement) and made the U.S. engage in the Kennedy Round. European governments agreed to participate in tariff cutting because they expected large concessions from the U.S. for a relatively small reduction of discrimination." As Pierre Uri stated already in the late 1960s, "The establishment of the European Community gave the initial impetus to the Kennedy Round; its bargaining power has thawed American tariffs which had remained frozen for twenty years; and its existence induced some of its members to accept massive cuts in their previous levels of protection." Andreas Dür, *Theorizing the Contagious Effects of Regionalism: European Integration and Transatlantic Trade Relations, 1957–1963*, Dissertation, European University Institute, San Domenico di Fiesole, 2000, pp. 51–2.

20. One may add that European integration was one of the factors that boosted, as of the 1960s, direct investments by major American companies in Europe. There was a precautionary motive (to avoid potential tariff discrimination) and a growth motive: the combined impact of regional and global trade liberalization created a strong upward conversion in the European economy – among European countries and between Europe and the United States.

21. Cf. Horst Ungerer, "Political Aspects of European Monetary Integration After World War II," Paper Presented at ECSA Conference, Charleston, S.C. May 13, 1995.

22. Cf. Horst Ungerer, *A Concise History of European Monetary Integration: From EPU to EMU*, Quorum Books, Westport, Connecticut, 1997; Tommaso Padoa-Schioppa, *The Road to Monetary Union in Europe*, Oxford University Press, Oxford, 2000.

23. Cf. Tommaso Padoa-Schioppa, *The Road to Monetary Union in Europe*, Oxford University Press, Oxford, 2000 and Tommaso Padoa-Schioppa, *The Euro and its Central Bank*, The MIT Press, Cambridge, Mass. 2004.
24. For example both Robert Mundell and Paul Volcker shared this view.
25. Of course, the siren songs of UBS and their relentless search for bigness, led them to forget Swiss this basic wisdom, that used to be the rock-solid foundation of the exceptional economic, financial and social performance of Switzerland. The direct and indirect long-term damage that UBS and the mentality for which it had become the unfortunate symbol have caused to the Swiss economy will take at least a generation to absorb and to compensate.
26. For this argument cf. Otto Hieronymi, "In Search of a New Economics for the 1980s: The Need for a Return to Fixed Exchange Rates," *Annals of International Studies*, Institut Universitaire de Hautes Etudes Internationales, vol. 12, pp. 107–26, Geneva, 1982.
27. Group of 20, Working Group 3, *Reform of the IMF, Final Report*, London, March 4, 2009.
28. The so-called Basel rules have proven insufficient to forestall the crisis. Basel Committee:
    "From a supervisory perspective, the main contributing factors that came together to form a perfect storm include

    - A large amount of pre-crisis, system-wide liquidity, which led to excessive risk taking;
    - Inadequate measures to contain leverage, maturity mismatches, risk concentrations and the erosion of liquidity buffers over the credit cycle;
    - Regulatory gaps, which left important segments of the financial system under regulated;
    - Poor incentives in regulatory frameworks;
    - Poor underwriting standards;
    - Outsourcing of the due diligence process to the rating agencies;
    - Fundamental shortcomings in financial institution's governance, of which the current risk management shortcomings, are just a symptom.

    The crisis, which has re-concentrated risk in the banking sector, has resulted in financial market stress and massive deleveraging of historic proportions, with increasing spillover to the real economy. The speed and scale of these developments have been nothing short of astonishing." Nout Wellink, "The Importance of Banking Supervision in Financial Stability," Keynote Address by the President of the Netherlands Bank and Chairman of the Basel Committee on Banking Supervision, at the High Level Meeting "The Role of Banking and Banking Supervision in Financial Stability," Beijing, November 17, 2008, BIS.
29. According to Daniel Tarullo: "(W)here a regulatory sphere includes significant transnational activity, the effectiveness and efficiency of national regulation may increasingly depend on bilateral, multilateral, or even supranational cooperation. Basel II reveals the potential hazards as well as benefits of one approach to such arrangements. But its ultimate lesson is that something different must be tried, not that sustained and cooperative efforts should be abandoned." Daniel K. Tarullo, *Banking on Basel. The Future*

of International Financial Regulation, Peterson Institute for International Economics, Washington, DC, August 2008, p. 284.

30. Cf. Otto Hieronymi, "The International Financial Institutions and the Challenge of Transition and Reconstruction in the Former Communist Countries of Central and Eastern Europe," in Miklos Szabo-Pelsöczy (Editor), *Fifty Years After Bretton Woods*, (Sixth Conference of the Robert Triffin-Sziràk Foundation, Brussels 1994), Averbury, Aldershot, 1996, pp. 129–40.

31. Quoted in Shalendra D. Sharma, *The Asian Financial Crisis. Crisis, Reform and Recovery*, Manchester University Press, Manchester, 2003, p. 285. See also Sharma's analysis of the evolving international financial architecture in the wake of the Asian crisis, op. cit. pp. 284–339.

32. Otto Hieronymi and Daniela Bensky, "The Outlook for the Post-War Western Model of International Order and the Prospects for Perpetual Peace," *Paper presented at 8th International CISS Millennium Conference*, Paris, June 13–15, 2008.

33. Otto Hieronymi, "The Outlook for International Economic and Political Order: the Role of Japan and Europe," in *Kudan Square*, Institute For International Economic Studies, Tokyo, no. 17, March 2004, pp. 8–11.

34. On the link between the efficiency of the market economy and the role of solidarity cf. Otto Hieronymi, "'The 'Social Market Economy' and Globalisation: The Lessons from the European Model for Latin America," in Emilio Fontela Montes and Joaquin Guzmàn Cueva (Editors), *Brasil y la Economia Social de Mercado*, Cuadernos del Grupo de Alcantara, 2005, pp. 247–300; Jagdish Bhagwati, *The Wind of the Hundred Days, How Washington Mismanaged Globalization*, The MIT Press, Cambridge, Mass., 2002; Jagdish Bhagwati, *In Defense of Globalization*, A Council on Foreign Relations Book, Oxford University Press, 2004; Wilhelm Röpke, *The Social Crisis of Our Time*, William Hodge, London, 1950 (First German edition 1942); Wilhelm Röpke, *Civitas Humana. A Humane Order of Society*, William Hodge, London, 1948; Wilhelm Röpke, *International Economic Disintegration*, William Hodge, London, 1942; Marcelo F. Resico, *La Estructura de una Economia Humana, Reflexiones en Cuanto a la Actualidad del Pensamiento de W. Röpke*, EDUCA, Buenos Aires, 2008.

3
The Global Financial Crisis, Central Banking and the Reform of the International Monetary and Financial System

Michael Sakbani

3.1   The origins of the crisis

The current financial crisis originated in the years 1999–2007 as a result of a combination of several factors. During the first five years of the 2000s, there was an extraordinary boom in the housing market, in particular in the United States. The overhang in the supply of housing opened up for financial institutions, which were flushed with liquidity obtained from the global market, the possibility of extending vast numbers of mortgages at attractive rates.[1] The housing boom enabled them to double their portfolio of mortgage lending over its share ten years before; mortgages reached a plateau of 40–50 percent of their total loan assets after 2001. The second factor was the historically low interest rates set by the major Central Banks. The third was the accelerated pace of financial innovations in the context of rampant deregulation. The fourth was the virtual disappearance of the inflation fear from the screens of Central Banks. This latter was no doubt the contribution of the extraordinary growth of cheap Chinese imports in all world markets and the healthy growth of productivity in almost all the economies. Lastly, The international payments imbalances as manifest by the Chinese, South Korean and the Republic of China surpluses created a floating mass of capital in pursuit of financial investments any where in the global economy.

The demand for housing equity during the last decade and a half was at an historical high in every major country. In the United States, the number of housing units sold in 2005 reached a peak of 1,283,000 compared to an average of 609,000 in 1995–2000. More than 6.4 million units were sold in the five years up to 2006.[2] However, such an expansion in real estate equity would not have taken place had it not been for the availability of cheap mortgages made possible by the rather loose monetary policies of the United States from 2001 to 2004, and the consequential low interest rates.

Banks and other financial institutions, operating under loose regulations in the context of global liberalization, fed the housing boom with mortgages containing initial grace-periods of up to three years, minimal down payments and low initial interest payments to be adjusted later to market rates. Furthermore, many of these mortgages were extended to borrowers ordinarily considered not credit-worthy or, at the very least, borrowers who incurred debts beyond their capacity to pay back. But in so doing, the lenders observed the old rule that the higher the risk, the higher the reward. Thus came to be the subprime mortgage market a market whose borrowers could only pay back their debt if the rate of increase of housing prices continued to outstrip the rate of debt service so that they could refinance these loans or sell the houses at big profits.

Naturally if this was done under the old rules of mortgage lending, they would have had to hold them on their books and eventually would have run out of funds. But from the late 1980s, financial innovations made it possible for mortgage lenders to unload their loans to pools, which transformed these personalized, non-negotiable obligations into masses of repackaged derivative securities guaranteed by the mortgages. The amalgams of mortgages in the pools have the statistical predictability of large samples (see the discussion in section II below). Two major institutions, active in gathering mortgages, guaranteeing those on bank books and passing through what they bought, were the US public supported institutions Freddie Mac and Fannie Mae, which emitted roughly half of these papers, giving the illusion that they were government backed.

Financial institutions unbundled such mortgages and then bundled them anew, according to their characteristics, in the form of structured papers sold on the global market. The papers were circulated in the global financial markets with scant evaluation of their risk, no consideration of the leveraging involved and an oblivion regarding their potential illiquidity in case of system crisis. Moreover, as a result of the re-bundling, holders were hardly able to identify the primary mortgages on which they were based at issue. Like a herd, the Banks simply followed each other, buying these lucrative securities and garnering in the process big profits on their income statements, while hiding the eventual risks as contingent liabilities. The investment managers thus fell into the trap of the fallacy of composition, so well known in the history of the real bill-lending theory.[3] The non-transparency of these new instruments and their massive quantum even trumped the rating agencies, which evaluated them for each bank separately without ever considering their systematic risk. The rating agencies thereby operated as paid agents for the institutions that hired them and not as agents informed about the market risk and the state of all institutions. In addition, guarantees on such paper were sold by insurance agencies to various banks and the insurers were financed by other banks.

After the crisis erupted, the International Monetary Fund (IMF) estimated the size of these securities at more than $945 billion, while Goldman Sachs put them at more than $1.0 trillion.[4] In September 2008, the IMF revised its estimate to $1.4 trillion.[5] On January 28, 2009 the IMF once more revised its estimate to $2.2 trillion. In effect, nobody seems to know the real volume of these papers.

There were many culprits: the greedy banks and other financial institutions with their irresponsible and uninformed behavior, the equally greedy borrowers, the absence of appropriate regulations covering all the financial institutions involved, the lacunae of vigilant supervision at both state and federal levels, the non-regulated and non-transparent character of the financial innovations, the failure of the rating agencies to do their job and finally the loose monetary policy of the Greenspan era in the years 2001–2004. Mr. Greenspan, testifying on October 23, 2008 before a Congressional Committee, admitted his error in believing that investment mangers would exercise prudence in their operations and accepted that the regulatory system was loose and fundamentally obsolete.[6]

3.2   The financial crisis of 2008 unfolds

The crisis erupted in 2006, the first year in which prices declined. By August 2007, the annual decline exceeded 7 percent. The unsold inventory of houses was 39 percent higher in 2007 than a year before.[7] Naturally, the housing price decline rendered refinancing mortgages at higher interest rates rather difficult. The financial institutions, which had for long goaded the borrowers to take on mortgages they could not afford, now turned into parsimonious bankers. It should be recalled that in 2005 the Federal Reserve started to tighten monetary policy and raised interest rates seven times in one year. These hikes were of course carried through to the sub- prime mortgages, all of which were on a floating rate. Gradually, mortgage borrowers came to realize that unless they could borrow or refinance, they could not carry on with their debt. At the higher interest rates, the capital value of many mortgages started to exceed the resale value of the house. This opened the door to defaults and foreclosures. In the process, banks started to classify sub-prime mortgages as non-performing assets. The leveraged mortgage bonds and other derivatives, which were previously prized, now became risky and balance sheets became vulnerable. The crisis of the banks started in the United States and then, in the environment of globalized markets, spread to banks' balance sheets all over the world. As of the middle of 2007, banks began to realize the gravity of the risks of their balance sheet assets and started to feel the pinch of capital inadequacy. This was soon reflected in retrenchment on lending.

Concurrently, as the US economy and other economies teetered on the edge of recession, the stock markets all over the world turned bearish. In the second half of 2007 and up till end February, 2009, between a third and a half of the value of assets on the world stock exchanges was wiped out. More ominously, since March 2008, major investment banks and major integrated global banks and other financial institutions have been threatened with collapse unless they can receive huge injections of capital or are bought by solvent banks. Citibank, the United States' biggest bank, got a $27 billion injection from foreign sovereign funds followed later by $40 billion from the US government and UBS, the world's fifth biggest bank, got a $37 billion capital injection from similar sources plus $35 billion from the Swiss National Bank late in 2008. Other banks, in less egregious cases, rushed to raise their capital in order to write down, or off, billions of dollars of leveraged mortgage-based paper. However, not all banks were successful in their rush to raise capital. The market dried up in the face of Bear-Stearns March 2009. The US Federal Reserve had to step in to lend against collaterals and extend loan guarantees for Bear-Stearns. The situation was saved by JP Morgan Chase who acquired the bank for $10 a share. Merrill Lynch, the second largest investment bank in the United States, had better luck: the Bank of America bought it for a bargain price. On top of these banks, Freddie Mac and Fannie Mae, the two giants of mortgage pools and guarantees, holding more than $550 billion of mixed-quality mortgages, were saved from collapse and bankruptcy by the US authorities putting them into public conservatorship.

At any rate, the financial crisis did not stop there. In September, the market faced the imminent collapse of Lehman Brothers, another century-old institution; it was not successful in either borrowing or finding a buyer. The Federal Reserve shrank from stepping in because of the cost involved and, according to Chairman Bernanke, there were no appropriate collaterals.[8] The excuse of the Treasury was the lack of Congressional authorization. One should not discount ideology as well. Hence, Lehman applied for protection under Chapter 11 of the bankruptcy act.

Lehman's collapse sent severe shocks through all the markets. On Monday 15 and Tuesday 16 September, the NYSE lost more than 900 points (more than 8 percent of its capitalization), and similar percentage losses were recorded in other stock exchanges all over the world; in the global market all stock markets seem correlated.[9] In the week following September 15 started, AIG, the world largest insurance group with a global network covering non-bank insurances, lending insurance, insurances of retirement plans, protection of construction contracts, covers for health insurance schemes and various other asset protections, revealed that it needed a staggering $85 billion to be saved. Once again, in view of the world-wide repercussions and the direct threat posed to the safety of the financial system, the Federal Reserve came to the rescue. This time, and it was an historical first, the Federal Reserve rescued a financial institution outside both banking and its control; surely a precedent in the annals of monetary policy.

The fear that had gripped investors and manifested itself in the volatile and depressed stock exchanges was still not broken by all these dramatic rescues. Stock markets seemed to reason that the basic underlying problems remained untreated. Despite the announcement on Wednesday 17 September of a hurried pooling of $85 billion by the world's biggest banks to aid banks in need of refinancing and mobilizing a fund of $180 billion by the world's major Central Banks, stock markets still nosed down in Europe and Asia on the Thursday, amidst rumors that Morgan Stanley and Goldman Sachs, the two remaining independent US investment banks, were looking for buyers. Furthermore, the credit market literally stopped lending and the economy faced the specter of a credit lockout. By this time, it had become clear that the ad hoc approach was not working. Late in the day, a rumor spread that the US Federal government was at last considering a direct attack on the underlying housing problem by establishing a Resolution Trust Company (RTC) with sufficient resources to acquire and liquidate most of the non-performing mortgages. Indeed, during the weekend, President Bush announced his intention to set up a $700 billion agency to deal with the underlying problems.[10]

Europe, in particular the United Kingdom (UK), has also been in the grip of the same crisis since March 2008. The Bank of England took over the illiquid assets of Northern Rock, a major mortgage bank, at the beginning of the summer. At the behest of the Bank of England, Lloyds Bank agreed to purchase HBOS the mortgage giant which owns the Halifax Bank and the Royal Bank of Scotland, two institutions that teetered on the edge. At the end of September, Bradford and Bingley, another big bank, was taken over by the Bank of England. After unfathomable dithering, the British government announced on 8 October $87 billion in bank capital injections plus credit support facilities up to $420 billion.[11] On the continent, October saw the Belgian and Dutch governments taking action to save Fortis, a big mortgage bank. In October, the Germans had to step in to save Hypo-Real Estate, the mortgage giant, by extending $48 billion. On 5 October, Germany announced that it would guarantee all individual saving deposits in all its banks.[12] So did Ireland, Greece, Austria, Denmark and Iceland.

European and Asian officials outside the UK were quite slow to realize the extent of the crises. They thought initially that it was limited to a few banks. As they realized that the crisis was global, they started to float various ideas: the Dutch Prime Minister suggested a plan of $450 billion for Europe financed by a percentage of the GDP of EU members. Similar thoughts were attributed to French officials. On 4 October, President Sarkozy hosted the heads of governments of the four largest economies in an emergency meeting on the crisis. This meeting produced an agreement to take coordinated but independent national action by the members as they see fit. It called for an international conference in the form of a G7 meeting and a meeting of the heads of states of Europe to look into the situation. It was revealed that the European Central Bank had established a swap line with the US Federal Reserve of $240 billion to deal with system action and that the European Investment Bank has laid down $40 billion of loan facilities for small and intermediate businesses. The Europeans announced that five proposals for revamping the regulatory system would be presented to the College of Regulators in a short time. They also petitioned the EU to waive the Treaties restrictions on budget deficit limits.[13] And, not to be ignored, China's package at $860 billion represents 8 percent of its GDP, which is considerably larger in relative terms than the US package.

3.3   Analysis of the rescue plans: A new Central Banking

There are now several rescue plans, of which the most important are the US rescue plan, the British rescue plan and the variety of plans announced by other members of the EU, as well as rescue plans announced in November by China, Japan, and a host of other countries.

The US Treasury rescue plan, whose first draft was rejected, was approved by the Senate in a second draft which attached to it tax benefits amounting to an extra $50 billion, and an increase in limits of the FDIC deposit insurance to $250,000. In essence, the rescue plans aim initially at breaking the fear factor by assuring depositors and financial investors. Next, depending on the country, they seek to reestablish confidence in the banking system by removing from balance sheets the "Troubled Assets" so that banks and other financial institutions can utilize the funds received to resume their lending, especially, inter-bank lending. Finally, they aim at restarting the credit system of the economy. The US rescue plan is embodied in the Emergency Economic Stabilization Act of 2008 (hereinafter EESA), which entered into application the day after it became law on October 3, 2008.

The G7 meeting referred to above took place in Washington on the margin of the annual IMF-World Bank meetings. At the meeting, the Europeans discussed their plans with the United States. According to press reports, the EU Finance Ministers told the US officials that they prefer their method of direct capital injection over just buying troubled assets. Next day, the US Secretary of Treasury announced that he will use the EESA to buy stocks in the financial institutions, an idea long objected to in Washington.

The IMF meetings produced an international consensus to extend help and support to emerging countries and other developing countries suffering from the twin blow of recession and high food and fuel prices. In October, the IMF approved programs for Poland, Iceland and Pakistan. Several other countries, notably Turkey, are under consideration.

Right after the G7 meeting in Washington, the EMU members plus Britain conferred in Paris at the level of head of states and Prime Ministers and agreed to launch coordinated action in specific steps taken by each member according to its own conditions. By Monday 13 October, actions were announced by France, Germany Italy and the UK, which had actually preceded all of them.

The European Rescue Plans are multifaceted: they involve capital injections, funding outlays as well as guarantees for inter-bank lending. In addition, the measures provide help to banks in their lending operations. The scale is massive: France mobilized €320 billion for funding and €40 billion for capital injections. Germany mobilized a total of €480 billion for both. The UK mobilized $87 billion for capital injections and $420 billion for potential funding. Other countries: Italy, Spain, the Netherlands followed later. At the going exchange rates, this mobilization adds up to about $1.9 trillion of potential commitments. The multiple approaches of the Europeans, i.e., bank capitalization, inter-bank funding and guarantees and co-financing bank commercial lending, is the most comprehensive rescue package in place. President Sarkozy, as the current head of the EU, also announced that Europe will consult with the United States about reforming the international financial system in the weeks ahead.

The EESA raises a host of technical, economic and political issues.

3.3.1   An overriding issue

The first and foremost issue is whether the Rescue Plans are needed and justifiable at all. Many conservatives do not condone shielding firms from market discipline. During the week of negotiating the EESA in the United States, no alternative plans came up; there were suggestions to allow private insurances to do the job. However, such suggestions are not viable at this juncture and their time-line would be disastrous. Populists do not approve of shackling tax payers with the cost of the mistakes made by highly paid financial executives and do not, despite all the evidence, connect the crisis on Wall Street with the functioning of the real economy and the safety of public savings and pensions. Whatever the merits of these positions, the economic facts require action to stave off many potential disasters to the United States and the world economies. *The Economist*, basing itself on IMF estimates, put the total outlays of the rescue plans at 7 percent of the GDP of the countries involved, whereas the damage to the real economies is estimated at 16 percent.[14] The cost of not acting is therefore substantially greater than acting. Obviously, modern economies cannot operate with locked-up financial markets. It should be pointed out that, in the event, the rescue plans were structured in a way – see below – that might recuperate tax payers' money.

3.3.2   Technical issues in the US plan

The EESA creates a troubled asset relief program (TARP), under the supervision of the Secretary of the Treasury (Secretary) to establish vehicles to purchase, hold and sell troubled assets. The law provides for two approaches to deal with troubled assets: purchasing them from the institutions holding them (section 101) and/or extending guarantees to cover such assets (section 102).[15] This is surely a preferable market solution, but it takes time to work out and is less direct than the EESA.

It can be argued that, in addition to TARP, two more avenues are authorized under the EESA, which are, in our opinion, more effective. The first is to extend loans or guarantees of loans to banks with attached suitable conditions and the second is to recapitalize banks with a view to reestablishing capital adequacies. The suitable conditions may involve bank restructuring, provisions on foreclosures and new risk-evaluation methods. The capital injection is more powerful than purchasing troubled assets in that it implies under the prevailing capital adequacy norms a 1–11 leveraging, that is, for every dollar capital a possible $11 credit. This idea, according to press reports, was discussed but rejected in Washington as a kind of socialism. After meeting the Finance Ministers of the G7 in Washington on 10 October, Secretary Paulson, however, indicated that he is studying it. As a historical precedent, Sweden nationalized temporarily its banks in 1991 and got out of its crisis in record time.

The Treasury announced on 12 October that it will acquire shares in nine major banks and that it intends to allocate $250 billion for such acquisitions. The equity is in non-voting stocks, warrants and bank preferred stocks. It is possible that equity debt swaps can be made a part of the plan. In effect, the Treasury thinking has gone into four mutations before the ideological veil was lifted. The first was accepting the idea of TARP. The second was agreeing with Europe that injecting capital was more effective than buying troubled assets. The third was accepting the idea that participating in lending and guaranteeing interbank lending were what was required. The fourth mutation is setting in but is not yet played out. This is to place EESA in the context of an integrated program of macroeconomic stimulation and rescue of house owners. In such a program, in addition to expansionary action, EESA would deal simultaneously with the entire spectrum of credit provision, including consumer lending. In addition, it must deal with the restructuring of non-performing mortgage loans at reduced interest rates, extended payment periods and, if need be, reduced values. On November 12, 2008, Secretary Paulson announced that he is indeed changing direction on EESA, the third such change.

Assuming that a mixture of all four approaches will be employed, we will proceed to discuss the issues that would arise.

Regarding the pricing of troubled assets, it should be borne in mind that the financial institutions involved have not collapsed. Therefore, their assets are worth something between their book values and fire-sale values. Unlike the RTC experience of the depression years, the assets involved have values unknown by the markets. Therefore, one of the first tasks of EESA is to authorize the Secretary to find a mechanism for defining and acquiring troubled assets and establishing a market price for them. This cannot be done without differentiating their risks and categorizing them accordingly. If the Treasury were to price the troubled assets too high, there would be undue gain for the banks and other institutions. If, on the other hand, the price were too low, that would discourage healthy, but affected, banks from participating in TARP and harm its successful conclusion. It would in addition encourage private bidders to purchase such assets at low prices thereby accrue private benefits from the Treasury rescue. Most likely, the price would be determined by setting up a reverse-bidding auction, i.e., one buyer and many sellers. Assets of the same risk would then undergo a market price discovery through these auctions. The Secretary is to report to the Congress, within 45 days from the entry into effect of EESA, on the mechanisms and valuation methods adopted.[16]

Another problem is to help banks in a way that stops unnecessary foreclosures. If mortgages remain on the books at historical cost, the underlying problem for the house owners will not be resolved. If they are drastically down valued, both the institutions involved will suffer and the non-defaulting borrowers will bear a moral hazard penalty. The EESA provided for a variety of relief measures based on capitalizing mortgages at the present value of a loan to the tax payers. The provisions amount to refinancing and restructuring the troubled loans of those who are willing to continue holding them. There are in this respect forbearance provisions to keep people in their houses while the process is engaged. However, through the middle of March 2009, this does not seem to be working.

Another technical hurdle is to choose assets to be unloaded. The troubled mortgage assets were estimated by Secretary Paulson at only 5 percent of total mortgage assets.[17] Providing a level playing field for all banks implies that all institutions should be included. Several months already into the crisis, banks and other financial institutions are now in a position to present the Secretary with the assets they consider troubled. The available empirical knowledge regarding the size of the assets still outstanding on the books – without capital write-offs – is estimated at $760 billion for US institutions.[18] The EESA was approved to the tune of $700 billion: an initial authorization to the Secretary of $250 billion, with $100 billion extra placed under the authority of the President and the remaining $350 billion subject to congressional approval.[19]

3.3.3   Analysis of the economic issues

It is remarkable indeed that the US Treasury was caught in the crisis without preparation, without policy forethought and without appreciation of the true situation. Secretary Paulson's first proposal was a sorry three-page paper which proposed granting him absolute and unfettered power to spend $700 billion buying his former colleagues' assets. The rescue package that emerged is by no means a great plan. However, it is detailed, flexible, supervised and politically attuned. And it was the only plan on the table.

The first economic issue is the scope of the monetary intervention and that of the fiscal one. Monetary intervention directly affects inflation and interest rates and thus the dollar exchange rate and, in the process, the balance of payments. It is likely that, in the short term, the dollar might be boosted if the action plan is perceived positively. However, in the long term, there is little doubt that the dollar should weaken. But this is all relative to what happens to other currencies. The inflationary consequences are for the short run irrelevant, but not so in the longer run. The fiscal action affects the US budget deficit and, therefore, the gap between US national investments and savings as well as the size of the US public debt. This, in turn, affects adversely the long-run dollar exchange rate and the Balance of Payments and crowds out private investment. Expanding the size of the public debt to $11.2 trillion augers future tax increases and shifting the burden to future generations.

The fiscal action would be more effective if it is done with global coordination because that would protect exports, thereby reducing the size of the required stimulation of internal demand. However, there is a problem of global resource transfer involved. While we still do not know how much of the fiscal layouts will actually be spent on sorting out the credit system and the real economy, the announced plans imply adding trillions of dollars to fiscal expenditures and taxing or borrowing that much from various sources. If such massive expenditures are to be financed by taxes, then consumer spending in the developed economies must retract by a good fraction of such layouts for a long time to come. This means a reduction in the standards of living and an adjustment in the disposition of the national product. If, on the other hand, all is borrowed then if the borrowing is from domestic sources, consumption declines but the lenders make claims on the public sector. Thus, there would be forced savings but at the cost of crowding out private investment. Moreover, future taxes will increase and/or there would be a shift in tax burden to future generations. If the borrowing is from foreign sources, that would mean increasing foreign debt and placing limits on exercising sovereign foreign policy. In the long run, borrowing abroad will not be sustainable without paying back through extra exports or paying with real assets. A middle solution between these two poles would only modify the quantum of adjustment in the standards of living of the developed economies. In sum, we are witnessing the acceleration of the shift in economic wealth and political influence to nations outside the developed West.

The monetary action has global implications. These concern international inflation and the global pattern of payments deficits and the relative valuation of currencies. The misalignment of currencies has been part of the present crisis. However, there is, at present, no global authority in the IMF to cope with these problems.

The monetary action has changed the theory of Central Banking. Central Banks acquired in this crisis assets of banks and of financial institutions outside their traditional purviews. They also modified the scopes of their discount policies or bank window policies by financing private commercial papers. In effect, Central Banking was used in the crisis for the purposes of financing institutions. Thus, the traditional scope of monetary policy through controlling interest rates or monetary aggregates has been significantly modified. In addition to operating on the liability side of the Central Bank balance sheet by increasing or decreasing its liabilities to the public and banks, monetary policy has added operating on the asset side by changing the composition of the assets to include new lending and new credit operations. Moreover, Central Banks, including the European Central Bank (ECB), have shifted their stance on inflation and cut interest rates in a coordinated manner down to 0–2 percent, the lowest in fifty years.

The fiscal and monetary actions also have implications for resource allocations, market efficiency and the role of governments in market economies. The latter two issues will be treated below. Regarding economic efficiency, the question is the impact on efficiency of not allowing markets to penalize the derelict institutions. More fundamentally, how can one be sure that their behavior will change and their inefficiencies removed? A good suggestion is for the Secretary to demand of participants restructuring as a quid pro quo for help when he deems that warranted. The other side of this issue is already alluded to in the above discussion of crowding out, to wit, the impact on the economic growth of transferring resources from private to public investments at higher secular trend of interest rates.

By mid-January 2009, there has been no visible credit expansion by banks. If the financial system does not resume inter-bank and other lending, authorities everywhere must be prepared to intervene in a more direct and forceful way. For example, they may consider extending guarantees on all inter-bank lending, or even create, for a short period, a clearing house run by the Central Bank for inter-bank lending. They may also announce that, as an exception to the discount policy, they would grant access to the Central Bank windows for discounting commercial loans including mortgages. Still another avenue is to allow Central Banks to make, under certain conditions, direct loans to businesses and/or extend short-term guarantees for such loans. Another avenue is to authorize the Central Bank to purchase business debt papers, such as Commercial Papers and other high-grade money market instruments whose market has dried up. This step is already decided by the US Federal Reserve, which additionally doubled the size of its discount window funds.

To enhance confidence, many countries, including the United States, have increased substantially their bank deposit insurance coverage. To avoid beggar-thy-neighbor practices, this measure should be coordinated internationally.

In sum, four types of direct policy actions on the financial-monetary front are called for: a direct removal of troubled assets, a direct injection of liquidity and guarantees, a direct capitalization through guarantees or purchasing stocks, and a direct treatment of the mortgage-housing problem. In this context, the Treasury might consider, as a part owner of banks, to demand that they recapitalize, restructure and modify every mortgage loan in which the capital value exceeds the resale value of the property, provided that the loans are not taken up at their book values.[20] Moreover, as part owner of banks, and provider of capital, the government should attach specific and clear cut, appropriate conditions forcing the banks to lend as a quid pro quo for help received.

Beyond these immediate finance-credit problems, there is the underlying macroeconomic recessionary condition of the United States and other economies. The circularity between real economic performance and the health of the financial system calls, in our judgment, for a global stimulatory action. In the October meeting of the IMF, it was agreed to take such actions and, further, the IMF was instructed to extend financial help to countries affected by the rise in food and other commodity prices. As regards the US economy, it is commonly agreed that a stimulatory package is in order. With the exception of the export sector, the investment and consumer sectors are experiencing significant expenditure shrinkage. The available data show investment spending shrinking since July after a modest increase in the second quarter. Data on economic indicators show that consumer spending, accounting for two thirds of total spending and long the stable mainstay of the US economy, declined 3.15 percent from May to August 2008.[21] In the production sectors, with the exception of the export sector, energy and some services, all other sectors are experiencing relative decline. Leading the list is the construction sector: house prices declined by 16.3 percent in September 2008 compared to a year before, and housing starts declined by 6.2 percent in August on top of 12.4 percent in July.[22] The orders for products of the manufacturing industries experienced their lowest levels in six years, dropping by 5.5 percent in July and August. The car industry expects declines in sales ranging from 15 to 30 percent compared to the previous year sales. In the second week of November, the car industry announced that its sales were, relative to income levels, the lowest since 1946 and GM announced that its cash position is in dire straits. The Industrial Production Index declined 111.51 in June to 110.3 in August.[23] Many consumer-related service industries, such as insurance and of course the financial service industry, are in decline. The data show also that unemployment hit 6.1 per cent, a six-year high on Tuesday 23 September. In the nine months to September, 750,000 workers lost their jobs. On 7 November, the US Bureau of Labor statistics announced that unemployment increased by 240,000 in October, bringing the jobless rate to 6.4 percent, the highest in 14 years. And November was even crueler with 533,000 more losing their jobs.[24] If one were to extrapolate the unemployment trend and include in the official statistics involuntary part timers and those who dropped out of job search, one would be talking about nine and a half to ten percent unemployment.

Thus, by any yardstick, the US economy, after a good performance in the second quarter, was in recession in the third and fourth quarters of 2008. With the combined effects of the credit crisis and an expected deceleration in exports, the decline has accelerated in 2009. Early in November, the IMF reported that it judges the United States; the United Kingdom and the Euro zone countries all to be in recession. On January 29, 2009, the Chief Economist of the IMF, Monsieur O. Blanchard, forecasted for 2009 a decline in the United States of 1.5 per cent of the GDP, a decline in Europe of 2 percent, in the UK of 2.8 percent and a world-wide growth of only 0.5 percent. Therefore, the case for a coordinated stimulus has become persuasive.

For the United States, the necessary fiscal stimulus can be estimated in three ways: replacing the amount of expected decline in the GDP by fiscal expansion; adding the two deficits in the current account and the investment saving balance; and using Okun Law to estimate the expenditure necessary to reduce the rate of unemployment from 9 to 5 percent, the US full employment rate. Any of these ways would yield a stimulus in the neighborhood of 8 percent of the GDP. This implies some $1.1 trillion. President Obama's package calls for more than $800 billion stimulus in fiscal 2009. This is a harrowing amount of expenditure with major long-run negative implications under the prevailing national saving rate and external balance of the United States. Coming on top of all the other fiscal commitments, the situation would call for a major commitment to return to fiscal discipline in the long run.

The US fiscal stimulus must aim at more than replacing lost expenditure. The current crisis should serve the purposes of effecting major structural changes in the US economy, in the fiscal and budgetary structure of the Government and in the tax system. There is a manifest need for public investment in the US infrastructure to underpin long-run productivity. There is obviously an urgent need as well to invest in new technologies friendly to the ecological system and to prepare for the post-oil era. Recent fiscal stimuli of tax cuts and expenditures were not of this type and the recent growth of the US economy has been consumer and construction driven rather than investment driven. But all this need not be done in one go. It is advisable to phase in the stimulus package over three phases: in the first phase, urgent filling of the expenditure gap; in the second phase, the United States goes for investment in infrastructure and for economic restructuring; in the third phase is the turn of necessary and worthwhile expenditures, such as health care reform. In the process, the future posture of the US public budget must be faced as a critical issue. This involves reviewing and restructuring the US entitlement programs and their financing, and undertaking an overdue reexamination of the US budget priorities, which should include eventual reduction in all forms of military and other national security spending.

The package should initially have direct spending elements in view of their short propagation lag and their superior multiplier effect; the effect on unemployment reduction of spending one dollar exceeds by some 25 percent the effect of one dollar tax cut. The empirical evidence shows that tax reductions have larger spending effects when they take the form of increases in disposable income rather than lump sum tax hand outs, which are mostly saved.

The first that comes to mind are the spending plans already prepared by state and local governments, including some urgent infrastructure projects. Another element is to lengthen the period of drawing benefits by laid-off workers and tax breaks to small businesses hiring workers. Still another suggestion is to extend extra food stamps programs to beneficiaries. Help in the form of tax breaks and even direct loans and guarantees to small businesses should be an early priority. Another avenue is reductions in payroll taxes. At this point it is sensible to integrate the TARP and the stimulus program, as well as help to affected sectors and industries, all in one multifaceted multi-period approach.

Naturally, there is the question of the duration of the recession. The data since 1972 indicate that the length of global recessions has been 12–16 months compared to 6–9 months when confined to the

United States. This would imply that even with a fiscal stimulus, the recovery of the US economy would take place some two to three quarters after EESA restores the health of the financial system. That implies no recovery before mid-2010.

Similar facts and reasoning would also apply to the major European economies; the case for fiscal stimuli in Europe is quite convincing. On 24 October, the UK officially announced that its GDP dipped down 1.5 percent in the third quarter of 2008. Even though the Europeans insisted on 9 October that fiscal policy remains in the national domain, they turned around on 14 October and announced coordinated fiscal stimuli. Such coordination is necessary to avert world-wide inflation and produce an inconsistent pattern of external payments. Finally, on November 6, 2008, the IMF reported that the UK, the Euro zone and several other countries were, in its judgment, in recession. The IMF followed that on January 28, 2009 with a forecast of a drop in Europe's GDP of two percent and 2.8 percent for the UK in 2009.

3.3.4   The political issues in the United States

The political problems are manifold. First of all there is a cross economic one concerning the security of tax payers' money. The US government and tax payers are potentially out of $650 billion for the rescue operations in place. The EESA will add immediately $250 billion followed, if needed, by another $100 billion. Consequently, the Congress put into the EESA provisions requiring the involved institutions to issue in favor of the Treasury both warrants for non-voting preferred stocks in the firms, and promises to pay the difference (if positive) between the realized value of the asset and the Treasury purchase price. Such stocks would be offered without dilution of capital. If most institutions recover, it is possible that the tax payers might get their money back and hopefully garner a profit.

The control and oversight authority for the disbursement and the disposition of the assets is a major political issue everywhere. The EESA of 2008 created a Stability Oversight Board (SOB) composed of five members including the Secretary, the Chairman of the Federal Reserve, the Housing Secretary, the Chairman of SEC and the Director of the FHFA, under an elected Chairman who turned out to be the Chairman of the Federal Reserve. The Secretary reports periodically to the SOB, which in turn reports to the US Congress.[25] Regrettably, up to the writing of these lines in January 2009, there has been little information on where the $350 billion already drawn out of the TARP has been used, under what conditions and with what stipulations. Moreover, by the end of 2008, there was slim evidence of changes in the lending of banks and the treatment of the housing loans. Hence tax payers have so far little to show for their spent money, beyond rescuing financial institutions.

There is, as well, a problem of national resource allocation in all of this: is the rescue of the derelict institutions a better choice than spending the tax payers' money elsewhere, for example, on the decaying US physical infrastructure, on investment in health care, education and research and developing a new ecological technology to reduce the demand for carbon fossils fuels. Many would argue that the alternative is a better investment. Another political problem is the potential benefits accruing from the rescue to bank stock-holders and bank executives at the public expense. Many voices are heard asking for limits on salaries and bonuses for departing executives in the rescued institutions and a maximum on salary increases.[26] The EESA places two limits: for the institutions taken over, a limit of $400,000, and for those on their own there would be no tax deduction on the salaries and golden parachutes. In the same vein, the European rescues, for example in France and in the UK, provide strict limits on compensation together with penalties on the management of institutions seeking help. By comparison, the United States still seems too lax about executive compensations.[27]

3.4   The rise and fall of the model of global liberal finance

The current global crisis might mark the end of an era in the history of financial capitalism. The prevailing model of deregulated, liberal and open financial capitalism was ushered in the mid-1980s with the coming to power early in the decade of Mrs. Thatcher in the UK and President Reagan in the United States. This model was no doubt given impetus by the manifest success of open market economies and the concomitant manifest failure of the state controlled ones. While it is not possible to impute the success of the economies concerned to this sole reason, the margin of empirical difference was undeniable and persisted for a decade. The growth of financial flows world wide together with the growth of international trade and transnational corporation investments and other Foreign Direct Investments (FDI) were superior to the growth of national incomes every where.[28] The economies, which opened themselves to this new brave world, reaped rich benefits. Therefore, many observers came to the conclusion that the liberal open model was the only successful choice on the menu.

The United States offered the most successful example of this model in application. And of all the US economic institutional set up, the financial system was the best performing and most esteemed. The global trend was therefore to copy the American model and push liberalization and globalization to the limits. Hence, the world witnessed a gathering wave of deregulation and globalization in the second half of the 1980s, which accelerated in the 1990s and came to rule the roost thereafter.[29]

In the United States, the protestations of non-bank financial institutions against regulatory barriers that they faced, coupled with the rather stagnant performance of commercial banks in the 1990s, convinced the US Congress and Administration to overhaul the financial legislation and do away with the barriers erected by the Glass-Stiegel Act of the depression era, removing in the process the distinctions between banks and other financial intermediaries and institutions.[30] At the end of the second term of the Clinton Administration, the President signed into law the Gramm-Leach-Bliley Modernization Act of 1999, thereby removing distinctions among financial institutions.[31]

The act allowed US banks to become supermarket banks, grouping under the same institutional roof retail and wholesale banking, investment banking and other intermediary financial services. This is more or less the European system, but with less regulations. In the global era, banks started a massive consolidation and globalization process turning themselves into mega-size global institutions. However, banks were not the only beneficiaries of this liberalization. Other financial institutions previously not as regulated as the banks, also jumped on the band-wagon and started offering diversified financial services on a global scale. The stage was therefore set for the double digit annual growth of the financial industry. This growth was propelled by the multiplicity of financial innovations offering a bewildering variety of financial products. This imparted momentum to the securitization of the financial industry and, thanks to the revolution of information and communications, the global scale operation of banks.

Among the innovations was the coming of age of derivative products, whose market is estimated by the IMF to be in excess of $22 trillion, and which now account for 22 percent of US bank income. Such products are treated as off-balance sheet items carrying contingency risk, which yield income but do not burden capital so long as they continue to perform. The innovations retouched also mortgage loans. In the late 1980s, Merrill Lynch and Michael Millikan at Drexel Bank transformed mortgage loans from personalized assets with non-predictable flows into derivative paper based on the statistical properties of large samples: predictable inflows and outflows and standardized uniform sample characteristics.[32] Investment banks saw a great opportunity in acquiring papers based on mortgage pools and then repackaging them at several times gearing ratio and selling them under the splendid neutered name "Structured Financial Vehicles." These papers were sold to financial buyers all over the world.

It should be remembered that the underlying mortgages came from banks, which were regulated, and non-bank institutions, which were much less regulated and supervised. In the pools, the loans were mixed and nobody could access their differentiated risk and thus price the constructed derivatives in relation to their true risk. The pools enabled the banks and the other lending institutions to unload their loans. Had stricter regulation and more realistic risk evaluation standards been applied, the circulation of the resultant derivative securities would have been attached to differentiated risk rating in respect of the issuer: prime papers, essentially issued by regulated banks, and the sub-prime papers issued largely by non regulated lenders. In all probability, this risk segmentation would have limited their quantum and reduced their circulation in the global financial markets.

Does the crisis mark the end of the liberal financial model and a return to regulations and national financial markets?

On the September 22, 2008, Morgan Stanley and Goldman Sachs applied to the Federal Reserve to operate under its umbrella as bank holding companies. That certainly signaled the end of investment banking as Wall Street knew it. But investment banking is essential for underwriting securities, arranging mergers and acquisitions, extending financial services and advice as well as for financing big projects. Those functions will remain and continue to be performed by institutions which call themselves banks but not Investment Banks. What is likely to emerge is a reasonably supervised and regulated structure, which will continue to operate globally. President Sarkozy of France was speaking for most when he said, at the European summit of the four biggest economies on October 4, 2008, that a reform to bring about an entrepreneurial capitalism and not a speculative one is called for. Perhaps the future system will be a market-based multi-standard banking system, some of which is more regulated than the other, but all of which is largely safe and global.

The crisis threw into sharp relief the indispensability of the state's role in a market economy as a regulator, a last resort provider and a custodian of the financial markets and people's savings. In essence, there is now a common realization that markets are too important to be left operating on their own. There is also an equal realization that it is legitimate for government to interfere in the markets, not only when there is market failure, but also when the political interests and stability of the country requires it. President Sarkozy's National Fund for safeguarding the French economy, announced on October 23, 2008, is a case in point. The world seems to have come to closure of the Reagan era of ribald financial liberalization.

3.5 Toward new international norms for financial regulation and bank supervision: Reforming the international system

In the light of the above, it would be reasonable to say that the global financial crisis would not have occurred with the ferocity we have witnessed if proper financial regulations and supervision had been in place.

For a number of years, these issues have been under consideration in the Basel Bank of International Settlements (BIS) and the Basel Committee on Banking Supervision (BCBS). The two bodies studied the risk of derivative securities and other instruments of structured finance along with other contingent liabilities and their relationship to bank capital.[33] The BIS produced in 1988 the financial convention Basel I, while the BCBS produced in 2003 Basel II. Basel I has been incorporated into the regulations of about 100 countries, while Basel II is still under consideration. This work proposed norms for estimating risk and measuring capital adequacy in the new global environment. It also covered best practice norms for banks and international markets. The BCBS proposed examples of standardized accounting norms for banks and models of financial auditing and supervision. Moreover, it developed agreed methods for estimating asset value. It also established modalities for supervision and bank examination. In recent years, the BIS has also become a major center of data gathering and dissemination.[34]

The work of the BIS and the BCBS furnishes a good basis for revamping the regulatory system in the United States and for making sure that such an overhaul is done on a world-wide scale. The salient features of a possible new system, which incorporates the lessons of this crisis, can be summarized as follows:

- Uniformity of international standards: the surest bank behavior is to exploit differences and gaps in regulations. In the current global market, this means that no regulations are enforceable if they are not done on a global scale. Similarly, nation-states would accrue unfair advantages if they adopt different standards from their partners. In October 2008, Ireland and Greece gave 100 percent insurance cover for deposits in their banks, a move that was immediately contested by other EU members and matched within two days by Germany, Austria and Denmark.

- The new regulatory system must cover all financial institutions and not just depository institutions. In other words, it should be based on regulating the type of financial function, regardless of who is doing it. The aforementioned European summit promised to submit to an international conference a comprehensive scheme for a college of supervisors of all institutions.[35] It is doubtful that there would be agreement on one international authority. However, international coordination is both imperative and feasible.
- In line with the recommendations of the BCBS report, the new system may consider the proposed measures to strengthen prudential oversight of banks and other financial institutions and adopt best practice models for this supervision.
- The new system must establish common international models for asset-risk valuation. The BCBS considered three asset risks: market, credit and operational. It devised rules for weighing various asset risks and relating them to bank capital adequacy ratios, thereby setting the regulatory auditing standards.[36] However, all that should now be revisited to factor in the evolution of risk in the global system. In other words, the emphasis on micro-prudential risk management, should be coupled with a macro-prudential risk evaluation, which factors in cyclical and systemic factors
- The new system should strive to establish common financial accounting standards for examining, auditing and supervising all financial institutions.
- In view of the gross negligence of the rating agencies in the lead up to this crisis, the new system should factor in changes in the role and uses of credit ratings and in the standards applied by these agencies in their work. It should also demand that the credit rating agencies consider system risk. There is also a manifest need to make these agencies transparant in their work, adherant to internationally agreed standards and secure their financing by bodies independent of their client under examination.
- Put in place agreed modalities to strengthen the responsiveness of authorities to systemic risk, and set robust arrangements for dealing with stress in the international financial system. In this context, given the enormous size of consolidated banks, there should be provisions for dealing with banks and non-depository financial institutions whose size is too big to allow to fail. According to

The Economist of 7 November, of the $13 trillion bank assets, six institutions hold 75 percent of the total. Consequently, there should be rules on how to take over such institutions and procedures for the final resolution of troubled non-depository institutions. More generally, the new system must set ways for the oversight authorities to burst finance bubbles.[37]

- Establish internationally standardized system for data definitions, gathering and electronic dissemination to all participants and to the public at large.

While the BIS forum has been quite active over the last ten years, the IMF and other international financial and monetary organs have been notable for their passive presence. In a global economy with global financial markets, an international authority is essential for solving and dealing with any global problem. Resolving the current crisis is impossible through the lonc action of the United States. Yet, the prevailing international monetary system has no such locus of authority. The IMF, from its inception, has had no bank of last resort function and no resources of its own to create international liquidity in order to cope with large-scale crises. The international reserve system it runs is essentially a pool of sovereign contributions of national currencies, dominated by the major reserve currencies and subject to the sovereign control of their governments. The IMF's surveillance functions under Article IV are essentially limited to balance of payments issues.[38] It is therefore expected that, contrary to all logic, it is irrelevant in the current crisis. However, the BIS forum cannot substitute for the IMF because its membership is limited to the ten major countries plus Switzerland. More importantly, none of the results of its work are mandatory on member states, let alone other countries. It takes no leap of imagination to conclude that international monetary reform should be a major item on any intergovernmental future agenda.[39] President Sarkozy of France and other heads of states said as much in the current session of the UN General Assembly, which coincided with the crisis.

In the years since the Washington Consensus, the International Bank for Reconstruction and Development (IBRD) and the IMF have become unconditional advocates of deregulation, openness and market liberalization.[40] Their policy recommendations, emphasizing unfettered openness and liberalization, proved ineffective in foiling the Asian crisis of 1998, and in some cases, such as Malaysia, irrelevant.[41] Worst, they could neither predict nor stop the crisis.[42] Thereafter, the importance of these institutions and their relevance to a global financial system was dwarfed by the size and the availability of private and regional lending institutions. Now it is only countries with no market access or access on onerous terms and conditions that resort to them. Consequently, their relevance has been put in question.[43] In the aftermath of the current crisis, the role of these institutions and their philosophy must be reconsidered. While it is unrealistic to expect that they will ever be a substitute for national authorities as banks of last resort,[44] they can be very helpful and effective if they move in concert with the BIS to provide a true international forum for international coordination in the areas of regulations, practice standards and bank data reporting. They can also break new grounds if they make themselves loci of advanced warning of system crisis and the forum of coordinated response. This is precisely what the October meeting of the IMF council produced: agreement to coordinate a common action by all member states to deal with the crisis. The EU secured the agreement of the United States to convene in Washington, on November 15, 2008, an international conference of 20 major countries to discuss reforming the international system. Similarly, the Euro-Asian summit held in Beijing concluded, on October 24, 2008, with a call to use the upcoming Washington meeting to launch the discussions about international monetary and financial reforms. The stage seems therefore set for an exercise that might be as ambitious as the C.20. However, one should not raise expectations too high, as monetary reform has been a taboo in the United States for over thirty years.

A considerable literature on international monetary reform has developed over the past three decades with a wealth of ideas and proposals.[45]

Notes

This paper was partially supported by a research grant from Webster University-Geneva.

1. For a detailed discussion of the US housing market see Elise, Luci (2008), "The Housing Meltdown: Why Did It Happen in the US," BIS Working Papers no 259, September.
2. The statistics are forming Wikipedia (2008), "The United States Housing Bubble," http://en.wikipedia.org/wiki/United_States_housing_bubble, September 2008.
3. The fallacy of composition refers to the observation that real bills guaranteeing bank loans have little market if all banks proceed to liquidate them at the same time. See any standard money and banking text on the real bill theory and the fallacy of composition, for example, Mishkin, F. S. (2008), *The Economics of Money, Banking and Financial Markets*, McGraw-Hill, international edition, eighth edition, Ch.16, p. 420.

4. IMF (2008), *Global Financial Stability Report*, Washington DC, April. See also the story in the *International Herald Tribune*, April 8, 2008 on the estimate of 1.2 billion made by Goldman Sachs.
5. *Economist, The*, (2008), "When Fortune Frowned, A Special Report on the World Economy," October 11, p. 4.
6. In 2002, the House Democrats brought to the attention of Allan Greenspan, the Fed Chairman, the dangers of the behavior of the unregulated mortgage lenders and asked for putting up regulations. According to Congressman Barney Frank, the Chairman refused the idea of regulating markets; interview on CNN, September 20, 2008.
7. Wikipedia, *The United States Housing Bubble. http://en.wikipedia.org/wiki/United_States_housing_bubble.* September 2008.
8. Statement of Bernanke, Ben (2008), Statement before the *New York Bank Association*, NY, October 14.
9. Wikipedia, *The United States Housing Bubble. http://en.wikipedia.org/wiki/United_States_housing_bubble.* September 2008, for data on stock market developments of the respective days.
10. The most widely observed stock index, the Dow Jones Industrial of New York, recouped close to 800 points and the CAC-Quarante of Paris soared 9.6 percent of its value, whilst the London FT-100 gained 5.6 percent on Friday. In Frankfurt, the DAX gained 3.9 percent. The Asian markets were more impressive: the Hang- Sang recorded 9.6 percent gain and the Nikkei 3.8 percent. See; www.Reuters/finance/economic, Friday, September 19, 2008.
11. Forty four billion of this amount will go to support the capital of eight endangered banks and the rest for other possible use if and when necessary.
12. *The International Herald Tribune*, October 6, 2008.
13. For the full text, see: http://www.politsite.com/act.pdf.
14. *The Economist*, "When Fortune Frowned," p. 4.
15. Ibid., pp. 6–8.
16. Ibid., section 102, p. 10.
17. This is the estimate made by the US Secretary of the Treasury in the Senate hearing on Tuesday, September 23, 2008.
18. *The Economist*, "When Fortune Frowned," p.4.
19. With the disclosure in January 2009 that City Bank and Bank of America have more troubled assets than previously known, these estimates look short of what will be needed.
20. This idea was raised by Senator Hillary Clinton in her primary campaign. At the time, the cost to the Government of this proposal was seen prohibitive. However, now that EESA provides $ 750 billion, the price is no longer untenable.
21. Data from US Economic Statistics Administration (2008), *Economic Indicators*, 2 October.
22. US Census Bureau, data announced on September 30, 2008.
23. Board of Governors statistics as released by the Reserve Bank of St. Louis, Economic Indicators, September, 2008.
24. UNCTAD, *World Investment Report*, Geneva, 1997 and 2007.
25. With November figures the jobless rate climbed to 6.7 percent. However, the figures in the text do not include workers converted involuntarily to

part time work, those no longer drawing unemployment benefits and those who quit the labor force. If these are included then the unemployment rate should exceed 9.0 percent.

26. See UNCTAD, *Globalization and Liberalization*, Geneva, 1996, Chapter I; also. UNCTAD, "Global Financial Integration and Related Domestic Liberalization Policies," in *Globalization and Liberalization: Effects of International Economic Relations on Poverty*, New York and Geneva, 1996. See also: Sakbani, Michael (2006), "A Re-examination of the Architecture of the International Economic System in a Global Setting: Issues and Proposals," UNCTAD, Discussion Paper, no. 181, Geneva, pp. 5–7.

27. The Glass-Steigle act established fire walls between commercial banks and other financial institutions in order to remove conflict of interest and financial pyramiding, which was rampant in the prior decade.

28. It came to public attention, that after receiving billions of tax payers' money through the TARP, many financial institutions: AIG, City Bank, Merrill-lynch and others, have put aside billions of the received funds for executive bonuses!!

29. See the analysis of the act known as the Gramm-Leach-Bliley Modernization Act of 1999, in Mishkin, *The Economics of Money, Banking and Financial Markets*, Ch. 10, pp. 268.

30. For an entertaining narration of this innovation and the personae involved, see, Lewis, Michael (1990), *Liar's Poker*, Penguin, New York.

31. See for the Reagan era, Michael Sakbani, "The Liberal Financial Order in Crisis: Examination of the Rescue Plans and the Reform of the International System," in www. networkideas.org, October 2008.

32. BCBS, The New Capital Accords, GIS, April, 2004; Cornford, Andrew (2004), "Basel II; Vintage 2003," *Journal of Financial Regulations and Compliance*, 12 /1, February.

33. Cornford, Andrew (2006), "The Basel Committee's Proposal for Revised Capital Standards," G24 Discussion Paper Series, no. 3.

34. Cornford, Andrew (2005), "Basel II, the Revised Framework of June 2004," manuscript.

35. Cornford, Andrew (2008), "Basel II at a Time of Financial Peril," *TWN Global Economy Series*, March.

36. Ibid.

37. BCBS (2006), *International Convergence of Capital Measurement & Capital Standards; A Revised Framework Comprehensive Version*, BIS, Basel.

38. The last systematic exercise in IMS' reform was the work of the C.20 in 1972–4. The report of the C 20 was approved by all IMF members except the United States and Germany. Two more partial attempts were effected in 1981 and 1993 to no results. For a review of the C 20 and IMS reform in general, see Sakbani, Michael, (1985), "International Monetary Reform: Issues and Proposals," UNCTAD, *Trade and Development*, no. 6, pp. 172–94. See also Williamson, John, (1979), *Failure of International Monetary Reform*, Nelson, Sunbury-on-Thames.

39. Joseph Stiglitz, the Nobel laureate, is a leading critic of the Washington Consensus. The WC represents the collective views of many economists, gathered around the Bretton Woods institutions as to what should be the correct model of economic policies. Briefly, it consists of following liberal

market policies opened on the world along with full liberalization of the financial sector and full acceptance of globalization. Stiglitz and others like him do not agree that the liberal model followed by the IMF and the World Bank, is applicable in every case, and in the same way. On this view, it is argued that country specific circumstances and the complexity of the development process would call for nuanced and multi dimensional paradigms suited to the particularities of various countries. In particular they disagree with the Consensus regarding the role of government and the unadulterated application of the liberal model. See Stiglitz, Joseph (2002), *Globalization and its Discontents*, Norton and Company, New York. Doni Rodrik, of Harvard University, expresses amazement as to how the IMF can still maintain a one-fit-all model, now that we begin to understand how and why things work in some countries but not in others. See Rodrik, Doni (1999), "Governing the Global Economy: Does one Architectural Style Fit All?" in *The Brookings Institution Trade Policy Forum, Conference on Governing the Global Economy*, Harvard University, April. On empirical grounds, it is rather simplistic and blatantly false to argue, after the 2008 crisis, that the WC views have a great deal of relevance to the real world.

40. Ethan Kaplan and Doni Rodrik (2001), *Did the Malayslan Capital Controls Work?* Harvard University, J. F. school of Government, February.
41. See Sakbani, Michael (2006), *The International Economic System under Globalization: System Problems and Reform Proposals in the Monetary System*, International Development Economic Associates Studies (IDEAs), www.networkideas.org, January, part ii, Governance of International Flows.
42. Soros, George (1997), "Avoiding a Breakdown," *Financial Times*, London, 31 December. Also, Idem (1998), *The Crisis of Global Capitalism*, The Public Affairs Press, N.Y.
43. Summers, Lawrence (2000), "International Financial Crisis, Causes, Prevention and Cures," *Papers and Proceedings*, American Economic Association, New Orleans, May.
44. See Fischer, Stanley (1999), "On the need for an international lender of last resort," *The Journal of Economic Perspective*, 13 (4), pp. 85–104.
45. See Michael Sakbani, Reform Proposals, section II, pp. 10–23. Copyright © 1999–2008, Google.

4
The Role of the IMF

Daniel Kaeser

I am very honored to have been called back from retirement to write about the role of the International Monetary Fund (IMF) in a book on Globalization and the Reform of the International Monetary System.

The IMF and the World Bank, the so-called Bretton Woods institutions, were established at the end of the Second World War in order to create a new economic and monetary order. The new order had to prevent the return to the national policies that were responsible for the worldwide and protracted economic crisis of the 1930s. During that period, individual countries tried to improve their economic situation by introducing measures that harmed other countries. They devalued their currency in order to improve their own competitive position, and they introduced exchange controls and different kinds of tariff and non-tariff barriers to restrict the imports. This induced other countries to retaliate, with the result that international trade almost completely collapsed.

In the international economic and financial architecture that was created at the end of the Second World War, the task of the World Bank was to help countries damaged by the war to rebuild their economies and to support the development of poor countries. As for the IMF, it had to be the pillar of the new order. The Fund's Articles of Agreement – or Statutes – spell out its purposes and its role. Today these purposes are still governing this institution. Thus they are worth quoting here:

"The purposes of the IMF are

1) To promote international monetary cooperation through a permanent institution, which provides the machinery for consultation and collaboration on international monetary problems

130

2) To facilitate the expansion and balanced growth of international trade, and to contribute thereby to the promotion and maintenance of high levels of employment and real income and to the development of productive resources the of all members as primary objectives of economic policy.
3) To promote exchange stability, to maintain orderly exchange arrangements among members, and to avoid competitive exchange depreciation.
4) To assist in the establishment of a multilateral system of payment in respect of current transactions between members and in the elimination of foreign exchange restrictions which hamper the growth of world trade.
5) To give confidence to members by making the general resources of the Fund temporarily available to them under adequate safeguards, thus providing them with the opportunity to correct maladjustments in their balance of payments without resorting to measures destructive of national or international prosperity.
6) To shorten the duration and lessen the degree of disequilibrium in the international balance of payments of members".

It has been noted that the Fund is no longer asked to watch over a system of fixed currency parities. The so-called Bretton Woods monetary system, which served the world economy well for more than twenty years, collapsed with the gold exchange standard at the beginning of the 1970s, in the wake of the Vietnam War. Since then the Fund still has to promote exchange stability and to prevent competitive exchange depreciation, which usually trigger retaliatory measures.

Attention has to be drawn to the fact that member countries are not requested by the Fund statutes to liberalize capital transactions (contrary to current payments). Nevertheless, the Fund is promoting the liberalization of capital transactions, which has positive effects on the growth of the world economy, but also contributes to crises, because some emerging countries are unwise or ill-advised in the management of their external debt.

The rest of this chapter will address three topics. Under the first topic will be the instruments that the Fund can use to play the role assigned to it by its Statutes as mentioned. Under the second topic, the credibility crisis, which the Fund was experiencing recently, will be commented on. Finally, the question raised will be what role the Fund may play in the solution of the present crisis and in the new financial order.

Let us discuss first the instruments that the Fund can use to fulfill its statutory purposes. Supported by the staff of the Fund, consultation and collaboration on international monetary problems take place at ministerial level in the International Monetary and Financial Committee, which usually meets twice a year. Discussions on international monetary problems also take place among the 24 executive directors, senior representatives of member countries, who are in continuous session at the Fund headquarters in Washington.

The economic, monetary and financial behavior of each member country undergoes, usually every year, an examination by the Fund within the framework of the so-called bilateral surveillance. A Fund mission will visit the country to hold talks with government and central bank officials, bank and financial market regulators, legislators and members of non-governmental organizations. The mission's report is discussed by the Executive Board, which will transmit its conclusions and advice, which are not binding, to the government of the member country. Most countries now accept to have a summary of the conclusions released to the press.

The Fund conducts, also periodically, global or multilateral surveillance exercises, which show the economic, monetary and financial interaction between countries and address potential risks for the world economy. Multilateral surveillance is carried out by the Executive Board, then by the International Monetary and Financial Committee on the basis of two reports prepared twice a year by the staff. These are the World Economic Outlook and the Global Financial Stability Report.

Coming to the lending activity of the Fund, the Articles of Agreement provide that the IMF has to lend financial resources to member countries in difficulty, in order to give them the opportunity to correct the maladjustments in their balance of payments without resorting to measures destructive of national or international prosperity. In other words, the role of IMF credits is to soften the shock of inevitable austerity policies and to discourage countries in difficulty from taking protectionist measures. In order to be able to cope with different members' problems, the IMF can revert to more than ten different lending facilities. Unlike central banks and commercial banks, the IMF lends financial resources without asking for guarantee or collaterals. Its safeguard is the conditions attached to the lending: the borrowing country shall pledge to implement a tight program of economic and financial policy. The rationale for this is that the success of the program will get the borrowing country out of trouble and give it the financial leeway necessary to reimburse the Fund. When drafting the conditions should the Fund ask for a quick fix or should it impose structural reforms on the borrowing country? This is a matter of controversy.

Finally, one should mention that the Fund is devoting about a quarter of its budgetary resources to the provision of technical assistance to less advanced member countries in order to enable them to implement its policy recommendations.

As issue number two, we have to address briefly the credibility crisis that the IMF has had to face in recent years. The Fund has been seen as an undemocratic institution, lacking transparency and account- ability. Economic programs imposed upon borrowing countries relied on an ultra-liberal philosophy, causing economic over-adjustment and social suffering. To escape the Fund conditionality, emerging countries preferred to tap into the financial markets, so that the amount of Fund lending declined dramatically. This depleted the Fund's main source of income, which used to be the charges levied on the use of its financial resources by members.

Pressed by its membership and by stockholders, the Fund was, and is still, working hard to surmount this crisis. It is tightening the screws of its own corporate governance and its information policy is becoming one of the best. The Fund improved its own financial situation nota- bly by trimming its expenses, improving the management of its own reserves, and preparing to sell part of its gold with a view to investing the proceeds. Some progress has been made toward a fairer repartition of quotas and voting rights of members but much remains to be done. Like other international financial institutions, the Fund does not follow the principle "one country, one vote." The Fund is based on quotas, which represent the contributions of members to the organization's financial resources and determine their voting rights. A big country with a strong balance of payments position, which can be asked to contribute large amounts of financial resources, will not accept being given the same quota as a small deficit country, which is likely to bor- row from the organization. However the relative country situations can change dramatically over time, making corresponding quota adjust- ments necessary. Selective adjustments of quotas are painful and diffi- cult, because this is, in percentage terms, a zero sum game: what is given to the ones is taken away from the others!

The IMF lost part of its credibility for two reasons. First, as we said, it postponed for too long a major realignment of quotas. Second, its decision-making process has been perverted. We will return later on to the first topic. In order to understand the perversion of the decision- making process, it is necessary to have a look at the composition of the

Fund's Executive Board. There are 24 seats on the Board. Eight countries (China, France, Germany, Japan, Saudi Arabia, Russian Federation, United Kingdom, and United States) have a seat of their own. The other 16 seats are held by groups of countries, or constituencies, whose composition is based on vicinity or affinity links. As a result of this architecture, each member country is represented on the Board, either directly or indirectly through the elected head of its constituency. There are large differences in the voting power of the 24 seats. In the view of the founding members of the institution, the far-reaching mandate of the Fund, with a diverse membership and differing interests, called for a cooperative framework in which policy would be set by all and for all. There was an understanding that nothing would be decided until everything was agreed. That is why the rule of consensus decision making was adopted for issues that do not require qualified majorities in order to protect the interests of the minority shareholders.[1]

This cooperative approach was doomed when the Head of States of France, Germany, Japan, the United Kingdom and the United States decided in 1975 to meet regularly to mend the world's affairs. As time went by, Italy, Canada and the Russian Federation were invited to join the Summit, which includes now eight members. The Summit is to a large extent masterminded by the eight Finance ministers who meet regularly and constitute the G8. The Summit and the G8 that fit into each other like Russian dolls have a definite bias, because the Finance ministers and their alternates, being usually former or prospective bankers, have a clear empathy for the banking community and its agenda. This comes to the fore in the persistent push for financial deregulation and liberalization of capital movements.

As the G8 countries command practically half of the voting rights in the Fund they can – with the support of a few English speaking countries – impose their views upon this institution and its management. Hostile to substantial Board discussions, they have the tendency to send junior people to sit on the Executive Board and to feed them with ready-made position papers written in their Ministries. Imposing their will from outside, the G8 countries undermine the cooperative character of the institution. Furthermore, in order to retain their command over the institution, the G8, apart from minor changes, oppose the large quota realignment needed to give the new economic powers the strong position that they deserve to have within the Fund.

Instead of loosening their grip on the Fund, the G8 countries prefer to have informal meetings with the Group of 20, which they created in 1999 in order to be able to discuss matters of common interest with emerging countries with access to the international capital markets. The Group of 20 leaves in a limbo large parts of Europe, the former Soviet Union, the Middle East and Africa. It has no legitimacy to speak and act for more than 160 sovereign countries that are not members of it. The IMF would have this legitimacy because all member countries are represented in the Executive Board. The major shareholders of the Fund will perhaps realize that it would be worthwhile to restore its credibility by bringing the quotas in line with economic realities and by making it again a cooperative institution.

This being said, one has to admit that the Fund, with its highly qualified and disciplined staff of roughly 2000 economists and other academics, its organization that allows it to screen regularly 185 member countries, and its expertise in financial matters, is an outstanding institution. Thanks to the improvements of its own governance, the Fund is now in a better position to play an important role in the resolution of the present crisis. But which role?

The crisis creates two major problems. The first problem that should be addressed urgently is the risk of default by sovereign countries. Some countries with access to the international financial markets made or were induced to make the same kind of mistakes as the American subprime borrowers. They are now looking for help. Other countries have been badly hurt by the rise of the prices for oil and imported food products, even if the prices have receded from their peak level. The Fund, which already promised not to impose harsh conditions upon borrowers hit by the crisis, has to step in, possibly with other creditors, to restore the solvency of the countries in trouble.

The second problem is to reform the financial system. There is obviously a broad agreement to rely heavily on the IMF to this end. In its communiqué, dated October 11,2008, the International Monetary and Financial Committee called on the Fund: "given its universal membership, core macro-financial expertise, and its mandate to promote international financial stability, to take the lead in drawing the necessary policy lessons from the current crisis." Once new rules relating to all segments of the financial market are drafted and agreed upon by the membership, the Fund will be well placed to monitor their introduction in the framework of its bilateral surveillance. It will also have to evaluate their regional and global impact within the framework of its multilateral surveillance. It remains to be seen if the Fund will be given enough power to influence the behavior of large countries, for instance when it tries to reduce the disequilibrium in the balance of payments of major members. One can deeply regret for instance that the United States, contrary to other major countries, refused to submit to the Financial Sector Assessment Program, claiming that the American Financial sector should anyway be the standard for the rest of the world.

Note

1. Van Houtyen, Leo (2002), "Governance of the IMF; Decision Making, Institutional Oversight, Transparency, and Accountability" IMF Pamphlet Series No. 53.

5
The Financial Landscape – Seen from a Converging Country

Péter Ákos Bod

5.1   The scene before the storm

A dynamic and seemingly successful decade of financial expansion came to an end in the world when the international financial turbulences erupted in 2007 and became global in the fall of 2008. This decade was interrupted temporarily by the burst of the "technology bubble" after 2000, yet the big picture of international finance looked impressive until 2007. Over that decade, many *emerging markets* managed to absorb sizable funds, and could thus maintain a fast economic growth rate for a long time. Others ran huge trade surpluses, building up impressive international reserves, and financed current account deficits in other countries, in particular the United States (US). Investment banks, equity firms, institutional investors, and transnational corporations turned to China, India, the former planned economies in Europe with interest, as these markets became known to offer profitable business opportunities.

Benefits were mutual: foreign investors' rates of return in these markets were typically much higher than in mature core markets; meanwhile overall financial conditions continued to be supportive for a number of emerging markets (mostly in Asia, Central Europe, and Latin America) in terms of ease of access to funds and cost of funding. Yet, market players active in these emerging markets and the authorities concerned must have known all the time that fast economic growth and increased dependence on borrowed funds makes for as risky a combination as slow growth in core economies with increased dependence on borrowing. The international investors, however, had a problem throughout that decade: excess liquidity burned their pockets. As for the regulators and risk analysts, they could gain some comfort from the statistics: international trade boomed during this period, the world economy grew at an assuring rate of 5–6 percent a year, sovereign ratings kept improving. In short, there was not much to worry about the financial sustainability of these emerging markets.

The optimistic mood and factual data seemed to support each other: trade and financial flows remained strong between the developed world and the (limited) number of successful emerging nations, underpinning the general view that both parties benefited from liberalized foreign trade and financial openness (even if historic data do not fully support such optimistic views[1]). The International Monetary Fund (IMF), the international lender of last resort, had a very quiet period in its otherwise busy history: no new client turned to it for funds in emergency.

The mood changed abruptly by the end of 2008. Surprisingly, the financial crises of 2007–8 erupted not in the periphery of the world economy, but at its very core: in the United States. Much has been said about the reasons and factors leading somewhat unexpectedly to the subprime crisis in the American economy.[2] Yet, it is equally surprising how less obvious targets were instantly hit by the financial turbulences: Iceland, a rich and developed country, and Hungary, a member state of the European Union (EU) since 2004. These were the first two European countries in three decades to turn to the IMF for funds to avoid financial collapse in late 2008, soon followed by smallish Latvia, a Baltic state, and then the Ukraine, not a member of the EU.

The banking and financial crisis of tiny Iceland could be regarded an accident, or a sad but understandable consequence of bankers' over-lending.[3] Compared to that, the Hungarian case looks more puzzling and thought provoking in the whole context of global financial order: the size of the country is larger, and its economy is closely connected with other emerging markets in the region as well as with the core economies of Europe.

When the first pieces of news appeared about the troubles with Hungary, the market understanding was that what was happening to Hungary could possibly unleash a domino effect among some other indebted emerging economies of Central and Eastern Europe. This aspect must have been one of the reasons why, in November 2008, the Bretton Woods institutions (the IMF and the World Bank) swiftly put together with the EU an impressively large 20 billion euro lending facility for Hungary, a medium-size country with a gross domestic product (GDP) of about 100 billion euro, when the country was suddenly hit by a set of negative shocks.

What follows is, first, a review of the events during, before and after the financial turbulences in 2008 involving European emerging

economies in general, and in particular Hungary, once the "local wonder child" in the region, and a showcase in transition from planned
to market economy.[4] Then obvious questions are raised. What are the
factors that led a country to the brink of bankruptcy during the international credit crunch? Why Hungary, a champion of privatization
and market liberalization?[5] How come that membership in the EU does
not protect a member state from serious imbalances that may trigger
speculative attacks on the currency? What are the lessons from what
happened in this particular country, and in the way international institutions, rating agencies, Western governments and other influential
market players reacted to the events?

5.2   Fat years

It is with reason that bankers and fund managers were so eager to commit monies for countries such as Hungary, Poland, Croatia, Romania,
Estonia and other former planned economies throughout the decade
preceding 2008. Market players regarded Central and Eastern European
(CEE) countries as *top of the class of the emerging market category*: fast
improving physical and institutional infrastructure, growing asset
prices, liberal economic policies, openness to trade and financial flows,
high economic growth.

These countries were not only promising emerging markets but they
also belonged to the group of *transition economies*, that is, nations in
transit from central planning to market-based regimes. What decades
of central planning had left behind was, among other factors, a rather
educated labor force with low wages, and an adequate level of technical and scientific sophistication. At the same time, pent-up demand for
consumer goods and infrastructure services (housing, banking, insurance, and telecommunication) offered great growth opportunities for
businesses. All these factors made the new European democracies an
obvious choice for foreign direct investments (FDI).[6]

Analysts knew very well in the late 1990s that these countries
were soon to become members of the EU – again a factor that added
to the appeal of these markets in the eyes of strategic investors. EU
membership certainly represents a big plus from investors' viewpoint:
a European legal system, relative political stability, the countries' access
to pre-accession grants and later sizeable EU funds and, perhaps most
importantly, free trade within the EU.

The CEE countries certainly benefited from their status as European
emerging and accession economies. Inflows of EU pre-accession funds were

not particularly high before 2004, yet even a modest cash surplus with the EU helped ease the current account balance. After their entry into the EU in May 2004, the eight former planned economies (Poland, Hungary, Slovakia, Slovenia, the Czech Republic, Estonia, Latvia, Lithuania) did receive significant infrastructure and regional development funds, amounting to two to three percent of GDP. Similarly, Romania and Bulgaria, parties to accession in 2006, received EU funds of the same proportion.

But inflow of EU-funds was only one factor among many. What really changed the savings-investment equation in most CEE countries was the inflow of FDI. FDI inflows took off in some CEE countries such Hungary and the Czech Republic – "early birds" – already during the early and mid-1990s.[7] After a decade of rough transition, in about the year 2000, net FDI inflows in most CEE economies became as high as five or more percent of GDP, particularly in high growth Slovakia, Romania and the three Baltic countries.

Institutional investors found these markets promising already in the run-up to EU accession, and set out to buy underpriced CEE financial assets, particularly government securities, and shares, land, and real estate. Their investment decisions were underpinned by improving sovereign ratings granted by credit rating agencies. The new EU members seemed to be on a path to gradual long-term convergence to the level of advancement of older EU members. Yes, countries in this region could be referred to as *converging economies*.

Thus, CEE countries – similarly to some other "top" emerging markets – had experienced for a long time easy access to foreign funds. One of the interesting consequences was that the *current account* (CA) constraints on economic growth became soft if not suspended altogether. Previously, even the most acknowledged investment target economies had to reckon with a certain limit to incoming financial flows. International institutions, rating agencies and investment analysts would issue warning signals should the current account deficit pass a given size (say, five or more percent of GDP). Domestic authorities would also feel prompted to implement corrective policy changes at more than five percent of CA deficit.

This rule of thumb became quickly neglected or forgotten in European emerging markets – with some justification. The received wisdom was that if CA deficit was mainly financed by foreign strategic investors and transfers from the EU, a "sudden stop" or reversal of capital flows is unlikely to happen. Unlikely maybe, but certainly there remained obvious risks with high CA deficits and high foreign exchange debt, should market mood change direction.

This is exactly what happened in 2008. After the financial troubles in Iceland, analysts and the press kept wondering who would become the "next Iceland." Hungary, with similarly high foreign debt/GDP ratio, became a potential victim of the sudden stop of foreign and domestic funds financing the national debt. The specter of national bankruptcy appeared suddenly in October 2008.[8]

5.3   Membership in EU – does that matter?

Why had EU membership not protected Hungary from the accumulation of excessive foreign debt and other disequilibria? It would be logical to assume that accession to the EU and membership of the Union protects a country from getting into unsustainable macroeconomic situations.

First of all, accession to the EU is conditional on attaining a given institutional order and absorbing the vast body of EU laws (called "acquis communautaire"), but not on formal macroeconomic entry criteria. Yet, the pre-accession negotiation process is typically long enough to give time for the applicant to correct macroeconomic disequilibria and to prove to the European community that the country concerned keeps its macro-finances in order. Once a country joins the EU, there are two particular institutions to protect a member state from a too high deficit and an excessive national debt. One is the Stability and Growth Pact, the other is the so-called Maastricht criteria of entry into the euro zone.

The *Stability and Growth Pact* (SGP) adopted in 1997 is an agreement by EU member states to conduct their economic policy in a manner that ensures fiscal discipline within the Economic and Monetary Union (EMU).[9] SGP is in essence a rule-based framework for safeguarding sound public finances in member states – an important requirement for the EMU to function properly and to protect the common European currency.

Under the Pact, member states have to submit annual convergence (or stability) programs, presenting how the authorities intend to achieve or maintain sound fiscal positions in the medium term. The Pact determines that national annual budget deficits shall not be higher than 3 percent of GDP, and gross public sector debt shall not exceed 60 percent of GDP (or should at least approach that reference value), or else the *excessive deficit procedure* (EDP) will be triggered. If EU authorities determine that the deficit is excessive (breaching the 3 percent of GDP threshold of the Treaty) the European Council issues recommendations to the member state concerned to correct the excessive deficit, and sets a time frame for doing so. Non-compliance with the recommendations may trigger further steps, including the possibility of sanctions for euro area member states.

From the above it would be logical to conclude that the new member states of the EU are well protected from too much budget deficit and thus excessive indebtedness under the Pact. But that is not the full picture. At the time of their entry into the EU, most new members ran annual deficits higher than 3 percent of their GDP. Some states, Hungary in particular, even increased the size of the public sector deficit after becoming a full member. One should note that the legal text contains specific sanctions only for euro zone countries, that is, for those already using the common European currency. The text is opaque on sanctioning a member state with a currency of its own.

Frankly, the EU authorities (the Commission and the European Council) did not seem to be concerned for a long time about the public sector deficit in former planned economies. Benign neglect by the EU was initially justified inasmuch as it is in the best interest of the new members to reduce excessive public sector deficit, for at least two reasons: first, not to crowd out private sector investments during their much desired catch-up process; and second, because new member states intend to enter the euro zone.

Here comes into the picture the other key EU institution: a set of quantitative conditions of entry into the euro zone. The conditions are based on Article 121(1) of the European Community Treaty: member states that are about to adopt the euro need to meet certain criteria known as the "convergence criteria" or "Maastricht criteria" as they were agreed upon by the EU Member States in 1991 in the Dutch town of Maastricht as part of the preparations for the introduction of the euro.

The convergence criteria are formally defined as a set of macroeconomic indicators:

- Relative price stability, to show that inflation is already controlled in the candidate country. Tolerable inflation is determined as consumer price index not being more than 1.5 percentage points above the rate of the three best performing member states reference value.
- Soundness and sustainability of public finances, through limits on government borrowing (not more than 3 percent of GDP) and national debt (reference value: not more than 60 percent of GDP).
- Exchange-rate stability, through participation in the Exchange Rate Mechanism for at least two years without severe tensions

- Long-term interest rates, to assess the durability of the convergence achieved by fulfilling the other criteria: long term government bond yields shall not be more than two percentage points above the rate of the three best performing member states in terms of price stability.

Now, whatever one thinks of these particular criteria and reference values as adequate measures of readiness for entering the euro club of countries, it is certain that if a country meets the above criteria, and later as a club member honors the deficit regulation of the SGP, it will avoid excessive deficits and debts.[10] For a former planned economy with a relatively high national debt, it would be particularly advantageous to enter the euro club with its low interest rate and good sovereign risk rating. In this context it sounds logical to expect a new member state to regard entry into euro zone as a national priority, and to make efforts to fulfill the Maastricht criteria.

Some governments did so: two out of eight former planned economies entering the EU in 2004 successfully fulfilled the criteria and joined the euro zone before the 2008 crisis hit them: Slovenia in January 2007 and Slovakia in January 2009 (after having fixed irrevocably the exchange rate of the domestic currency some months before the January 2009 change-over to euro).

Other governments failed to do that. In 2001, the then Hungarian government still aimed at entering the euro zone in 2006 but, one year later, the new government moved the target date to 2008 and declared instead a very costly "regime change in welfare"; a year later the target date had to be extended to 2010, as the country could not meet the reference values, particularly the deficit target. Public sector deficit caused problems in other former planned economies, to a lesser degree. See Chart 5.1.

By the summer of 2006, the EU became concerned about the serial fiscal slippages of the Hungarian government, and demanded an update of the Hungarian convergence program. Under the threats from Europe, the Hungarian authorities dutifully compiled a new convergence program, projecting a marked improvement in deficit figures.[11] Yet, the revised program still failed to set an official euro zone entry target date. When the international credit crunch hit the country two years after that, Hungary stood there without a clear position on such a key policy issue. This was the worst slippage in the region but not the only one; some other countries were also behind their original schedule to enter the euro zone.

The conclusion is that EU membership in itself does not prevent a government from making serious policy mistakes. A far too obvious

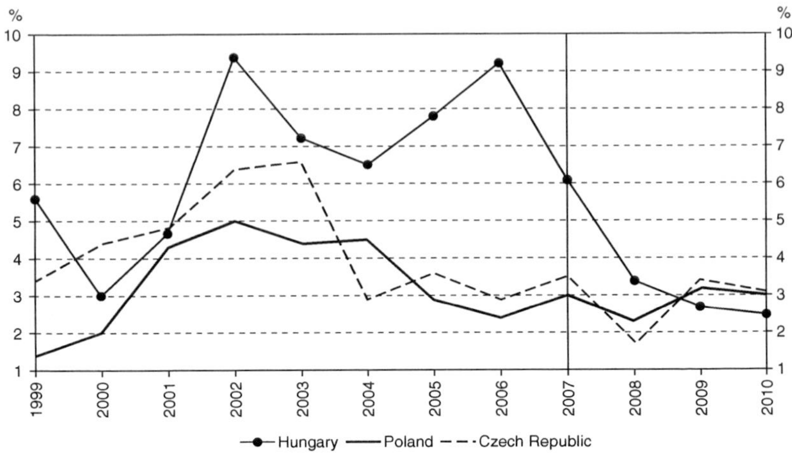

Chart 5.1   Budget deficit in CEE countries.

case is Hungary. Public sector deficit climbed to a record high in 2002, an election year before accession, and overspending did not stop after 2004, the year of accession to the EU: the government deficit amounted to close to 10 percent of GDP in 2006. Had Hungary not been a member of the EU, the capital markets would probably have stopped financing the huge and fast growing debt long before 2008.

5.4   Path dependence and adjustment fatigue in transition champions

Bad policies and irresponsible governments are part of the picture but there seem to be more general factors explaining the deficit and debt situation in CEE countries. Strong popular demand for government services and welfare transfers, on the one hand, and weaknesses in collecting state revenues, on the other, would understandably lead to a structural budget deficit. But the persistent deficit itself is a consequence and symptom of the accumulation of social imbalances in the transition process. Economic growth and thus real convergence to the European average, and speedy transition, as the case was with new EU members, helps but would not automatically solve the socio-economic problems of transformation.

The process of transition from planned economy to market-based economy is understood to be tough on the general public, shaking up the whole society, and eliciting justified demand for government protection and welfare support. Yet obvious questions can be raised here: why do some governments in transition countries still keep public spending under control while others build up costly public sector debts in otherwise good times? Why did certain governments decide to spend on welfare transfers even at the price of postponing entry into the euro zone?

Ironically, the states with particular deficit and budget problems are those CEE countries that had been in the vanguard of transition for a long time: Hungary or Poland. In general, the "old" ex-communist countries maintain large and costly public sectors with concomitant budget deficits, while new nation states born after the collapse of the Soviet Union or of other artificial entities (Yugoslavia, Czechoslovakia) have a much leaner public sector: Estonia, Latvia, Lithuania, Slovakia, and (less so) Slovenia. Leaner states in these cases have proven to be more suitable frameworks for high economic growth, as exemplified by the phenomenal growth in the Baltic region or in Slovakia.

It is certainly noteworthy that a previous transition champion has become a growth laggard: Hungary, which had the reputation of being more open economically, financially if not politically even under the old, communist-ruled, regime. The country was also regarded as a successful reformer at the time of the regime change in 1990, and turned out to be remarkably successful in absorbing foreign direct investments even during the first complicated years of the transformation in early 1990s.

Still, the premature opening of an economy to global trade and capital flows comes at a price. Unilateral market liberalization exposes the unprepared economy to competitive forces – this is exactly what happened to Hungary under the so-called reform-communist period in the 1980s, well before the political regime change. State-owned companies under a semi-closed, state-controlled economic system were no match for competitive market players: Socialist Poland and Hungary during the 1970s surprisingly quickly ran into trade deficits and, consequently, current account deficits. The opening to the West, well before the return to democracy and free market economy took place in 1989–90, had led to international indebtedness. Poland had to declare bankruptcy in 1981; Hungary just managed to avoid insolvency in the 1980s.

This legacy did not disappear with the regime change: foreign debt accumulating under the reform-communist period later weighed heavily on democratically elected governments. Interestingly enough, countries under orthodox communist rule did not inherit such a burden from their past.

The fact that some new democratic regimes had to face huge foreign debt partly explains why the first governments after the regime change followed an economic policy intended to please the creditors: the international financial institutions and capital market players, even if domestic conditions would have justified a more cautious attitude to structural changes. Some advisors and analysts noted already at the time that instant trade liberalization and too fast privatization would backfire in terms of jobs and market shares lost to competitors, and fire-sale privatization was to be avoided.[12] Yet, pressures from international financial institutions, donor governments and the foreign press proved to be rather influential in shaping government policies: transition in Hungary, like in some other, but not all, CEE countries, took on a radical nature.

The consequences are certainly mixed in Hungary. Foreign-owned firms contributed through net exports to the increase of the GDP. However, high productivity FDI, by its nature, does not create large number of jobs. Moreover, HR departments at foreign-owned firms can choose among numerous applicants, and they are not eager to employ older or less skilled workers; thus FDI-driven modernization provides no answer to the problems of mass unemployment. Foreign firms are reluctant to invest in depressed areas of the country. As a consequence, in the absence of a vibrant local entrepreneurial class, unemployment – particularly outside the capital city and growth poles – remains high.

In such an open, FDI-dependent economy, low employment may coexist with high industry growth and excellent export figures – this is the case in Hungary and, to various degrees, in other CEE countries. But, there are also obvious social repercussions: the unemployed and the under-employed expect welfare services from the new democratic regime. If governments yield to popular demand, and political parties respond to the expressed will of a large part of the electorate, then the size of the public budget becomes too large, unless strategic goals such as nation building or an early entry into the EU and later into the euro zone prove to be politically stronger than welfare considerations.

Chart 5.2 indicates that European countries differ a lot in respect of the relative size of the state measured by the revenue collected (horizontal axes) and by public spending as percentage of GDP (vertical axes). Public sector size does not determine competitiveness of the economy: there exist internationally competitive countries with big government (the Nordic model) and similarly competitive countries with relatively small government (the Baltic countries, Ireland, Slovakia).

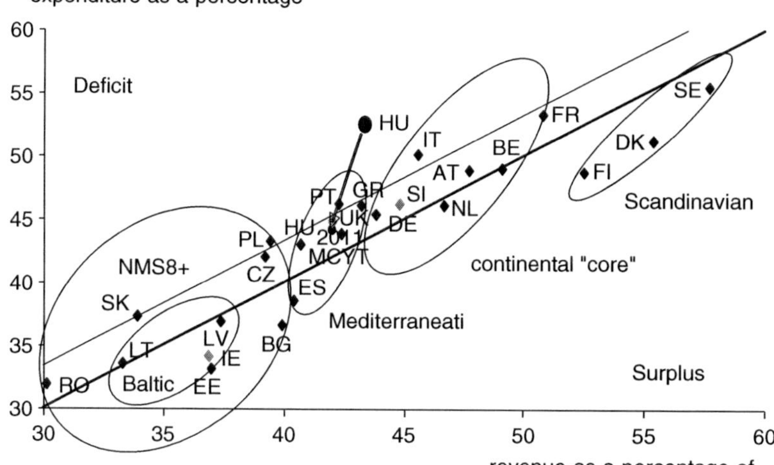

Chart 5.2   Revenues and expenditures of states in Europe

The Hungarian figures on government revenues, spending and deficit are surprisingly high, placing the country in a rather awkward position on Europe's fiscal map. Seeing this position, it is less surprising now that the financial turbulences hit this particular country. History is of course an explaining factor: Hungary was not only a full employment planned economy before the regime change (where the general public got accustomed to extensive welfare services) but also heavily indebted. Therefore welfare (pension) expenditures and debt service expenditures were always sizeable cost items burdening the economy from the very start of the regime change.

However, the large size of public budget and its deficit are not the only variables that can drag down the economy and risk its development. During the international credit crunch, it is the total foreign debt exposure that counts the most, that is, debts of firms, banks, and the households in addition to the government debt. Public sector debt certainly aggravates the case if it is partly or significantly externally financed.

Unfortunately, this is exactly the case with some CEE countries. Particularly those economies built up a big stock of foreign exchange debt where the domestic interest rate level was consistently high. Expensive borrowing in domestic currency prompts all economic agents, including the government, to borrow in lower rate foreign currencies. Such practice, of course, involves high foreign exchange risk, and may lead to a certain dollarization (or euroization) of the economy. Interesting enough, borrowing in (lower interest rate) foreign currency is not specifically an emerging market practice; even in euro zone Austria, a measurable part of household borrowing was made in Swiss francs before the crisis hit Europe.[13] While Austria was an exceptional case, taking out loans in foreign currency became typical in most CEE countries, where the level of the domestic interest rates remained consistently much higher than interest rates in Swiss franc, yen, or euro.

High interest rate levels may be due to a variety of reasons, but one key factor is the conduct of fiscal policy. This certainly is the case with Hungary: the country ran for a long time high public sector deficits that were financed by domestic and foreign fund holders throughout the decade preceding 2007 – but at rather high Hungarian forint (HUF) interest rates.

With the passage of time, repeatedly missed fiscal targets and deteriorating debt figures generated doubts among investors about the sustainability of Hungarian economic policy. Under such conditions, the central bank (Magyar Nemzeti Bank – MNB) decided to maintain high interest rates in order to counterbalance the increase in sovereign risk and occasional nervousness about the public finance of the country. Strangely, high HUF interest rates tended to induce periods of appreciation of the forint, followed by similar periods of depreciation of the exchange rate, when market nervousness overcame the appeal of the high relative rates.

High forint interest rate levels, in turn, encouraged businesses and households to borrow in foreign currency – Swiss franc, euro, and yen. Commercial banks in Hungary, where market competition became sharper with the entry of a number of West European, American and other foreign banks, did not hesitate much to offer present and potential customers loan products (mortgages on homes, consumer and car finance loans) denominated in foreign currency. Funding to finance banking assets denominated in foreign currency came predominantly from the mother banks of the Hungarian subsidiaries, or through the international interbank market, at first on reasonable terms. However, the country's overall foreign currency exposure started to grow out of proportion.

Initially financial inflows were easily forthcoming, and consisted mostly of FDI, and less of bank loans. But with the passage of time, foreign investment turned somewhat away from Hungary, as the country lost part of its former appeal and other emerging economies offered even better deals. FDI is a non debt-creating kind of funds, but borrowing adds to indebtedness. In CEE countries, ongoing financial and real integration with the EU made it easier for domestic firms and banks to borrow internationally. This was also the case with Hungary whose external debt amounted to about 97 per cent of GDP by the end of 2007.[14]

5.5 The financial crisis

CEE countries, open to international trade and finance, are obviously sensitive to events in the financial world. The degree of financial integration in the banking markets of CEE countries is very high by any standard. Before the crisis hit the region, the consolidated market share of credit institutions with a nonresident parent bank amounted to 50–96 percent in individual CEE countries: over 90 per cent in the Czech Republic and Slovakia, between 60 and 80 percent in Hungary and Poland.[15] Most banks with cross-border activities in the region have their headquarters in EU countries.

Foreign-owned banks offer their customary financial products in CEE markets, such as mortgage and car finance loans. In this region, with a history of unsophisticated state-owned banking or no banking at all, these products represented a novelty; customers were not given much time to learn about the pluses and minuses of living and shopping on borrowed money. Household indebtedness had increased rapidly until the eruption of the financial turbulences. Loans to the private sector as a proportion of GDP practically doubled in the period between 2002 and 2006, particularly loans to households.

The rise in the indebtedness of families and private firms is essentially part of the catching-up process, following decades of a suppressed financial sector during planned economy. Yet, the speed of the rise in the obligations of the private sector adds to the financial risks both for the banks and the clients. With limited domestic savings, (foreign-owned) banks borrowed abroad in foreign currency and expanded their loan portfolio also in foreign currency, placing the foreign exchange rate risks on the clients. Clients did not seem to mind running that calculated risk: domestic interest rates significantly exceeded the rates of alternative loans denominated in foreign currencies, and exchange rates did not fluctuate too much. This was – while it worked – a rather smooth "carry trade," practiced by firms, households, and – somewhat strangely – the government in Poland, Hungary, Romania, and even more in those countries where, as a result of fixed exchange rate regime, becoming indebted in foreign currencies looked like a risk-free arbitrage (Bulgaria, the Baltic countries).

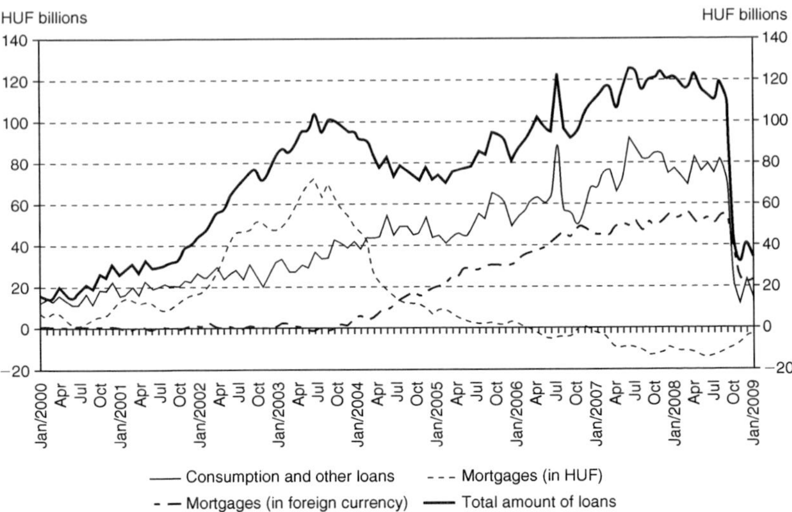

Chart 5.3　Net household borrowing in Hungary.

This is the context in which Hungary got into trouble in October 2008, as one of the first emerging market countries to suffer from the indirect consequences of the global credit crunch (see Chart 5.3). Indirect consequences, since the Hungarian financial sector was not directly exposed to "toxic assets" originating in American financial institutions. However, as the financial difficulties in advanced economies soon led to a decline in global liquidity and loss of appetite for risks, investors suddenly became concerned about emerging markets with high debt levels. There had been warning signs earlier that year: the increased volatility of the CEE currencies, and the fact that the Hungarian Treasury experienced a short episode of financial stress in March 2008, when demand for newly issued Hungarian bonds just ceased to exist for a week or two.

October 2008 was different, with three parallel shocks. One was again a "bankers' strike": issues of new Hungarian government bonds had to be canceled due to lack of demand, and bond yields on secondary markets shot up (see Chart 5.4).

Second, the domestic currency suddenly depreciated on the money markets. The Hungarian forint nominally floats freely. The central bank (MNB) does not set an official exchange rate target. Yet, as discussed above, large segments of society and businesses had become indebted in foreign currency: over half of bank lending to the nonfinancial sector was denominated in foreign currency (mostly euro and Swiss francs).

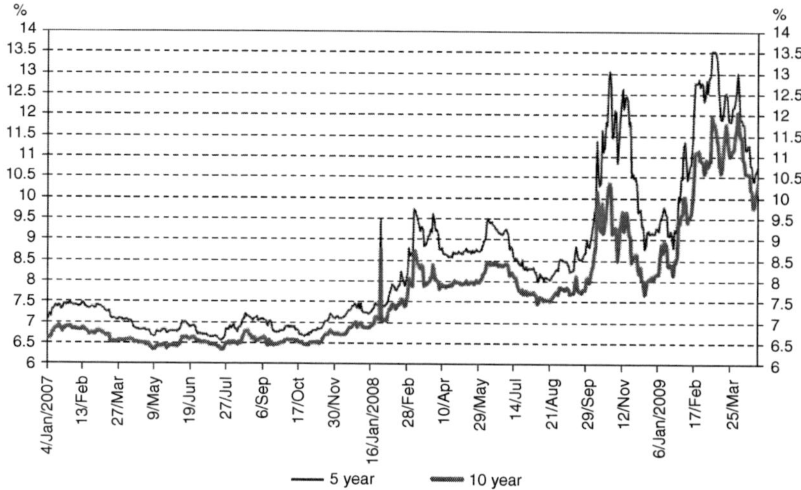

Chart 5.4   Yields on long-term maturity Hungarian bonds.

Indebted families and firms thus represented a constituency that authorities could not neglect. A drastic depreciation of the currency would lead to foreclosures, personal distresses, and widespread bankruptcies in small businesses, which in turn could shake the financial system. The foreign exchange positions of the banks were broadly balanced, but the domestic nonfinancial sector carried a high degree of exchange rate risk, which could translate into credit risk for banks. See Chart 5.5.

The third factor, influencing the government's decision to ask for external support, must have been the sudden freeze in cross-country cooperation in the European financial sector. West European parent banks (mostly Austrians, Germans, Italians) with sudden funding difficulties, or without adequate capital to weather the storms, behaved in a way which aggravated the situation in CEE countries from late 2008: some immediately closed their foreign currency credit lines to their subsidiaries, others even decided to repatriate free funds from subsidiaries in the region. Stopping the credits to high profitability CEE subsidiaries is not a sensible corporate policy, but some West European governments demanded that public funds and state guarantees that they offer to their banks should be utilized in the same country. This national policy regulation in effect forbade channeling state aid to entities outside the given national economy. As a consequence, the immediate outlook for CEE in general, and high debt Hungary in particular, immediately changed for the worse.

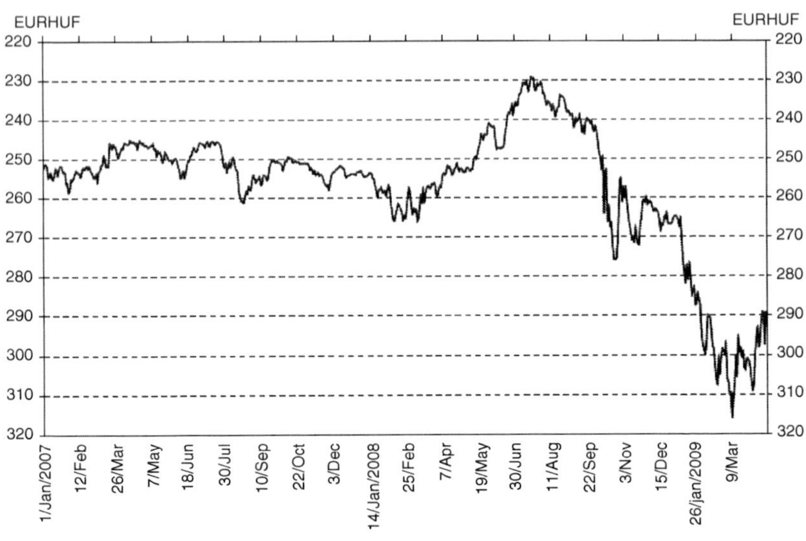

Chart 5.5   Forint-euro exchange rate.

The government turned to the IMF and the EU for financial support.
The IMF loan document described the situation as follows:

> Compared to other emerging markets, Hungary's higher "stock vulner-
> abilities" imply that a large amount of debt needs to be serviced and
> rolled over. Added risks include the large share of foreign currency
> lending by both domestic banks and subsidiaries of foreign parents.
> These exposures were hedged, but the use of foreign exchange swaps
> for this purpose exposed systemically important banks to significant
> rollover risk in the foreign exchange swap market. Past policy action
> has been insufficient to reduce these risks. In particular, fiscal and cur-
> rent account deficits of recent years did not come down sufficiently.[16]
> The IMF/WB/EU financial package was conditional on changes in the
> Hungarian economic policy, in particular, to implement a substantial
> fiscal adjustment to ensure that the government's debt-financing
> needs will decline; and to maintain adequate liquidity and strong
> levels of capital in the banking system. Ultimately, the program
> should help restore stability in the financial sector and create the
> conditions for an economic recovery.[17]

The language is in the parlance of the international financial institutions but the message is clear: "fiscal adjustments" in this context does

not mean *more* but *less* public spending. Accepting that, the Hungarian government promised the creditors a wage freeze in the public sector and a reduction of bonus payment to pensioners. Previously planned tax reductions were to be delayed even if the global deterioration of the business climate called for a fiscal easing under an anti-cyclical policy. However, over-indebted Hungary, being so dependent on IMF funds, was just not in a bargaining position to afford a bit of fiscal easing.

As a consequence, the economy would slow down even more, and the rate of unemployment would unavoidably increase. This is the price of avoiding the default on sovereign loans.

5.6   Lessons learned

One of the consequences of sweeping liberalization and speedy opening up to the Western socio-economic model during the regime change was the deep penetration of foreign-owned financial institutions into the CEE economies. The entry of foreign banks, brokerages and insurance companies undoubtedly increased the level of sophistication in CEE finance, and opened up channels for funds that would not had come to the region otherwise. Yet, in the period of global credit crunch, the simple success story became complicated as lessons were learnt about the behavior of foreign-owned banks. See Chart 5.6.

The previous view was that foreign owners of CEE banks provided an implicit safeguard of the health of the local banking sector, and also guaranteed abundant liquidity in hard currency. On both accounts, reality turned out to be different. The behavior pattern of international banks during the end-2008 liquidity crisis suddenly changed: profit generated before the crisis was repatriated from (high profitability) CEE subsidiaries; more importantly, a reduction or even a freeze of foreign exchange credit lines from Western headquarters was administered by some major banks. Such steps aggravated the evolving credit crunch in the domestic money and capital markets, and contributed to the change of direction of financial flows in CEE countries: outflows replaced inflows or, at least, the magnitude of net inflows shrunk drastically. As a consequence, exchange rates suffered, hence the deep depreciation of the Hungarian forint, Polish zloty, and Czech koruna in early 2009.

The sudden stop of these interbank funds led to a particularly grave situation in high public debt Hungary: the disappearance of some former major buyers from the Hungarian fixed-income markets provoked a near complete freeze of the government bond market (on longer maturities).

Eastern European banks
% share of foreign ownership in capital

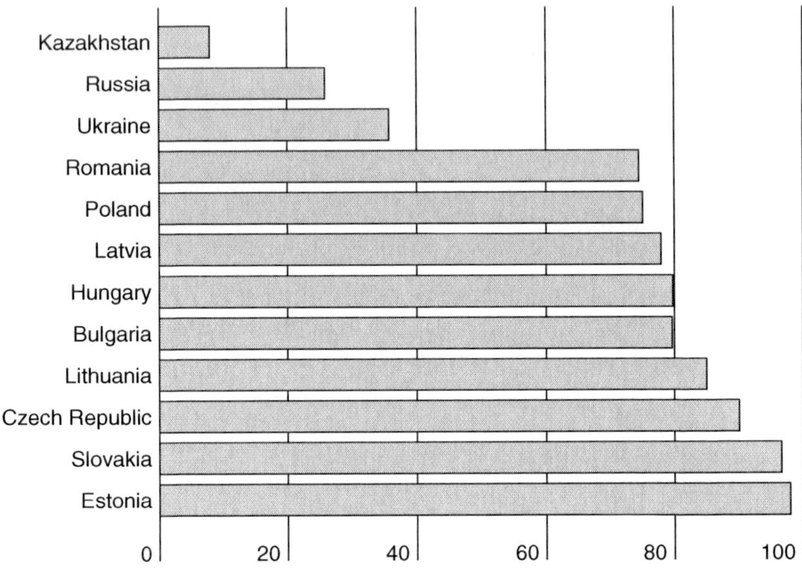

Chart 5.6   Share of foreign banks in CEE countries.

The deterioration of the economic situation in the CEE region, in its turn, had an impact on a number of Western banks. Euro zone banks had built a large exposure to Central and Eastern Europe over the years, representing about 90 percent of total foreign bank exposure to the region.[18] The Austrian banking system was the most vulnerable, with Central and Eastern Europe accounting for nearly half of its foreign loans; meanwhile Italian banks were exposed to Poland and Croatia, and Scandinavian institutions to the Baltic States. When Central and Eastern European currencies came under intense pressure in early 2009, rating agencies raised their concerns about the region's ability to finance its current account deficits. Financial turmoil in the CEE region could conceivable damage Western banks as well.

Too much dependence on foreign markets thus backfires in times of crisis. Hungary, a former transition champion, was among the countries to pay the price for large exposure to foreign funds. A big part of the blame for the high degree of indebtedness should go to irresponsible governments, but legacies of previous historical periods also had their impact on the macroeconomic conditions that had evolved by the time the crisis hit.

It is still not fully explained why membership in the EU could not save a member state from getting into grave financial problems. As the cases discussed above reveal, EU-wide institutions such as the Stability and Growth Pact or the entry conditions into euro zone are just not effective enough to provide a massive protective shield against systematic government mistakes. Policy coordination among member states have again proved to be slow and vague at best, just like in the case of a gas supply crisis in 2008, following Russia's cut of supply to Europe. The reaction to the global credit crunch also proved that the Union as a decision making body is not determined or efficient. True, in financial matters the EU consists of two sub-groups: those using the common European currency, and those outside the euro zone. In a currency crisis, this division becomes crucial: measures to strengthen the euro and to maintain the free flow of funds within the euro zone immediately weakens the position of EU member counties *outside* the euro zone.

In addition, it is not obvious whether the European Central Bank (ECB) should or should not fulfill the role of lender of last resort with non-euro member states, or at all. In the Hungarian (and later, for example, Latvian) case, the ECB reacted swiftly by offering foreign exchange facilities for the central banks of EU members states, even when the Commission was still hesitating. When it came to effective crisis management, the most important member states decided to follow their own, narrowly defined, national interests.

Lack of coordinated EU reaction urged Western banks operating in Central and Eastern Europe to club together to lobby the EU and the ECB to step up efforts to ease the credit crunch in the region. A group of ten banks, led by an Austrian bank, prodded Brussels and the ECB to extend support beyond the EU's new member states, such as Poland, as well as to prospective members, such as Serbia, and also to the Ukraine, which had few prospects of accession to the EU.[19]

Initially, the EU institutions played a (limited) role by joining the IMF in putting together an emergency financial package first to Hungary and later for Latvia. In addition, the ECB extended liquidity support to Hungary, and also to Poland, where the IMF was not involved. But the above mentioned Western banks wanted Brussels and the ECB to provide assistance to vulnerable non-EU members with high external financing needs (Serbia, Bosnia, Croatia, the Ukraine) – countries that could be swept away by the regional turbulences.

The reason why international banks active in the CEE economies, and the governments of the region had to turn publicly to the EU is that the official policy coordination mechanisms did not seem to work. The blame lies not solely with the Commission and the ECB: governments of member states pointedly reacted to the financial crisis in their own way – see the unilateral declarations of providing extra protection to depositors in the fall of 2008, or the fiscal packages to bail out and/or re-capitalize or even nationalize banks "of your own."

Lack of approved mechanism of crisis management in the EU, and poor willingness of member state governments to act together, opened the door for IMF actions when the crisis hit EU countries. The Fund had been searching for its proper role for some time; now it found duties to fulfill. The conditionality in the case of Iceland, Hungary, or Latvia, or non-EU clients such as the Ukraine or Belarus was shaped in the Bretton Woods tradition: fiscal correction, institutional reforms, strengthening the banking sector, devaluation of the currency – this time without excessive strictness. Still, it is open to discussion whether it is for the IMF to help remove clogs from intra-European banking channels, or reversal of flows between European core countries and converging Europe.

Heavy overexposure of an economy to global finance does not just happen; authorities allow it. Governments are always responsible for any excessive dependence on foreign savers. It is, of course, also true that global financial markets have been willing parties to the inundation of promising markets with funds. Abundance is followed by reversals, but such correction is a very costly cure for temporary overexposure; it is the responsibility of national and global decision makers to invent rules and institutions, and apply common sense policies that help avoid the mistakes that led to the global financial crisis.

It is important not to blame the mere existence of cross-country capital flows (that is, current account imbalances) for what happened to the world of finance. As Dooley et al. rightly underline, "The panic that hit in mid-September had its roots in US-originated securities (although in the UK, Spain, Iceland, Ireland, Hungary, and elsewhere the economic and financial problems have little to do with US-based assets). But it immediately affected credit markets in the rest of the world, perhaps due in some cases to a collapse of confidence in the dominant finance models, and it others to the knock-on effects in the real economy."[20] If international financial flows were believed to have caused the financial distress, advocates of protectionism would gain ammunition to their cause. The crisis would be deeper than otherwise and might spread to regions not yet affected, should the economic nationalist solutions gain support among decision makers.

Having said that, one has to acknowledge that governments, of economies badly hit by the fall-outs of the global credit crunch, are responsible for having committed serious policy mistakes or negligence. Hungary, for one, as a trade dependent country so closely related to major euro zone economies, should have already fulfilled the entry conditions and joined the rank of European countries using euro as legal tender. Better regulation of banks and non-banks active in mortgage, consumption finance and related businesses should have been a priority in countries with asset bubbles or gross misallocation of financial resources. But reduction of trade and financial flows across borders would only deepen the crisis.

One of the consequences of the financial turbulances has been the reappearance of protectionist tendencies in public policies (see the attempts to save carmakers and financial institutions in developed countries), and blaming international capital flows for the stresses in world finance. It may be tempting for politicians to blame some emerging economies for saving too much, thus contributing to access liquidity that provoked irresponsible market behavior, and blame cheap producers for crises in key industrial sectors. Yet, the world has become too interwoven for even "soft protectionism" to work well. Even well endowed West European financial institutions, with headquarters in a relatively well regulated social environment, have had to admit to too much exposure to high growth and high return emerging economies in Eastern and Central Europe and in the former Soviet sphere. But the other side of the coin is that these emerging economies are more exposed and vulnerable to what is going on in their major developed counterparts – this is a fact that the EU should care about.

Given the heavy commitments of the IMF in some of the new member states of the EU, the question is whether the decision making bodies of the EU (European Commission, the Council and the Parliament) are properly equipped to deal with financial crises within the EU. Farming out the job of restoring fiscal discipline in new member states to the IMF seems an admission of impotency.

Globally, the mood may turn against the free flow of funds across nations, but the reality for the emerging and converging economies is that they would be the first to suffer from slowdown in international flows. Multilateral financial institutions and groupings of powerful nations have to take steps to restart the cross border financial flows – without committing again the same mistakes that have been instrumental in creating the recent international financial mess.

Notes

1. Alan Winters (2004), "Trade Liberalisation and Economic Performance: An Overview." *The Economic Journal*, p. 114 (February).
2. See for instance Gary B. Gordon (2008): "The Subprime Panic." NBER Working Paper Series, w14398, October, pp. 1–38; BIS (2008): *Quarterly Review*, December, pp. 1–93; ECB (2008): *Financial Stability Report*. December, pp. 1–44. Gertrude Tumpel-Gugerell (2009): "The Financial Crisis – Looking Back and the Way Forward." Speech at European Economic and Social Committee and European Trade Union Confederation, Brussels, 22 January.
3. *The Economist* (2008b), "Kreppanomics. How a Banking Crisis Brought Down a Small Economy." October 9.
4. *The Economist* (2008), "A Magyar Mess," March 27.
5. See Hungarian transition indicators as defined by the European Bank for Reconstruction and Development (EBRD) in, among others, its 2008 Transition Report.
6. Péter Ákos Bod (2005), *A Great Transformation? Banking and Capital Markets in "Transition Countries."* MES –Schriftenreihe no. 3. Europa-Universitat Viadrina.
7. Péter Ákos Bod (1998), "The Social and Economic Legacies of Direct Capital Inflows: The Case of Hungary." In Bastian J. (ed), *The Political Economy of Transition in Central and Eastern Europe*. Ashgate, 1998.
8. *The Economist* (2008c), Who's Next? Oct 23rd.
9. Resolution of the European Council on the Stability and Growth Pact Amsterdam, 17 June 1997. Official Journal C 236, 02/08/1997 P. 0001–0002.
10. Münchau, Wolfgang (2009) is very critical with the criteria, particularly with the one on inflation.
11. Hungarian Government (2006), *Convergence Programme*. Budapest.
12. See Otto Hieronymi (1990), *Economic Policies for the New Hungary: Proposals for a Coherent Approach*. Battelle Press. Columbus – Richland.
13. Ewald Novotni (2009), "Real Implications of the Financial Turmoil –Strategies for Growth and Stability," BIS review no. 19.
14. IMF (2008), Hungary: Request for Stand-By Arrangement – Staff Report, November 28.
15. Éva Fisher (2008), "Challenges of Financial Integration in the Central and East European Region," MNB Bulletin, no. 12.
16. IMF (2008), Hungary: Request for Stand-By Arrangement, p. 5.
17. Ibid.
18. Adrian Cox and Peter Garnhem (2009), "Moody's Warns of Eastern Europe risk," *Financial Times*, February 17.
19. Stefan Wagstyl (2009), "Banks Ask for Crisis Funds for Eastern Europe," *The Economist*, January 21.
20. Michael P. Dooley, David Folkerts-Landau, and Peter M. Garber (2009), "Bretton Woods II Still Defines the International Monetary System," NBER Working Paper Series 14731. http://www.nber.org/papers/w14731.

6
International Institutional Reforms Between Economic Growth and Sustainable Development

Beat Burgenmeier

The current financial crisis has led to a worldwide recession overshadowing more fundamental problems of the international economic order. This contribution casts some light on those problems in addressing a paradigmatic change from economic growth to sustainable development. It is divided into six parts.

The first, introductory one illustrates the increasing environmental awareness. It refers to the main international reports shaping our understanding of environmental issues. The second one identifies three economic responses to the environmental threat from a conceptual and theoretical point of view. The third one recalls the different stages in the history of international institutions from the Bretton Woods agreements to the Washington consensus. The objective is clearly focussed on economic growth in promoting competitive markets worldwide. The fourth one traces this history further, from the Washington consensus to the emergence of the concept of sustainable development. The fifth one discusses the policy options for environmental protection, which can be derived from that history. It sets the stage for the sixth and final part, which concludes with the long-term trends that can be observed in the reform projects for reshaping existing international organisations.

6.1   Introduction

Beginning in the 1950s, our world started to experience damages due to pollution. In Switzerland, the outbreak of typhoid fever in Zermatt in 1961 was a landmark for public awareness of now widely accepted environmental problems. Each country experienced its own event in approximately the same time frame and it was no surprise that the question of a link between human activity and environment was raised. In 1954, the American administration under President Dwight Eisenhower gave a mandate to a panel of outstanding representatives of the academic community in order to examine the man made part of pollution. Two years later, the related report recommended a systematic enquiry into the possible link between human activity and environmental degradation and suggested it be documented, putting in place a complete database gathering all available information on observed environmental changes (Thomas et al., 1956). This report remained confidential and had little influence on public opinion.

Two decades later, a second report addressed to the Club of Rome, had a much stronger impact on public awareness of environmental problems. Meadows's report used a simple computer model of several interactive variables on key issues such as demographic and economic growth, food production and environmental degradation. It stressed that a positive economic growth path is incompatible with the target of pollution reduction (Meadows, 1972). The conclusion of this report is straightforward: in a world with limited natural resources, only the objective of zero growth is compatible with efficient environment protection. Though the public attention was very much attracted and alarmed by this conclusion, the practical consequences were very weak.

The oil-shock – a more than hundred per cent increase of the oil price in 1973 – followed by the stock market crash, put a sudden end to a period of thirty years of economic growth. It was even regarded as the first real recession since the Great Depression. The target became not 'zero growth' but policies stimulating the economy. Nevertheless, international organisations started to integrate more systematically environmental issues in their priority setting. OECD launched an initiative for a 'quality growth' project, assembling twelve indicators of economic growth. The United Nations Environment Programme (UNEP) organised the first international conference on the human environment in 1972 in Stockholm, deciding an action plan and adopting a declaration. It stipulates that 'the concept of "no growth" could not be a viable policy for any society, but it was necessary to rethink the traditional concepts of the basic purposes of growth' (UNEP, 1972).

The follow up of this conference led to an intense exchange of information in several working groups, which lasted several years, where several intermediate reports have been published, but only the final one, published in 1986 became the universally praised landmark under the title 'Our common future' also known under the title 'Brundtland report', which coined the concept of sustainable development (WCED, 1987).

It defines this concept as a 'development that meets the needs of the present without compromising the ability of future generations to meet their own needs'. This definition obviously includes an appeal for inter-generational responsibility. This report not only refers to the link between the economy and the environment, but also includes a social dimension, insisting that without significant poverty reduction worldwide, there will be no efficient environmental policies.

It invites the international community to reform the economic order by strengthening multilateralism and to set the target less on economic growth than on sustainable development. As Hermann Daly has since shown, there are significant differences between the two (Daly, 1990). Indeed, the report focuses on development and not so much on economic growth. It is directly related to the spirit of the Stockholm Conference, which acknowledged environmental concerns on the agenda of international policy making.

The Brundtland report offered the background to the first Earth Summit in Rio de Janeiro in 1992, where an action plan for the twenty-first century in a participatory local setting was adopted. The slogan 'act local, think global' was born. The collective decision-making process is now based on multi-criteria analysis, where the different interacting criteria are weighted through an active participation of all actors of our society in consultation and decisions relating to sustainable development.

The last report we would like to mention, in order to document the growing public awareness for environmental issues, is the Stern report, named after Sir Nicolas Stern, second permanent secretary of the English Treasury department and director of the governmental economic services (Stern, 2007). Its main finding is that an active policy preventing climate change is less expensive in economic terms than the clean-up and repairing of damage. It had a tremendous impact on public opinion and political leaders. It contradicts in a very convincing way all those who denied the urgency of action. Its main finding is to show that the pursuit of economic growth without climate change policies will lead to cost evaluated to five per cent of GDP in a direct and 11 per cent in an indirect way, taking into account all externalities involved.

However, this report is going around in circles, as we are back to the Thomas report where only the link between the economy and the environment matter. It addresses neither the zero growth debate nor the social dimension of the concept of sustainable development. It shows that economic costs are still the main benchmark for any reform of the international economic order taking explicitly into account environmental issues and there is actually no way to escape this logic. The Kyoto Protocol reflects this fact quite well. It only mentions economic instruments in order to achieve its target of lowering CO_2 emission.

6.2   Economy and environment

How did economic theory evolve over time in order to address environmental issues? Three main approaches can be observed. Though they have been developed as a sequence in reaction to the observed environmental degradation, they continue to be simultaneously present in the actual policy debate.

The first approach can be described as 'business as usual'. It counts on the relative price changes in competitive markets in order to re-allocate production and consumption patterns in relation to the increased scarcity of natural resources. It was the first obvious theoretical answer to the growing environmental awareness and was dominant until the 1960s. Economics is a science of scarcity after all.

The second approach is still market based but, in the face of increasing pollution, its central idea is to change the calculations of the main economic actors, obliging them to take into account all costs, namely also those which they inflict on third parties. Pollution is seen as the expression of a market failure, which needs to be corrected. This approach is known as 'environmental economics' and is still one of the main references in policy making. However, the fact that the market seems to be myopic in facing environmental problems does not justify State intervention under any circumstances. Private action can also lead to the internalisation of external costs and the principle of subsidiary suggests an intervention more on an international than national or local level.

Therefore, the correction of market failure need a concerted action internationally and enforces the need for reform of the international institutional architecture.

Finally, the third approach arose in the 1980s along with the growing popularity of the concept of sustainable development. It is still not well understood, as it claims to change the perspective. Instead of an external treatment of the environment to the market, it treats the market as an externality to the environment. The consequences are twofold:

- It focuses on the analysis of ecosystems and their complex interactions, which should be better understood in order to determine their carrying capacity for a growing economic activity.
- Environmental protection policy should be in alignment with the concept of sustainable development. Therefore, it should be a policy mix of economic instruments, clean technology and poverty reduction tools. A single oriented approach is not able to cover

the whole range of reforms. The new regulatory needs have to be defined not only in an interdisciplinary way, but also call for new international governance.

This conclusion has not been put into practice so far. The institutional changes, which intervened in the last fifty years, rather supported economic growth worldwide as a 'one fits all' solution. The resulting antagonism between economic growth and sustainable development is striking and puts the reform agenda for the whole international economic order under stress.

In contemporary regulatory practices, top priority is given to the economy and an inferior status to environmental and social policies. Given this hierarchy, it is hardly surprising to find so-called economic instruments being extended into social and environmental domains while still respecting the priority accorded to economic growth and stabilisation policy. As a result, instruments of social and environmental policy have a place in international policy agencies (cf., OECD, 2001) only to the extent that they do not interfere with economic objectives. We refer here to the post-World War II (WWII) period that was characterised not only by a reform of the economic order through the Bretton Woods agreements, but also by a growing consciousness of inequalities in development and of worsening pollution.

As the economic approach to instruments for environmental protection was given privileged status by the Kyoto Protocol, it is now widely promoted at international as well as national levels. However, application is rather timid. Economic instruments run into a serious problem of social acceptance. Indeed, our knowledge of environmental protection needs and opportunities are not very effectively put to work. Scientific uncertainties are certainly present, but we know enough about the origins and the effects of most polluting agents to justify action and to seek reforms of society's regulatory systems. For example, even a common sense principle, that of 'precaution', is more present in reform rhetoric than in concrete actions to reorganise current economic practices. This rhetoric is the consequence of major changes, which intervened within the international organisations after the breakdown of the Bretton Woods agreements (e.g., Burgenmeier, 2008, pp. 23–30).

6.3   From the breakdown of the Bretton Woods agreements to the Washington consensus

After the breakdown of the Bretton Woods agreements in the 1970s, two contradictory – and necessarily conflicting – trends emerged. The first seeks to generalise the precept of market efficiency and notably affirms – for want of better – the flexible exchange rate system as a cornerstone of the new international order. The second insists on the environmental dimension of development as a fundamental component in the search for a new international economic order. The former pushes for liberalised markets at the world scale and has led to the Washington consensus. The latter seeks to correct market failures and is exemplified by the signature of the Kyoto Protocol.

6.3.1 Breakdown of the fixed exchange rate regime

The Vietnam War gobbled up more and more of the United States' financial resources during the 1960s that were, as well, characterised by social movements affirming the critical importance of environmental problems. These movements often opposed the Vietnam War but, more fundamentally, they were also pacifist movements that opposed the energy nuclear option.

The historical facts of the 1960s are well known. The United States became increasingly indebted relative to the rest of the world, which accumulated dollars (or promises of dollars) in counterpoint to the American debts contracted to finance the anti-communist effort. In the face of these mounting borrowings – all convertible into gold under the Bretton Woods agreements – the United States in 1971 suppressed unilaterally the convertibility of their national currency into gold and, with a single stroke, undid the whole international economic order that was the outcome of multilateral international negotiations in the post-WWII years. From the beginning of the 1970s, the world thus entered a new phase where the ideology of a new world economic order was fed by a primitive liberalism conflating the rules emerging as outcomes of multilateral negotiations with the principle 'might is right' – a confusion repeated without limits in the different forms of economic imperialism. The revival of neo-liberal currents is a clear sign of the need for legitimacy of the strongest, leading to the following simple affirmation: the misfortunes of humanity are solved by economic growth.

6.3.2 The Washington consensus

During the 1980s a sort of consensus emerged, more as a convergence of viewpoints than a formal agreement. This consensus centred on the sort of policies that should be pursued by the three Bretton Woods institutions. The World Bank and the International Monetary Fund (IMF) converged in their appreciation of development problems (it doesn't much matter if the adjective 'sustainable' is added or not) by insisting on the importance of respecting macroeconomic balance conditions. We can note in passing that these conditions imposed on Third World countries concerning mainly balanced budgets and balanced current account, continue to be flouted by the United States. Access to loans has been made conditional in seriously constraining ways, with little regard for the fact that the conditionality has often worsened the lot of the poorest components of society. The respect of macroeconomic balance conditions was seen as the way to guarantee an optimal growth perspective which, following the 'trickle down' principle, was supposed to end up improving conditions for even the poorest strata of society.

This strategy did not take sufficiently into account the rapid development of financial markets, which have perhaps been the most profoundly influenced by technological innovation in computing and communication. By virtue of an integration of financial markets at the world scale, it has become very easy to operate horizontal transfers of wealth and income generated through economic growth, thus completely sidelining any 'trickle down' process. What has taken place is the emergence of a network of little growth islands across North and South countries alike. The problems of social inequalities tend to spread as a systematic accompaniment of the economic growth ideal at the world level.

We see, in summary, a process of simplification along four lines:

- The first is the reduction from the utilitarian principle of 'the highest level of well-being for the greatest number' to the objective of economic growth obtainable via 'free' (supposedly efficient) markets at the world scale.
- The second reduces the treatment of social inequalities to the objective of economic growth, through the assertion that 'more is better than less'.
- The third reduces the challenges of development to a problem of economic growth circumscribed by the respect of macroeconomic balance for internal as well as external balances.
- The fourth is to place confidence in economic growth as a mechanism to allow reduction in pollution levels, of which climate change is one of the clearest expressions.

Confronted by this reasoning which seeks to fix all ills – unequal economic well-being, precarious social justice, under-development and environmental degradation – by a single strategy in line with the Washington consensus, there are evidently other social movements that highlight contradictions and limits of the Washington consensus in a dialectical manner.

The first seeks to correct market failures and starts from the precept that the objective of the Washington consensus pushing for a highest possible growth path can be reconciled with those of poverty reduction across the world and better protection of the environment. Thisreconciliation is pursued through some formulations of sustainable development and is expressed in, for example, the international negotiations leading to signature of the Kyoto Protocol.

The second insists on a fundamental opposition between the objective of economic growth and that of environmental protection. This opposition opens up the question of rethinking radically the concept of economic growth and its pertinence for guiding societal ambitions.

6.4   From Bretton Woods to the Brundtland report

The Bretton Woods agreements put into place in 1944 sought to resolve problems, foreseen by the future victors of the Second World War, concerning the transition from a world economy largely oriented to production needs dictated by armed conflicts, towards a peacetime economy. An economy controlled by rationing, exchange rate controls and strict regulations would have to be converted into an economy where economic actors could once again decide for themselves their opportunities for commercial activity. This transition from a war economy towards a free-exchange economy needed rules that the Bretton Woods agreements defined through an institutional framework built on the three pillars of the General Agreement on Trades and Tariffs (GATT), the IMF and the World Bank. This framework was oriented towards the freeing up of international trade, its financing, and also the needs of reconstruction and of economic development. Each institution was to play a specific role and found itself, one way or another, confronted by the rising awareness of environmental degradation (as an unwanted side-effect of economic growth and development) from the 1960s onwards. It was impossible to ignore the growing pollution problems and so the Bretton Woods institutions had to find ways to respond to the challenge, without, however, modifying their fundamental priorities. They were not conceived for this task. Environmental problems were largely unheeded at the end of WWII and each of the Bretton Woods institutions was set up to help establish the post-war international economic order and not to save the environment.

6.4.1   GATT and the environment

The first of the Bretton Woods pillars was specifically for the liberalisation of trade in the narrow sense. The GATT had as its main objective to reduce customs barriers and break down obstacles to international competition erected by governments. It was a question of exploiting every prospect of gains from trade, putting faith not only in the benefits of increased volumes but also in the prospects of better inter-country specialisation. Environmental protection was not yet a theme in 1947 and there is allusion to it only indirectly within Article XX of the original agreement. The point (b) of this article covers measures necessary to protect human, animal and plant life and health, which is really quite vague. The point (g) refers to measures for conserving non-renewable natural resources, in terms of restrictions on internal production and production, which once again is rather vague.

There is a clear hierarchy. Free exchange carries the day over environmental protection, which remains ill defined. For the latter to have the same standing, it would have been necessary to enlarge the competences of the GATT to include also the barriers to international trade (and to gains from trade) coming from the private sector, which would have made the GATT the competent instance of a worldwide mechanism for coordinated competition policy. In the absence of this, international trade remains forcibly sub-optimal. Market failures due to imperfect competition and those due to the 'external effects' of pollution reinforce each other and make difficult any comparison of international trade in welfare terms through time. Although the freeing up of international trade undoubtedly gives rise to a substantial welfare gain, the rising pollution associated with economic activities works in the opposite direction – without, however, being able to compare the two effects, the gains and the losses not being expressed in the same units of measure. In effect, over time international trade has evolved from one sub-optimal state to another.

In the real operations of the GATT, the focus of attention has been much more on gains from trade than on the negative effects of pollution. The standpoint of the GATT for a long period was to consider environmental protection as a protectionist argument used to obstruct efforts to liberalise trade. As recently as 1982, it considered the American ban on imports of tuna from Canada as a violation of Article XX (g) because the United States did not itself limit its national tuna production and consumption. It was not until 1992, when the United States sought to protect dolphins in the Eastern Pacific Ocean, that a change of position took place. This case has entered the history of the GATT as the 'tuna-dolphin issue' since it implied protection of this sea mammal species, which was frequently caught in tuna fishing nets. The reversal is not total, but has led to more clearly defined rules for species protection. Since that time, there have been many other cases and there are by now more than 200 recognised cases, including some agreements with quite major consequences. Examples are the conventions on international trade in endangered species in 1973, on substances provoking degradation of the stratospheric ozone layer in 1987 and on international trade of wastes in 1989.

With the extension over the years of the GATT to include services (GATS) and intellectual property, it is the World Trade Organisation (WTO) that, since 1995, has taken over the leading role, making it still more difficult to address environmental problems. The need to extend the GATT objectives was felt notably with the evolution of economic activities towards the tertiary sector, partly as an outcome of the Uruguay round of negotiations which substantially cut customs duties from 1986 to 1994.

As regards services, one particularly sensitive domain, from the environmental point of view, is that of transport. With most of the transport modes at an international level, there has been inadequate attention given to the social costs associated with their environmental nuisance effects. And there is no doubt that the internalisation of these social costs in transport costs would lead to significant price increases and establish a new 'barrier' to international exchange.

As regards intellectual property, patents are now equally subjected to international competition, which has immediately given rise to a major philosophical question. To what extent does or should the environment, notable in its variety of life forms, fall within the scope of private property rights? Given that the working of competitive markets is dependant on a clear definition of such rights, this opens up the debate of the 'commoditisation' of nature.

The controversy on this point has contributed without any doubt to the highly publicised opposition to the WTO such as street protests surrounding recent WTO meetings. While this contestation is nourished from several different and sometimes contradictory sources, it does force the international community to think about the necessity of reforms to the architecture of the global economic order. Possible outcomes for the environmental domain are either an explicit place in WTO negotiations, as seemed to be sketched out since the 1996 ministers' conference held at Singapore, or the creation of a new international organisation charged specifically to address environmental problems. Questions such as the monitoring of standards, the implementation of policy instruments and their coordination at international level – notably arising from the Kyoto Protocol on the limitation of green house gases – need to find a clear institutional response as the protocol reaches its implementation phases.

In the meantime, the GATT morphed into the WTO deals uncomfortably with environmental questions. Its decision-making process engages a delicate balance of interests, and it can be expected that more and more 'exceptions' to the free-trade principle will be admitted for environmental reasons. So it is only a question of time before the exception becomes the rule.

6.4.2   The IMF and the environment

The second pillar of the international economic order established by the Bretton Woods agreements was the IMF charged with assuring the financing of international trade. This agency is thus the expression of the monetary side of the classic dichotomy between real and nominal flows in international exchanges. It was given an exchange rate stabilisation function, because the Bretton Woods agreements envisaged a regime of fixed (but adjustable) exchange rates, with adjustments motivated for reasons of structural imbalance. The anchor of this exchange rate stability was the American dollar, which was exchangeable for gold – the so-called gold standard. This situation thus reflected from the outset the political hegemony prevailing in the post-war period, and hinted already at the heavy weight that the United States would exercise in the years to follow on the evolution of the world economic order, notably as regards the place given to the environment.

Of course, the link between the environment and the IMF is neither direct nor clearly visible. This agency had, in appearance, nothing to do with the environment. Its objective was to put at the disposal of the world economy a sufficient quantity of international liquidities to allow trade liberalisation to occur without constraint. However, given the primordial role of the dollar as the principal form of international liquidity, this exchange rate system contributed not only to the 'dollarisation' of international economic relations but also to reinforcement of the American role in these relations. Through its heavy influence on the international economic order, the IMF has promoted a strongly monetary vision of international relations, a bias that equally has led to monetary evaluation of the environment being seen rather too much as a cost for the economy and not as an asset. A non-monetary valuation of the environment would also have meant that the natural environment should be kept out of the market sphere – an absurd proposition given the strategic importance of international trade in certain natural resources necessary for economic growth, such as oil.

In 1971, following a unilateral decision taken by the Nixon administration, the dollar was declared no longer exchangeable for gold (viz., the end of the 'gold standard'), a decision stemming directly from the growing size of the American debt, which reflected in turn the Vietnam War. The fixed exchange rate regime broke down and the relative values of national currencies were freely determined on foreign exchange markets. For want of anything better, this 'flexible' exchange rate regime has become the new international monetary order, thus making superfluous the maintaining of a compensation fund for excessive fluctuations in exchange rates. The IMF therefore had to redefine its role and, in this context, identified for itself the task of managing international debts and liquidities – a mission subsequently referred to as the 'lender of last resort' in situations of acute international monetary crisis (which indeed were always possible given the fundamentally unstable nature of the foreign exchange markets). As a result, international economic relations have become riskier and must cope with levels of uncertainty much higher than those prevailing during the gold standard period.

Although, today, the debates around environmental protection reinforce the uncertain universe within which economic decisions are taken at the international level, this does not count for much in the face of the uncertainties of a strictly financial nature that characterise the international economic order. However, in order to reduce the risks of international monetary crises, the IMF came to impose increasing conditionality in its loans to countries having difficulties meeting its obligations. These conditions related, in the first instance, to matters of macroeconomic performance, such as internal and external balances and also budgetary balance, which touched directly and indirectly on the public financing for social and environmental purposes; these conditions thus touching on challenges of 'sustainable development' for countries said to be 'on the development path' (or under-developed). As a consequence, the identification of conditions brought the IMF closer to the World Bank on several points. From the initial situation of funds with a purely monetary purpose, there is a slippage towards problems and challenges of development. From there, it is only a small step towards environmental problems whose financing evidently poses all sorts of problems.

6.4.3   The World Bank and the environment

The third and last pillar of the international economic order established by the Bretton Woods agreements had to do with economic development. The authors of this agreement were fully conscious that the liberalisation of international trade on its own was not an adequate mechanism for managing the transition from a wartime economy to peacetime one. The scale of destruction and the scale of inequalities in the Third World countries were too great to imagine that free trade on its own could be a remedy. In addition, there was the need to manage the colonial heritage, which itself required some transition rules on the political plane.

The Bretton Woods agreements therefore envisaged a third international body, called the International Bank for Reconstruction and Development (IBRD) which subsequently became better known by the name World Bank. As its name indicates, this was to be a bank whose primary task was to finance investment projects for, on the one hand, the repair of war damages to economic infrastructures and, on the other hand, to promote development in Third Worlds countries. Environmental protection did not figure explicitly in its statutes, but entered bit by bit into the evaluation of projects and more generally into World Bank practices. A programme on population, energy and the environment has been launched and procedures for taking the environment into account have become more and more mainstream. However, it was not until 2001 that an authentic environmental strategy was defined, which would serve as a guideline for the definition of projects and their financing. The World Bank has, at the same time, moved closer to the IMF through offering payment facilities for the global environment as part of its increasingly diversified portfolio of projects and instruments for pollution reduction.

6.5   Options for an internationally coordinated environmental policy

There are four main policy options, which are illustrated in the following table (see Table 6.1) showing the related 'decision tree' for international reorganisation patterns.

We find here again the three approaches, which were discussed in the second part of this contribution. The 'business as usual' option corresponds to the period before the generalised public awareness of environmental problems in the 1950s. The option 'reactive policies' corresponds to the period beyond, where the policy response to

Table 6.1 Options for environmental policies

Options	Objectives	Instruments	Consequences
'Business as usual'	Efficient markets	Relative price change	Optimal resource allocation
Reactive policies	Clean-up, repairing	Direct controls, technology	Equal treatment
Proactive policies	Prevention	Market based (taxes and emission trading)	Change of consumer preferences and of technical progress
Policy mix	Adaptation and mitigation	Combining several instruments	Conformity with sustainable development

environmental damages could only be in actions such as clean-up and repairing. The 'proactive policy' option has been promoted since the 1960s. It has found considerable support from international organisations. However, the achievements do not relate to this supportive rhetoric, as the introduction of market-based instruments does not easily find political support.

The main reasons, which lay behind this lagging support, are twofold:

- Market-based instruments refer to two fundamentally different concepts in public philosophy. If the environment is seen as public good, the following two main characteristics apply. It is available (the 'non exclusion' criterion) and is accessible to everyone (the 'non rivalry' criterion). The State as the guardian of those criteria derives its legitimisation for raising environmental taxes. This instrument is not mentioned in the Kyoto Protocol, because it lays in the competence of the Nation-State.

  If the environment is seen as an economic good lacking clearly defined propriety rights, new markets can be organised by defining such rights in the form of permits or emission certificates. The market sets their prices and evaluates at the same time their environmental cost. This instrument is explicitly mentioned in the Kyoto Protocol. The choice of instruments is biased. In the first case, national competence is at stake. In the second case, multinational negotiation promotes a private approach to environmental protection policies.
- Special interest groups oppose an incentive policy as long as already decided investment is not written off. Real capital is only gradually mobile and can only be reinvested in clean technology as a result

of a preventive strategy, if this fact is fully understood. Therefore, the promotion of market-based instruments needs clearly designed modalities, such as long advanced announcement periods and gradually introduced instruments.

Finally, the option 'policy mix' imposed itself as the result of fact constraints. Facing climate change, there is no choice left. Global warming is under way and needs a reactive, adaptive, and preventive mitigation strategy.

Therefore, the reform of the international economic order has no other choice than to put the promotion of a policy mix on its agenda. The meaning of such a programme has to be defined on all levels.

At the macroeconomic level, there is an already identified need for a reform of national accounting. Though the UN also recognises this need in promoting an 'international human dimensions programme on global environmental change providing the socio-economic science on climate, energy and sustainability' (IHDP), it never succeeded in replacing the well-established GDP-measure of economic growth by its index of human development. Moreover, the reform cannot count on a converging support of all groups. Some promote satellite accounts measuring environmental issues, leaving national accounting unchanged; others seek to replace GDP by indicators of sustainable development (e.g., Cobb and Cobb, 1994).

This division is symptomatic of this contribution about 'international reforms between economic growth and sustainable development'. Satellite accounts are in conformity with growth; indicators with sustainable development.

On a microeconomic level, internalisation of external costs is at the forefront of policy making. It includes full-cost pricing adding to the usual economic cost, the environmental and the social ones. It also includes investment in research and development and technology (Bourg and Erkman, 2003). It is completed by social policies, which are not only legitimated by international redistribution of income and wealth, but also by the promotion of 'capabilities', which offer an perspective for the poor to act accordingly to the principles of sustainable development (Sen, 1980).

We illustrated, in the second part of this contribution, the dilemma of 'international reforms between economic growth and sustainable development' by the growing antagonism between international free trade and environmental protection. This dilemma can only be overcome by applying these instruments in all markets operating internationally (e.g., Mol, 2001).

Finally at the level of the firm, sustainable management finds a growing support (Daub, 2005). It has found its application in nearly all functions and is present in any organisational diagram of a modern firm. One of the prominent applications is illustrated by new norms and standards promoting the social and ecological responsibility of the firm, such as ISO 26 000, which is under discussion. This trend can easily be extended to initiatives for socially responsible investment, which needs the cooperation of at least three groups of actors. The first group is mainly formed by pension funds seeking opportunities for 'green investment'. The second one concerns financial intermediates willing to change their evaluation techniques of firms using a multi-criteria approach, which takes into account all available information in the field of economic, environmental and social performances. The third one concerns the firm itself, which is exposed to a growing number of initiatives in the reporting of international norms and new forms of waste and resource management.

Therefore, reforms have to be extended beyond the existing institutions in charge of the international economic order. They have to strengthen this ongoing change in management techniques in adopting international, commonly applied standards. More fundamentally, it implies reform of international financial markets, which have to move from a short-sighted 'shareholder' to a long-term 'stakeholder' approach. In order to achieve this target, not only are reforms of international organisations such as IMF needed, but also of private organisations such as one promoting international accounting standards.

6.6 Conclusion

This reform agenda is ambitious. It claims a collaboration of public and private bodies of international cooperation. It addresses long-term trends and shows that the pursuit of economic growth can only be matched with sustainable development if there is an active environmental policy applied worldwide. This policy counts on a combination of several instruments. Its domain of application is not only confined to the real economy and its related international trade, but also to international finance. The fact that the UNEP is already promoting a programme of sustainable finance shows the direction in which the international organisations will move in the future (UNEP, 2008).

Finally, what will be the most appropriate reform for the system? Should the initial Bretton Woods architecture of three pillars be maintained or should it be replaced by a new order? In maintaining the existent organisations, reforms have to promote an endogenous approach to the environment in setting rules for 'greening' them. This approach raises a problem of coordination among international institutions, which cannot be treated in the same way as in the past, where the Washington consensus was the result of converging views on economic growth. Coordination between conflicting goals is more difficult indeed.

In moving to a new system, reforms still based on the existing three pillars approach lead to the creation of new international institutions in charge of the operational content of sustainable development. In any case, the maintenance of the existing order, claiming a 'one fits all' solution in setting exclusively economic growth as a target, has come definitively to an end.

7
Impact of Corporate Governance on Financial Markets

André Baladi

7.1 Introduction

The 40 percent global stock market collapse of 2008 affected pension funds and other institutional investors, as well as individual stockholders worldwide.

Recent history has demonstrated that when stock market conditions deteriorate, the importance of corporate governance soars as the main guardian of stock market investments.

Sir Adrian Cadbury, the renowned founder of the corporate governance movement in the United Kingdom, has defined corporate governance as the material obligations of a company toward shareholders, employees, customers, suppliers, creditors, tax and other supervisory authorities.

He added that corporations should also minimize possible adverse consequences of their actions on the communities in which they operate, and on the environment.

Corporate governance organizations aim to uphold corporate governance principles, foster the adoption of International Financial Standards (IFRS), safeguard adequate "one share one vote" shareholder voting rights, responsibilize corporate boards, and upgrade the services of audit rating agencies, corporate governance rating agencies, as well as securities exchange organizations and other concerned parties around the world.

However, they have failed to reduce the negative impact of the financial perversions which occasionally affect stock markets.

Hands-off regulations allowed certain bankers, savings and loans executives and hedge-fund operators to develop disastrous financial innovations such as negative-amortization mortgages and collateralized obligations, while ignoring fast-rising mountains of debt.

The result today is that free-market finance tends to be discredited, and several policy makers are invoking a return to the Keynesian doctrine.

John Maynard Keynes argued that governments should fight depressions with heavy spending, so as to stimulate the economy. However, a return to Keynesianism should ideally be complemented with the implementation of corporate governance principles.

7.2   Roots of the corporate governance movement

In 1637, the Dutch tulipomania generated the first ever recorded futures market collapse. The speculative bubble, which had started in 1597 and led to several short-sale bans as early as 1610, grew to a single tulip bulb being sold for the equivalent of two tons of butter.

Long before Charles Mackay published in 1841 his *Extraordinary Popular Delusions and the Madness of Crowds*, Adam Smith wondered, in his 1776 *Wealth of Nations*, whether joint stock companies could really prosper, considering that their managers had few incentives to favor the interests of their widely scattered and often financially illiterate shareholders.

Actually, stockholders have been bilked throughout history, as demonstrated by the collapse of John Law's French Indian Company in 1715; the UK banking panic in 1825; the US banking panic in 1836; the Vienna stock market crash in 1873; the US market crash in 1907; the Black Friday stock market crash in 1929; the Chrysler rescue in 1980; the Black Monday stock market crash in 1987; the Long-Term Capital Management (LTCM) stock market failure in 1998; the Enron, Parmalat and WorldCom fiascos in 2001–03; the 2007–08 "subprime losses" of, among others, AIG, Bear Stearns, Citigroup, Lehman, Merrill Lynch, Soc-Gen, and UBS.

Corporate governance concerns emerged during the mid-1980s, when US pension funds decided to invest the majority of their stockholdings in index funds. Such long-term investments tend to be fixed over time, as their substantial indexed positions cannot easily be sold. US pension funds therefore set up the Council of Institutional Investors (CII) to defend their interests; Institutional Shareholder Services (ISS) founder, Robert A. G. Monks, challenged on behalf of shareholders the unethical behavior of certain corporate board of directors and chief executives; and US attorney Ira Millstein started to resolve corporate governance issues of major US corporations; while Sir Adrian Cadbury started to develop the first Corporate Governance Code.

American, British, Canadian, Dutch and Swedish pension funds joined forces, in 1995, with several corporate governance experts to create in Washington DC the International Corporate Governance Network (ICGN), with representatives from accounting firms, governance firms, law firms, banks, corporations, insurers, institutional investors, stock exchanges, and others.

7.3   "2008 Annus Horribilis"

Several financial commentators have paraphrased thus the 1992 statement of Queen Elizabeth, to describe the major global stock market losses in 2008.

Global stock markets were down by over 40 percent in 2008, according to the MSCI World Index. In the United States, the Dow Jones Industrial lost 35 percent, the S&P 500 39 percent, and the Nasdaq Composite 41 percent; the Dow Jones European Index lost 44 percent; in the United Kingdom, the FTSE 100 lost 31 percent; in Germany, the DAX lost 40 percent; the French CAC 40 lost 43 percent; Japan's Nikkei lost 42 percent (its biggest recorded loss); in China, the Shanghai Composite lost 65 percent; and in Russia, the RTS lost 72 percent.

According to the 6 November 2008 edition of *The Economist*, the Investment Company Institute (ICI), which assembles U.S. mutual funds, claimed that the latter had lost 20 percent of their assets in 2008, i.e., US$2.4 trillion. And US pension funds had lost a similar amount.

The Bank of England estimates that some US$2.8 trillion was lost in credit-related instruments, which dragged down the UK financial system in 2008.

Standards & Poor's estimates total 2008 global stock exchange losses at US$17 trillion.

According to the *Wall Street Journal* dated 2 January 2009, hedge funds performed even worse than the overall market. An index of 50 stocks "that matter most to hedge funds" lost 45 percent, including dividends.

Financial acronyms may have contributed to conceal a widespread speculative dilettantism. See Table 7.1.

Last but not least, the alleged US$50 billion Madoff "Ponzi Scheme," revealed on December 12, 2008 in New York, is likely to affect both directly and indirectly several thousand investors throughout the world – with losses estimated (according to the *Wall Street Journal* – wsj. com – of December 22, 2008) at US$7.5 billion for Fairfield Greenwich Advisors, US$3.3 billion for Tremont Group Holdings, US$2.7 billion for Banco Santander, and US$2 billion for Bank Medici.

The Securities Exchange Commission (SEC) conducted examinations at the offices of Bernard L. Madoff Investment Securities LLC throughout

Table 7.1   Financial Acronyms.

Alt-A (CDO linked to RMBS)	
ARS (Auction Rate Security)	CMO (Collateral Mortgage Obligation)
CDO (Collaterized Debt Obligation)	CPDO (Constant-Proportion Debt Obligation)
CDS (Credit Default Swap)	MBS (Mortgage-Backed Security)
CFO (Collateralized Financial Obligation)	MCE (Monoline Credit Enhancer)
CLO (Credit Loan Obligation)	RLN (Reference Linked Note)
CMBS (Commercial Mortgage-Backed Security)	RMBS (Residential Mortgage-Backed Security)

1992–2006, but never uncovered the fraud. According to the 6 January 2009 edition of the *Wall Street Journal*, the SEC intervened in 1992, 1999, 2004, 2005 and 2006. However, neither Barron's premonitory article by Erin Arvedlung dated May 7, 2001, "Don't Ask, Don't Tell", nor the interventions of Harry Markopolos (an executive at one of Madoff's rival companies) succeeded in persuading the SEC that Bernie Madoff could be front running for his wealthy clients.

The Securities Investor Protection Corporation (SIPC) has mailed over 8000 claim forms concerning this alleged Madoff investment fraud. According to the *Washington Post* of January 5, 2009, this fraud contributed to the US House Financial Services Committee recommending a major overhaul of the US regulatory system.

7.4   OECD pioneering corporate governance role

The Organisation for Economic Cooperation and Development (OECD) invited Ira Millstein and Sir Adrian Cadbury – with ICGN representatives, as well as several corporate governance professionals and institutional investors – to participate in the discussions of an Ad Hoc Task Force, which led to the adoption of the 1999 OECD Corporate Governance Code (updated in 2004), highlighting the following issues:

- Basis for an Effective Corporate Governance Framework
  The corporate governance framework should promote transparent and efficient markets, be consistent with the rule of law and clearly

articulate the division of responsibilities among different supervisory, regulatory and enforcement authorities.

- Rights of Shareholders and Key Ownership Functions
The corporate governance framework should protect and facilitate the exercise of shareholders' rights, for instance:
  - secure methods of ownership registration;
  - participate and vote at general shareholder meetings;
  - elect and remove Board members, and share in the profits of the corporation;
  - participate in, and be sufficiently informed on, decisions concerning fundamental corporate changes such as extraordinary transactions, including the transfer of all or substantially all assets, that in effect result in the sale of the company.
- Equitable Treatment of Shareholders
The corporate governance framework should ensure the equitable treatment of all shareholders, including minority and foreign shareholders. All shareholders should have the opportunity to obtain effective redress for violation of their rights.
- Role of Stakeholders in Corporate Governance
The corporate governance framework should recognize the rights of stakeholders established by law or through mutual agreements and encourage active cooperation between corporations and stakeholders in creating wealth, jobs and the sustainability of financially sound companies.
- Disclosure and Transparency
The corporate governance framework should ensure that timely and accurate disclosure is made on all material matters regarding the corporation, including its financial situation, its corporate objectives, its performance, its ownership, and the governance of the company.
- Responsibility of the Board
The corporate governance framework should ensure the strategic guidance of the company, the effective monitoring of management by the Board, and the Board's accountability to the company and its shareholders.

  Board members should act on a fully informed basis, in good faith, with due diligence and care, and in the best interest of the company and its shareholders.

  Where Board decisions may affect different shareholder groups differently, the Board should treat all shareholders fairly.

  Boards should consider assigning a sufficient number of non-executive Board members capable of exercising independent judgment to tasks where there is a potential for conflict of interest.

Board members should be able to commit themselves effectively to their responsibilities. Multiple Board memberships by the same person should be compatible with effective Board performance.

There are about 200 national and/or regional corporate governance codes worldwide, but only two major international codes: the OECD and the ICGN Codes. While the OECD represents member states, the ICGN represents investors. The OECD Code inspired the ICGN Code.

Since the OECD Corporate Governance Code was developed by governmental representatives and the ICGN Code by institutional investors, corporations might also be incited to develop their own Code. Suggestions were thus made for corporations to develop their own Code during the Corporate Governance Roundtable of the International Chamber of Commerce (ICC) on June 5, 2008 in Paris. Moreover, the founder of the Swatch Group, Nicholas Hayek, also hints at such an idea in the September 2008 issue of the Swiss monthly *L'Hebdo*. Developing a global joint OECD – ICGN – ICC Code framework would ultimately make a lot of sense.

7.5   ICGN corporate governance implementation initiatives

The ICGN is reported to be the premier global financial network, with members and participants holding equity assets of some US$15 trillion at the beginning of 2008. Should the value of the stocks traded on the stock exchanges with which the ICGN cooperates be included, the ICGN could be considered to assemble the majority of stock securities traded worldwide.

The ICGN is a non-governmental and not-for-profit organization set up to facilitate fruitful contacts, interventions and publications, so as to promote adequate governance practices around the world.

The ICGN has held major conferences and meetings throughout the world since its foundation in 1995 in Washington DC, sponsored by the CII. Annual Meetings were thus held in: 1996, in London, sponsored by the Corporation of the City of London; 1997, in Paris, sponsored by Paris Bourse; 1998, in San Francisco, sponsored by the California Public Retirement System (CalPERS); 1999, in Frankfurt, sponsored by the Deutsche Börse; 2000, in New York City, sponsored by the Teachers Insurance and Annuity Association-College Retirement Equities Fund (TIAA-CREF), the New York Stock Exchange (NYSE), and the National Association of Securities Dealers Automated Quotation (NASDAQ); 2001, in Tokyo, sponsored by the Tokyo

Stock Exchange; 2002, in Milano, sponsored by Borsa Italiana; 2003, in Amsterdam, sponsored by the Euronext Exchange; 2004 in Rio de Janeiro, sponsored by Bovespa; 2005 in London, sponsored by the London Stock Exchange; 2006 in Washington DC, sponsored by the CII; 2007 in Cape Town, sponsored by the Johannesburg Stock Exchange; and 2008 in Seoul, sponsored by the Korean Stock Exchange (KRX).

Mid-year meetings were held in: October 2004 in Wilmington (Delaware), February 2006 in Frankfurt, November 2006 in Mumbai, October 2007 in New York, March 2008 in Göteborg (Sweden), and December 2008 in Wilmington (Delaware).

The year-round activities of the ICGN are carried out by its various Committees, such as: Awards, Board Nominations, Accounting and Auditing, Corporate Governance Principles, Cross-Border Voting Practices, Executive Remunerations, Non-Financial Disclosure, Securities Lending.

The ICGN Corporate Governance Code was discussed throughout 1998–99, adopted in 2000, and updated in 2005.

7.6 The ICGN corporate governance code

The ten ICGN Corporate Governance Principles are,

Corporate Objectives
- Optimize long-term growth benchmarked vs. equity peer group.

Voting Rights
- Uphold the "one share – one vote" principle throughout the world.

Disclosure & Transparency
- Corporations should disclose all relevant material information on a timely basis.
- Corporations should disclose their systems of governance and whether they comply with a governance code.

Corporate Boards
- Split Chair and CEO functions.
- Majority of independent Directors.
- No reciprocal cross-appointment of Directors.

Executive Remunerations
- Avoid guaranteed high remunerations.
- Align the financial interests of managers with those of shareholders.

Strategic Corporate Focus
- Major strategic core business shifts should be made with prior shareholder approval.
- Shareholders should be allowed sufficient time for their evaluations, before exercising their voting rights.

Peer Group Benchmarking
- Corporations should strive to excel in specific sector peer group benchmarking comparisons, regarding their respective financial and shareholder return ratios.

Accounting and Auditing
- External auditors should be proposed by the Audit Committee of the Board, for approval by shareholders.
- Non-audit fees should be approved by the Audit Committee and disclosed in the Annual Report.
- A single global accounting standard should be developed.

Corporate Citizenship
- Impact of Al Gore's global warming campaigns.
- Corporate citizenship codes:
    - OECD Anti-Bribery Code
    - Social Accountability SA 8000
    - Environmental Certification ISO 14'000
    - U.N. Global Compact on Responsible Investments.

Corporate Governance Implementation
- Corporate governance disputes should preferably be addressed through dialogue, negotiation or arbitration, before resorting to class actions.
- Shareholders should have the right to sponsor resolutions or convene extraordinary meetings.

7.7   Main ICGN publications

Since its foundation, the ICGN has published several reports and best practice guidelines, such as

- Statement of Principles on Institutional Shareholder Responsibilities (2007)

- Securities Lending Code of Best Practice (2007)
- Executive Remuneration Guidelines (2006).

It has, moreover, issued a "Statement on the Global Financial Crisis," on the occasion of its December 10, 2008 Meeting in Delaware.

This Statement highlights the failure of regulators to secure fair and transparent markets. It particularly encourages shareholders to hold Corporate Boards to account, to ensure the prevalence of the "one share – one vote" principle, to limit executive remunerations, to reduce excessive reliance on credit-rating agencies, and to upgrade global accounting standards particularly regarding inter alia fair value and off-balance sheet issues.

7.8   Corporate governance rating agencies

A host of corporate governance rating agencies emerged over the past two decades, on the model of the three leading credit-rating agencies (Fitch, Moody's, and Standard & Poor's). The major governance rating agencies, favored by an international network, are generally considered to be (in alphabetical order):

- The Corporate Library (TCL), founded by Robert A. G. Monks and Nell Minow, in the United States.
- European Corporate Governance Service (ECGS) group, composed of leading European firms such as Corporate Governance Services in Spain, Deutsche Schutzvereinigung für Wertpapierbesetz (DSW) in Germany, Dutch Sustainability Research in Holland, Ethos Services in Switzerland, Pensions & Investment Research Consultants (PIRC) in the United Kingdom, and Proxinvest in France.
- Egan-Jones Proxy Services, in the United States.
- Glass Lewis, in the United States (it was recently acquired by the Canadian Pension Fund Ontario Teachers).
- Governance Metrics International (GMI), in the United States.
- RiskMetrics, in the United States (it recently acquired Deminor in Belgium, and ISS in the United States).
- Moody's and Standard & Poor's, in the United States.
- Proxy Governance, in the United States (it acquired Marco Consulting in the United States, and is reported to cooperate with Manifest in the United Kingdom).
- Vigeo, in France (it acquired Avanzi in Italy, as well as both Ethibel and Stock at Stake in Belgium).

7.9   Corporate governance monitoring organizations

The following five organizations – listed in alphabetical order – are considered to be the leading corporate governance monitoring organizations:

- The CII was founded in 1984 in Washington DC – www.cii.org. It assembles today over 500 representatives (mostly from major US pension funds) as General Members, as well as Educational Sustainers and a few Honorary International Participants. It organizes regular conferences and meetings with both US and international organizations. It also edits a string of publications and reports. Moreover, it played a significant role in the foundation of the ICGN
- The ICGN (cf. supra) – www.icgn.org
- The OECD (cf. supra) – www.oecd.org
- UNCTAD's Intergovernmental Working Group of Experts on International Standards of Accounting and Reporting (ISAR), in Geneva (cf. infra) – www.unctad.org and www.unctad.org/isar

The World Bank, the International Finance Corporation (IFC), and the International Monetary Fund (IMF) are also active in the global corporate governance arena, through conferences, publications and ad hoc interventions – cf. www.worldbank.org, www.ifc.org, and www.imf.org

7.10   UNCTAD's corporate governance disclosure endeavors

UNCTAD's ISAR corporate governance disclosure endeavors deserve to be covered relatively extensively. They concern the international deliberations, between 1999 and 2008, which assembled governmental representatives with accountants, auditors, credit raters, and corporate governance professionals.

During its 16th session in 1999, ISAR analyzed the role of accounting and auditing during the 1997 East Asian financial crisis. ISAR's conclusion was that the lack of reliable information on external financial exposures did not allow corrective actions.

ISAR then commissioned a study, which found that weak accounting and auditing practices were partly to blame.

The Asian crisis also brought a series of challenges to the audit profession. It raised the issue of the gap between public expectations of the audit process and the assurances provided by the profession.

Some of the large accounting firms were criticized for signing accounts prepared according to weak national standards, and for bestowing a level of credibility on company accounts through a reliance on their internationally recognized credibility.

The reliance on questionable accounting and disclosure practices, their approval by the board and their verification by the auditors arose from a variety of forces such as pressure to meet quarterly earning projections, support stock prices, executive compensation practices, complex corporate financial arrangements designed to minimize taxes and hide the true state of companies, compounded by the compromised independence of accounting firms.

During UNCTAD's 10th Quadriannual Conference of 2000 in Bangkok, Member States called on ISAR to promote increased transparency, including improved corporate governance disclosure.

At the 17th Session of ISAR in 2000, a review of corporate governance practices was requested, and the UNCTAD Secretariat organized a Corporate Governance Roundtable with the University of Geneva.

In 2001, at the 18th Session of ISAR, the identification of best practices in corporate governance was recommended. Through informal consultations conducted in a two-day workshop and via email, it was agreed that the research be focused on disclosure requirements, with a view to developing guidelines.

Investors surveyed by McKinsey identified accounting disclosure as the most important factor in influencing investment decisions. They stated that good financial accounting could be an important corporate governance tool.

After the 2001 corporate scandals, UNCTAD assembled in April 2002 an ad hoc group of experts, who discussed which items should be included in both financial and non-financial corporate disclosure best practices. Their recommendations for disclosure covered the following items:

- Financial disclosures
  Financial operating results, related-party transactions and accounting policies.
- Non-financial disclosures
  Corporate objectives, ownership structure, shareholders' rights, structure, role and function of the board, composition and functions of the board's committees, duties, qualifications, training and remuneration of independent directors, board evaluation, succession planning, material issues related to employees and other

stakeholders, independence of auditors, annual general meetings, timing and means of disclosure, and "comply or explain."

Their report, "Transparency and disclosure requirements for corporate governance" (TD/B/COM.2/ISAR/15), was discussed at the 19th session of ISAR. Delegations expressed appreciation to the ad hoc group for the quality of the report and emphasized the importance of ISAR's work, since the IASB seemed to regard corporate governance disclosure as being beyond its remit. ISAR experts debated the location of the disclosures, that is, whether they were to be in the annual report or in a separate special purpose report. Some experts expressed concern that a separate corporate governance report could lead to repetition of information, especially in relation to financial information.

The ad hoc group pointed out that the location of disclosures, although worth debating for the sake of harmonization, was not as important as the disclosures themselves. Possible options were to include a reference to some of the financial information already in the notes to the financial statements, to put all such disclosures in a separate section of the annual report or to provide a stand-alone report. There was also a lengthy discussion about which companies should make the disclosures: listed companies, and/or all entities of public interest including small and medium-sized companies? It was pointed out that the recommendations were relevant to all companies eager to attract domestic as well as foreign investment, regardless of their legal form and size. An expert from a developing country noted that, while there might not be stock exchanges in certain developing countries, there could be cooperatives, financial institutions and major enterprises playing a significant role in the economy. All these unlisted entities needed to provide adequate disclosures on their operations and governance. However, it was not practical to require such disclosures from SMEs, most of which were in the informal sector.

ISAR also debated the issue of transparency and its relationship to disclosure. Certain delegates maintained that the concept of transparency was broader than disclosure and should be dealt with separately. Transparency could cover corporate policy, rules and regulations, processes and procedures, specific actions of management and employees. A member of the ad hoc group responded that disclosure in itself constituted transparency. Another delegate maintained that in the case of Enron, even though issues were disclosed in notes to financial statements, the company was not transparent to its shareholders.

A number of delegates felt that it was important to consider the interests of all stakeholders, not just those of capital markets, and that issues of environmental and social stewardship should also be considered. Delegates also discussed issues regarding independent verification of corporate governance information. It was emphasized that there should be a statement about which information had been verified and how it had been verified.

In concluding the debate, ISAR agreed that the report provided useful information and a convergence of views on corporate disclosures. It also anticipated some of the new requirements, contained in the Sarbanes-Oxley Act of 2002, by the New York Stock Exchange and NASDAQ. The delegates suggested that the recommendations be supplemented with examples of best practice case studies.

These case studies were carried out throughout 2002 in Brazil, France, Kenya, the Russian Federation, and the United States.

These five countries were selected according to their global representativity, coupled with the availability of qualified researchers. Asia could not be covered in time for the publication of the study.

The following topics were covered:

- Country Background
  - Asset management framework.
  - Corporate governance framework and code(s).
  - Compliance with regional or international code(s).
  - Economic accounting-related regulations.
  - Compliance with international accounting standards.
- Financial Disclosures
  - US GAAP and IAS / IFRS accounting systems.
  - Evolution of national regulations.
- Non-Financial Disclosures
  - Corporate objectives.
  - Shareholders' rights.
  - Governance structures and policies.
  - Boards of directors.
  - Material issues regarding employees and other stakeholders.
  - Environmental and social stewardship.
  - Material foreseeable risk factors.
  - Independence of auditors.
- Annual General Meetings
- Timing and Means of Disclosure
- Best Practices for Corporate Governance Compliance
- Comprehensive References and Related Literature

In 2003, at the 20th session of ISAR, these case studies revealed a fair amount of consensus at the level of principles. A number of common features of corporate disclosure were identified:

- A consensus on the importance of corporate governance disclosures.
- Enforcement difficulties.
- Business preference for the voluntary approach.
- Impact of US rules, and the 2002 Sarbanes-Oxley Act, on other countries.
- Role of the audit committee and auditors to be examined further.
- Long-term convergence goal for the IFRS.
- Concern over access to reliable information.
- Inroads of significant social and environmental disclosures.

The following deficiencies were detected:

- Beneficial ownership was difficult to ascertain.
- Disclosure regarding the board of directors was limited (qualifications, biographical information, other directorships held).
- Information on board training and access to external advisors was lacking.
- Length of directors' contracts and severance pay could not be found.
- Disclosure on what other stakeholders consider "material" suffered from an absence of recognized standards or practices.
- Boards generally did not disclose that they had confidence in the auditor's independence, or disclose the interaction between the internal and external auditors.

The comparison of the disclosure requirements of the countries with the ad hoc group's recommendations gave cause for optimism. Several countries had legislations and regulations that corresponded well to ISAR's Transparency and Disclosure Requirements. However, corporate practices varied widely across the study group. Enforcement and legal recourse were of paramount concern. The case studies illustrated that disclosure had its limitations. No amount of disclosure or substantive regulation would be able to prevent individuals who are intent on defrauding enterprises from doing so. This does not diminish the importance of disclosure as an oversight tool. A well-conceived disclosure regime remains one of the most effective oversight tools available.

In 2004, at its 21st session, ISAR considered the status of the implementation of adequate corporate disclosure practices at the company level. The survey confirmed the difficulties of implementation in that, while there was increasing convergence among national and international codes and guidelines, the disclosure practices and content of disclosures among selected companies varied greatly. In general the highest scores were associated with disclosure of financial results, accounting policies, and various governance structures and mechanisms. The disclosure items getting the lowest scores were disclosure of decision-making, impact of alternative accounting decisions, use of an advisor to the board, and board performance evaluation. At the conclusion of the session, ISAR agreed to consider further development in the area of disclosures and to update its earlier work.

In 2005, at its 22nd session, ISAR considered updating its 2002 paper on Transparency and Disclosure Requirements. Based on case studies of best practices, the survey of implementation and recent developments, the paper had been revised. After discussion, ISAR decided to prepare its guidance for publication and disseminate it as widely as possible, to contribute to further convergence of disclosures, improve corporate transparency, and facilitate investment.

The purpose of ISAR's guidance is to assist the preparers of corporate reports in producing disclosures on corporate governance that address the major concerns of investors and other stakeholders.

The "Guidance on Good Practices in Corporate Governance Disclosure" was published in June 2006 (UNCTAD/ITE/TEB/2006/3), and the "Guidance on Corporate Responsibility Indicators in Annual Reports" in February 2008 (UNCTAD/ITE/TEB/2007/6).

UNCTAD also helped to organize several corporate disclosure conferences around the world, e.g., at the May 29–June 1, 2005 World Accounting Summit in Dubai; during the 11th Quadriannual UNCTAD Conference of June 14, 2005 in São Paulo; as well as at the "Investment and Good Practices in Corporate Disclosure" Conferences of 2007 and 2008 in Cairo, which were organized jointly with the Egyptian Institute of Directors (EIoD), in cooperation with, among others, the Egyptian Ministry of Investment, the International Finance Corporation (IFC), the Cairo Stock Exchange and US Aid.

7.11   Sovereign wealth funds

One of the first Sovereign Wealth Funds (SWFs) was the French Caisse des Dépôts et Consignations (CDC), founded nearly 200 years ago. The majority of SWFs tend to be in the Middle East, such as the Abu

Dhabi Investment Authority (ADIA) and the Kuwaiti Investment Authority. See Table 7.2.

The following 2008 stakes of SWFs were highlighted by the media:

- Barclays got US$9 billion from the Qatar Investment Authority with a group of Asian investors.
- Citigroup got US$7.5 billion from ADIA, and US$14.5 billion from Singapore Investment Co. and the Kuwaiti Investment Authority.
- Merrill Lynch got US$6.6 billion from Kuwait, and US$6.2 billion from Singapore.
- UBS got US$9.7 billion from Singapore, and US$2 billion from an unnamed Middle Eastern investor.
- Morgan Stanley got US$5 billion from China Investment Co.

While the OECD recommends restraint to incite SWFs to adopt a voluntary code of conduct, both the EU and the IMF are said to be in the process of requesting that SWFs disclose their assets, their investment strategies, and their possible political constraints.

Although the Middle East appears to be one of the main targets of EU and IMF criticism, such anxiety is unjustified considering the following achievements:

- The Hawkamah Corporate Governance Institute was founded in 2006 by Dr. Nasser Saidi, Chief Economist of the Dubai International Financial Centre (DIFC). The Institute organizes conferences, seminars and training sessions throughout the Middle East-North Africa (MENA) area, to develop corporate governance curricula focused on corporate transparency, voting rights, independent qualified Board

Table 7.2   SWFs assets (mid-2008).

	US$ million
Middle East	3000
Singapore	438
Norway	407
China	300
Canada	160
Russia	159
Hong Kong	140
Libya	50

Source: Author's estimates.

Directors, specialized Board Committees, as well as adequate court and dispute resolution mechanisms.

- The Cairo Stock Exchange, the Egyptian Banking Institute and the Egyptian Institute of Directors have developed a Corporate Governance Code.
- A corporate governance code was also recently promulgated in Lebanon, in connection with its Stock Exchange.

Moreover, the Middle East benefits from the patronage and/or the technical assistance of the long-standing American Universities based in Beirut and in Cairo, the US Center for International Enterprise (CIPE), the US Financial Services Volunteer Corps (FSVC), the ICGN, the International Financial Corporation (IFC), the OECD, and last but not least by the UNCTAD's ISAR Group of Experts in Geneva.

7.12   Securities class actions

Securities class actions are largely concentrated in the United States, where legal firms started to solicit the interventions of pension funds some two decades ago.

Table 7.3 shows the settlements achieved throughout 2006 by the five leading US securities class action law firms.

Despite the historical European cultural mistrust toward US class actions, several European plaintiff filings by US law firms were reported in 2007 (see Table 7.4).

Time will tell whether the alleged US$50 billion Madoff "Ponzi Scheme" is likely to incite a large number of investors located outside the United States to participate more actively in securities class actions – all the more so as the majority of affected banks were apparently based outside the United States.

7.13   Financial ratios

The 2008 financial crisis alerted the corporate governance community that it can no longer neglect the necessity to incorporate into its evaluation several key financial ratios, for example:

- Profitability: return on equity, return on invested capital.
- Leverage: debt-to-equity, interest coverage.
- Liquidity: current ratio, quick ratio.
- Management efficiency: days of sales and of payable outstanding, assets turnover.

Table 7.3   Settlements by leading US securities class action law firms (2006).

	US$ billion
Coughlin Stoia Geller Rudman & Robbins	11.5
Bernstein Litowitz Berger	10.8
Barrack Rodos & Bacim	7.9
Milberg Weiss	5.2
Heinz Mills & Olson	2.6

Source: RiskMetrics – SCAS 50 Power Ranking, November 6, 2007.

Table 7.4   European plaintiff filings by US law firms (2007).

Germany	50	France	6
Austria	13	UK	5
Italy	13	Luxemburg	4
Netherlands	7	Denmark	3
Sweden	7	Ireland	3
Belgium	6	Switzerland	1

Source: Institute of Social Studies (ISS), The Hague – quoted by Jeremy Wolfe, Financial Times, FTfm, November 26, 2007.

Ratios allow companies to be screened compared to their benchmark peers, e.g., food industry companies should be matched vs. other food industry companies, beauty care and toiletries companies vs. other beauty care and toiletries companies, steel companies vs. other steel companies, pharmaceutical ethical companies vs. other pharmaceutical ethical companies, pharmaceutical over-the-counter drug companies vs. other pharmaceutical over-the-counter drug companies, and so forth.

Indeed, financial ratio scores vary widely among different industries; financial or commercial services groups, and corporations should therefore be matched against their peers.

Conglomerates are difficult to benchmark. The former ITT Industries conglomerate, assembled by Harold Geneen during the 1970s, was a hodgepodge of unrelated businesses in insurance, auto parts, and hotels. Now that ITT is centered on a limited range of products, its profitability ratios have significantly outstripped those of the emblematical General Electric conglomerate, which was initially assembled by Jack Welch.

Actually, conglomerates were fashionable during the 1950s, when they could better protect their investors through diversifications in different businesses. Today, large institutional investors diversify their investments through a myriad of companies mirroring the main stock indexes, such as the DAX, Dow Jones, CAC, FTSE, MSCI, SMI, S&P. And individual investors can now diversify their stock portfolios through diversified mutual funds.

7.14   Stock exchanges

The familiar denominations "Bourse," "Borsa" or "Bolsa" prevail worldwide – mostly in Latin derived languages – to designate stock exchanges. Such denominations are reported to originate from the 700 BC Phoenician trading exchange "Byrsa."

The Tokyo Stock Exchange may ultimately consider teaming up with another exchange, as might the stock exchanges of Brazil, Russia, India and China (the so-called BRIC countries).

Table 7.5 shows the major stock exchanges, as we know them today, and their year of establishment, as reported by them.

The Cairo Exchange was rated fifth in the world in the late 1930s (after New York, London, Paris and Tokyo) in terms of capitalization of its listed companies. It is now struggling to regain part of its former status, by enhancing its corporate governance achievements.

Table 7.6 shows, according to information communicated by stock exchanges, the capitalization of listed companies in mid-2008.

We have witnessed a flurry of stock exchange alliances, mergers and technical cooperation agreements throughout 2008:

- NYSE Euronext negotiated technical cooperation agreements with both the Abu Dhabi Securities Market and the Doha Securities Market in Qatar, coupled with a stock participation with the former. It also acquired the American Stock Exchange in the United States and a minority interest in the Multi Commodity Exchange (the leading commodity derivatives exchange in India).
- Nasdaq OMX linked with the Dubai Exchange, which was renamed Nasdaq Dubai.
- The London Stock Exchange merged with Borsa Italiana.
- Deutsche Börse teamed with the Swiss Stock Exchange, to acquire the International Securities Exchange in the United States.

The growing consolidation of stock exchanges is contributing to the development of adequate global corporate governance practices. The NYSE Euronext Stock Exchange has benefited from the ICGN

Table 7.5   Year of stock exchange establishment.

	A.D.
Amsterdam and London	1600
Paris	1709
New York	1792
Geneva	1855
Tokyo	1878
Cairo & Alexandria	1903

Table 7.6   Capitalization of listed companies (June 2008).

	US$ trillion
NYSE Euronext	17.91
Nasdaq + Stockholm OMX	4.64
Tokyo Stock Exchange	4.04
London Stock Exchange + Borsa Italiana	3.17
Toronto	2.16
Shanghai	2.10
Hong Kong	2.09
Deutsche Börse	1.81
Spanish Exchanges	1.74

corporate governance conferences sponsored by Paris Bourse in 1997 in Paris, then by Euronext in 2003 in Amsterdam, while the NYSE sponsored the ICGN conference in 2000 in New York. Global corporate governance developments are periodically reviewed during the meetings of the International Advisory Board of the NYSE Euronext Exchange. It is so far the only major exchange to benefit from the fruitful feedback generated by such a Board, originally set up by Paris Bourse in 1995.

7.15   Major financial reform initiatives

Could the world economy recover by itself with a "laissez faire" approach? Or do we have to resort to a return to Keynesian interventionist policies?

An avalanche of public initiatives is emerging from the United States, the United Kingdom, France and the EC, as demonstrated by the following two examples:

A consortium of global securities market participants known as the "Global Joint Initiative to Restore Confidence in Securities Markets" was set up by the Securitization Industry and Financial Markets Association

(SIFMA), the American Securitization Forum (ASF), the European Securitisation Forum (ESF), and the Australian Securitisation Forum (AuSF). It published in December 2008 a report recommending reforms to help restore confidence in the securitization markets, which could be implemented without regulation or legislation.

This report recommends several major courses of action:

- Develop industry-wide standard norms for Residential Mortgage-Backed Securities, after attempting to disclose information on their underlying assets.
- Improve independent, third-party sources of valuations, and improve the valuation infrastructure and contribution process for specified types of securitization and structured products.
- Restore market confidence in credit-rating agencies by enhancing transparency in the credit-rating process.
- Establish a Global Securitization Markets Group, to report publicly on the state of the market and changes in market practices.
- Establish and enhance educational programs aimed at directors and executives with oversight of securitized and structured credit groups, as well as at investors with significant exposure to these products.

Moreover, the SEC has issued new rules for National Recognized Statistical Rating Organizations (NRSROs), to strengthen the Credit Rating Agency Reform Act of June 2007. NRSROs are now required to

- Publish credit-rating statistics, including upgrades, downgrades, and default rates – for one, three, and ten year periods.
- Provide details regarding whether, and to what degree, they verify the information they use to rate structured finance products.
- Disclose detailed information on their surveillance processes and rating methodologies.
- Publish a random 10 percent sample of their issuer-paid credit ratings and their ratings histories.

NRSROs will also be required to issue annual reports for the SEC on the number of rating actions that occurred during the year; document the rationale for any deviation from the agency's stated quantitative models used to determine a rating; and retain records of complaints regarding the performance of an analyst.

7.16   Quo Vadis corporate governance?

The future of corporate governance raises the following remarks:

- **Growing corporate governance awareness**
  According to the authoritative US publication *GlobalProxyWatch*, over 600 corporate governance related conferences were held worldwide throughout 2008. This is extraordinary, particularly when compared to the dozen annual conferences that were held in the mid-1980s only in the United States and the United Kingdom.

  A new generation of chief executives won't be allowed to run their banks like their more autocratic predecessors did. Board directors should now also worry about the risk of failing to challenge executives, or lacking the skills to do so.

  Plain speaking and simple concepts are likely to replace complex investment strategies, which were apparently not clearly understood by those in charge of supervising these strategies, whether at the US Federal Reserve, at the SEC, or at the Bank of England.

  Executive compensation structures will be shifted from a short-term to a long-term three year outlook, so as to avoid excessive short-term risk taking.

- **Growing corporate governance implementation**
  Corporate governance principles are now progressively either included in, or attached to, Annual Shareholder Reports of thousands of corporations worldwide. For instance the 2007 Corporate Governance Report of Nestlé covers a wide range of corporate governance topics.

  A host of prominent organizations refer today to adequate corporate governance practices, such as the CII, the Public Accounting Oversight Board (PCAOB), the SEC, the World Bank and the IFC in Washington DC; the ICC and the OECD in Paris; UNCTAD/ISAR in Geneva; the ICGN worldwide; and so on.

  Several academic institutions are also contributing to the development of adequate corporate governance practices, such as Harvard University, the Millstein Center for Corporate Governance & Performance at Yale, and Stanford Law School.

  Moreover, corporate governance rating agencies also exert a growing impact, particularly the Corporate Library, the members of the European Corporate Governance Services (ECGS group), Egan-Jones, Glass Lewis, Governance Metrics International (GMI), Proxy Governance, RiskMetrics, and Vigeo.

Corporate Governance Codes are progressively implemented by the efforts of the corporate governance community at major corporate governance conferences; at corporate AGMs; during meetings with corporate leaders, representatives of regulatory agencies, and the media; as well as via the publication of books, reports and articles.

The two major international corporate governance organizations – the ICGN and the OECD – are also likely to play a major role regarding the worldwide implementation of their respective codes.

- **Could one code achieve universal acceptance?**
  Although both the ICGN and the OECD Corporate Governance Codes are gradually recognized by all the cognoscenti of the corporate world, this does not necessarily mean that they will be fully practiced in the near future.

  Actually, corporations try to take advantage of the code (or sections of the code) which best suits the specific interests of their owners, their board of directors, their senior executives, and/or their other stakeholders.

  Ideally, one should aim at widely accepted corporate governance principles, similar to the 1948 Universal Declaration of Human Rights which set forth humanitarian principles. Wishful thinking? The future will tell.

- **Could corporate governance prevent major financial crises?**
  The emergence of corporate governance principles – and their adoption by leading institutional investors – could not prevent the 2008 stock market breakdown.

  One explanation could be that very few investors understood the complexity of the financial products developed by a group of creative financial gurus, bankers, hedge fund and other asset managers – although the 1998 collapse of LTCM should have alerted them.

  A second explanation could be that the clout of US pension funds (which promote corporate governance discipline, but only own a third of the US stock market) was perhaps over-estimated.

  A third explanation could be that too few corporate CEOs are familiar with corporate governance tenets, while too few pension fund CEOs and their governance advisors master adequate financial skills. UNCTAD/ISAR in Geneva is attempting to close this gap.

In any event, a UN Commission, headed by Nobel Laureate in Economics Joseph Stiglitz, has been set up to investigate the causes of the financial crisis and to suggest adequate remedies. This Commission is to submit its recommendations at the 2009 UN General Assembly in New York. The cognoscenti whisper that the UN might decide to organize, together with the World Bank, the IFC and the IMF, a Conference for redesigning the global financial system, on the model of the 1944 Conference which assembled delegates from 44 countries at Bretton Woods. The adoption of adequate corporate governance principles is likely to be recommended in the report of this UN Commission.

It could be worthwhile for investors to analyze the teachings of experts such as Peter Bernstein (*Against the Gods – The Story of Risk*, John Wiley, 1996), Roger Lowenstein (*When Genius Failed – Rise and Fall of LCTM*, Random House, 2000), and Nassim Nicholas Taleb (*The Black Swan – Impact of the Improbable*, Random House, 2007).

It is rumored that Taleb may have averted monumental speculative losses at a major global banking institution early in 2008.

His books are well-timed: the *Black Swan* sold over a million copies ahead of the 2008 financial crisis, and his previous *Fooled by Randomness* came out just before September 11, 2001.

After an MBA from the Wharton School and a PhD in management science from the University of Paris, he became an arbitrage trader at major banking institutions, such as Bankers Trust, Banque Indosuez, CS-First Boston and UBS.

He is Professor of Risk Engineering at New York University's Polytechnic Institute, and Visiting Professor of Marketing (Cognitive Science) at London Business School.

As a mathematical trader, he has explored how people misunderstand randomness and its impact on financial risk. At the heart of his thinking lies the most unlikely, but not totally impossible, event nobody seems to plan for. He illustrates this with the discovery of black swans in Australia, at a time when swans were "known" to be exclusively white.

He challenges the excessive reliance on financial "modeling," which does not require experience: models are spewed out by machines, often formatted by brilliant young mathematicians who are not always adequately versed in the byzantine complexities of financial markets.

While stock market downfalls in the past mostly affected individual stockholders, they now directly and/or indirectly affect the pensions of millions of retirees worldwide.

Several organizations are now focused on how to restore the credibility of stock markets. In the United States, the CII and the Center for Market Integrity of the CFA Institute are for instance considering setting up an Investors' Working Group (IWG) to ensure that investors' views are heard. Former SEC Chairs William H. Donaldson and Arthur Levitt Jr. are likely to co-chair the IWG.

Time will tell whether regulatory officials, economists, and corporate governance professionals versed in the history of finance can contribute to reduce the recurrence of financial crises, and thus reduce their impact on equity investments, particularly those of pension funds.

8
Banks, Their Role, and Responsibility in the Crisis, Their Future

Edmond Carton

The context of this volume is based around the theme of globalization and monetary and banking reform. The topic I was asked to write about seems particularly daunting, in the light of recent developments.

Given my background, as a long-time "practicing banker" for the past 35 years, I thought that it would be highly valuable to share, with the readers, my perspective on the current financial crisis. My viewpoints are not those of an economist, risk manager, strategist or even that of an academic. They have, however, been shaped by years of hands-on experience and a significant amount of time working "on the ground" within the finance industry.

In October 2008, I had dinner with a friend, a private banker, with 34 years of experience under his belt. He works here in Geneva, for a very large bank, and seemed genuinely concerned about the current crisis. It was during this time that he confessed to me, "I am not sure what I should do next. I no longer see a future in Private Banking. Our clients do not trust us anymore, and we continue to push products on them rather than advise, counsel, or assist them." I had to remind him that the world was his oyster and, with his level of experience and extensive résumé, he could do anything. To this he replied, "Well, I am thinking of going back to New York and joining a small commercial bank that has just begun to establish itself and needs people with experience, maturity and a high level of 'client-sense.'"

This conversation brought me back to the basics, in the past commercial banking was based upon the principle of "serving clients." It was under this mentality that I began my career 35 years ago, as a "credit officer," working for a well-known blue chip institution. Before I was even allowed to assume a junior management role, I had to complete a 16-month training program that was required and paid for by the bank. Throughout the training program, I learned about and researched every aspect of credit risk and was trained to properly identify "creditworthy borrowers" in need of bank financing.

With the strength of our balance sheets, we were there to assist our corporate customers in growing and acquiring new markets, upgrading their equipment, buying out weaker competitors, etc. Our first priority was to satisfy the client's needs and to make sure that potential risks were well understood and reasonable. It was also necessary to confirm that the borrowers were capable of sustaining leverage, while putting together the best possible solutions for satisfying the clients' needs, and, as a partner, sharing in the success created by ventures through direct and indirect rewards such as: spreads on loans, growth in deposits and other ancillary profitable measures of business.

Banks have always been a key part of the system and a necessary component of the economy. Traditionally, they were successful in balancing both their fiduciary and facilitator roles and upholding responsibilities to the business community, by paying back their shareholders and employees. These were the basic principles of commercial banking.

Those days, not so long ago, saw the finance world through a fairly simple prism. Concepts were straightforward. Risks, objectives, and instruments were clearly laid out and respected by most institutions. Bank balance sheets were, for the most part, transparent and in their fairly brief annual reports, banks would provide a history and mission statement for their clients and general public to review. All of their activities were well understood and their leverage, for the most part, remained around or within a reasonable 1–11 range. Most banks addressed community, regional, or national needs, and a few were considered to be international because they had branches in one or two additional money centres.

So one must ask, "What went wrong? Where does the responsibility of the banking sector lie in the financial crisis?" I know the previous question is very broad and I would like to be practical in addressing it. Rather than come up with elaborate and overly researched answers or become increasingly ambitious and propose solutions, I would simply like to share my own thoughts and observations.

According to a recent study prepared by the Boston Consulting Group and a survey of the current crisis: "The credit crisis is a consequence of aggressive risk taking by highly leveraged financial institutions, which funded unsustainable economic growth, particularly in the United States. Underlying this dynamic were three widely held misconceptions." The first was based upon the faulty assumption that the credit worthiness of borrowers, as per the "credible" reports of the rating agencies, was strong. The second and third were mistakenly believing that investors were sophisticated and that credit risks were also being widely distributed. The conclusions derived from this study can help provide us with a sense of clarity and a basis for understanding how we have arrived at the current situation we face today.

I would like to begin with a statement of the obvious: over the past 20–25years, banks' traditional balancing act, between purpose for its client community and profit, has shifted overwhelmingly toward the latter. Growth and profit, at all cost, and shareholders' interests have moved to the top of their priority lists and long-term rewards, traditionally generated from a "clients first" attitude, are now expected to come more and more rapidly. Over the last two and a half decades, the banking industry and finance, in general, went from the simple to the complex, the transparent to the opaque, and leverage of balance sheets (of all the actors of the economy as a matter of fact) surged and traditionally liquid activities became illiquid. The banking industry has became increasingly greedy, complacent and, with ever-growing revenues generated by new often off-balance sheet schemes, very arrogant. If these sentiments seem harsh, it is because they are accurate and expressed with a sincere amount of underlying emotion and concern.

First, I would like to focus on leverage and liquidity. For the past 15 years, "money-centre banks" and investment banks have increased their on- and off-balance sheet leverages to an average exceeding thirty times capital, with many better known institutions exceeding gearings of fifty times. Lehman Brothers and Bear Stearns' leverage topped one hundred before their shocking overnight collapse. There is no point in even discussing investment banks anymore. They have either been wiped out or "reclassified." At such high levels, institutions that are expected to withstand shocks brought about by economic cyclicality are unable to survive.

In the United States, average credit default rates are surging to levels that were previously only seen in the 1930s and now have the potential to reach double-digit figures. Leverage is also a forte of Governments. The deflation, created by the growing liquidity injected into the system by the US Federal Reserve (Fed) following 1987, was probably responsible for the following: while only one US dollar of leverage was needed to create US\$1 of GDP growth up until the 1990s, four dollars of debt was needed by 2005–06!

The Fed's deflationary measures following the 1987–88 and 2001–02 crises were highly influential in applying downward pressure, on the long end of the yield curve. The resulting consequences affected many bank's traditional methods of conducting business, most notably that of lending medium- and long-term funds and sponsoring themselves in the short term at lower rates. This resulted in most of them loosing their traditional and most stable source of revenue. (This was particularly strident when banks dealt with investor-grade borrowers demanding the lowest margins – or, even, disintermediating banks with, the now almost defunct, commercial paper market). The Fed's "easy money policy" and abuse of liberalism generated so much "false" liquidity that we now realize that everything has a cost. There is no such thing as a free lunch and easy money does not equal liquidity. Now where are the reserves that the banking sector needs to cushion the fall?

The roots of the current crisis, contrary to earlier ones, are financial and not economical. Most large "global" or leading regional banks are technically bankrupt and, in most cases, the only way out is through state rescue and bail-out packages. Nationalization is back and the banking sector is clearly being shaken to its core. Banks, along with the Fed, are definitively instrumental and have played a key role in contributing to and even fuelling the extreme magnitude of the problem.

Now, I would like to discuss *opacity*. Before the spring of 2008, if you asked any leading institution's top management how problematic was their survival, you would have faced a strong sense of denial, "chin-up," "we can endure," and "we've seen tougher times" type of responses. No one knew for certain the real depth of their problems and many were unable to measure the size of the risks that they had accumulated. At their peak, we are told that outstanding Certificate of Deposit (cds)/ Collateralized debt obligations (CDOs), and other similar structures were worth US$550 trillion, eleven times the whole world economy, more than thirty times the GDP of the United States (where these "contraptions" found their most fertile ground).

The lack of visibility, the *complexity* of these instruments, the multiplier effects and layering of counterparty risk, liquidity risk, market risk etc., created such a degree of opacity and uncertainty that, following the sudden demise of major Wall Street investment banks and major Scottish, Dutch or even global institutions, trust and confidence, cornerstones of the banking universe, disappeared overnight.

Where were the famous risk managers and all their expert advisement teams? They had been there but when they spoke up, nobody wanted to listen. The need to grow revenues through ever-increasing Value at Risk (VaR), more products, more "pushing" of complex structures ever illiquid, created a wall of denial. Nobody wanted to listen to the voices of caution. Compliance-wise the banks had done their jobs, they had hired risk evaluation teams but little was done to curtail the problems gathering, piling up in ever complex, illiquid opaque and unmanageable proportions. The banking system as a whole is now in gridlock. Trust and confidence need to be re-established, as well as government support.

Clearly it is time to see more liquidity, real liquidity. It is time for us to see rigor in risk management and to give it higher priority. It is time for us once again to use common sense and to return to simplicity, as well as transparency. In the banking world, if something cannot be explained to me in layman's terms, I will not invest in it, nor will I recommend it to my clients. We need to have a long-term perspective and the right kind of government involvement.

We need, for banks to regain their balance and their bearings, to bring back a degree of social commitment and stop conflicts of interest. We have moved away from traditional lending to "investment" banking so rapidly that it facilitated an explosion in rigid and complex structures. Originally, we were responding to legitimate needs. Now, these structures are mass-produced and pushed out for revenue's sake only. Banks are creating a need for them, when often there is not one.

Looking at the crisis from the perspective of Wealth Management, an important and sustainable contributor to many recently successful "global" institutions, we see that Asset Management has become mediocre (performance-wise) tracking or underperforming indices, at a higher cost and less liquidity to the investors; often a pipeline for the delivery of mass produced structured products. Are banks producing real Beta? What is the famous Alpha they so proudly purport to generate? In fact, through increased complexity and use of leverage, banks' Asset Management and Treasury divisions have become, in many cases, hedge funds in their own right.

A word on *competition*: we have seen such a proliferation of products, of new hedge funds, that competition has moved from an "oligopolistic" to a "perfect competition" environment. With exploding volatility, we find ourselves in a universe where the famous mean reversion and traditional asset pricing do not apply any more. We are in a world where pricing is set at the margin and where the law of supply and demand prevails. In other words, where financial assets behave like any other commodity. Where is the "true value" of a share? Can we suggest to investors to buy a share because it is cheap? We might as well try to catch a falling knife. Where, in these markets, is the true added value of the Asset Manager, in the true assessment of *risk*, in caring for the client's interests? Even today, as I write, products that have little to do with the concerns and needs of the investors are being produced in and pushed out of private banking "laboratories." It is urgent that banks start listening to their clients again!

I briefly mentioned *rating agencies* and their poor performance across the board. We should start by addressing the fundamental problem of their structure: conflict of interest. They rate issuers and are paid, for their efforts, by these issuers; the better the rating, the cheaper the issuer's access to capital and funding. This is an obvious conflict of interest. We have to address this issue immediately to restore faith in rating agencies.

Another issue to address are *human resource* practices and how banks have been hiring over the past 20 years. When I joined the banking industry, we had a few MBAs, mostly there were BAs and some had Bachelor of Science degrees in finance. There were also many lawyers, historians, sociologists, and political scientists. It was a very diverse mix that we do not see working the field anymore. We now have highly educated math PHDs, physicists, and statisticians who are working for companies, but where is their common sense? I do not want to be critical, but there is an imbalance. We need more common sense and reality going forward.

A word about the *crisis*: where are we today? In terms of the banking system, and in terms of the economic cycle crisis, are we in the eye of the cyclone? I think we are all holding our breath, praying that the worst is over. However, I'm afraid that we are smack dab in the middle of it. The warning signs have been here for over 36 months, if not more. We had our heads in the sand and turned a blind eye to them.

We are not used to the speed at which the crisis happened, or the way that events unfolded around us. There is total confusion, and we are unaware of how much risk there is and the loss that is likely to be incurred. The system is quasi-bankrupt and we are now searching for stabilization.

Speaking of *volatility*, as I just mentioned, it is impossible to price things in an environment where you move from a 15 percent annual volatility, to one that is 150 percent. But volatility is also a fundamental risk and a leverage-increasing factor. Ten times more volatility means that you are basically ten times more leverage exposed; asset managers did not take synthetic leverage into consideration.

We need to see a higher injection of liquidity and support from governments. It is absolutely necessary. Once government intervention and money have been approved, it will take time to trickle down to the beneficiaries.

From 1929–1936, 2000 American banks closed their doors. We must hope that the transition to stronger fundamentals will be made as painlessly as possible for the economic sector and banks. As the crisis expands to the economic sector, the suffering of banks will continue. This is the case because they are at the heart of the economic fabric. However, banks will remain part of our system and will continue to play an important role.

Where are we going?

Banks will be different! We are going to see some substantial change in ownership and re-capitalization.

Today "cash" is king.

The whole banking model is going to be reviewed.

We are going to have to come up with more creative solutions. For example, in France, I saw some creativity: Société Générale decided to go ahead and make a €25 million dollar loan to a midsize regional company. Instead of making a straightforward loan, they went ahead and did a convertible warrant, as a partner. Basically, they took an equity position in the company and provided a certain amount of liquidity, which contributed to the stable growth of the company. Becoming partners with clients means having a longer-term view.

Going back to basics, we have three aspects of business that are essential in banking: custody, deposit taking, and commercial and consumer lending.

Product pushing should be abandoned and off-balance sheet structures should be reduced. There should be no more lending without the appropriate risk offset. There will be new-purpose banks, maybe the return of the famous "banques d'affaires" or "merchant banks." There are certainly no more investment banks. We will have to see the restoration (absolutely necessary) of old values, real values for the sake of clients, as well as shareholders, and corporate governance instead of stifling restrictions.

How about user friendliness, service, flexibility, global reach, advice, and solutions! These are all areas where there is a need for improvement. Where are tomorrow's values? Where are tomorrow's champions? What about size versus nimbleness? Should there be global banks? What about ownership structures and re-nationalization? What about responsibility of shareholders, limited versus unlimited? Look at the success of the Swiss private banks where owners are responsible, in an unlimited manner, for their own businesses. It is rare to see them involved with off-balance and structured excesses.

There will be new specialists.

We are going to see more e-lending, a surge of microfinance, and the continued success of Sharia banking.

We should also look at demographics: East goes West, South goes global, and Brazil's Itau and Unibanco have merged. They are becoming a mammoth in Latin America. Where will they go next?

We need to exert *better* rather than *more* control. We need to monitor conflicts of interests regularly. What is the future of rating agencies? Their services cannot be paid by their clients.

Questions … questions. The answers are not around the corner.

9
Sovereign Wealth Funds: Strategies of Geo-Economic Power Projections

Gyula Csurgai

9.1 Introduction

Sovereign Wealth Funds (SWFs) are not completely new phenomena as these funds have existed for decades. For instance, the Kuwait Investment Authority was created in 1953, eight years before the independence of Kuwait, to invest its huge oil revenues. Abu Dhabi and Singapore have used SWFs for over 25 years. In recent years SWFs have been growing rapidly, by US$1 trillion a year, and in 2009 these funds all together control an estimated US$3.9 trillion, increasing to US$10–15 trillion by 2015.[1] As a source of huge and ready cash, SWFs are becoming increasingly well received in several countries hit by the financial crisis.

In recent years, concerns about the geo-economic influence of the SWFs have been growing, in particular in Europe and the United States due to some of the following considerations: possible penetration in strategic sectors of the domestic economy by foreign state-controlled funds, perception of the potential influence that these funds may have at the global scale, in particular in the context of an evolving distribution of power in international economic relations, concerns over a potential sale of strategic assets, transfer of vital industrial knowledge and expertise, and different issues of public security. As immediate or indirect state entities, SWFs are usually not covered by existing legal and regulatory requirements imposed upon similar entities, especially investment and pension funds. Public reporting by these funds is therefore sparse and non systematic in the majority of cases. Similarly, informal market knowledge about strategies and day-to-day transactions by SWFs is understood to be very low. Also, SWFs are not answerable to private shareholders.

Some of these considerations influenced US authorities to intervene and block the takeover by the China National Offshore Oil Corporation (CNOOC), of US oil major Unocal Oil Company in July 2005. In 2006, the US administration made a similar move to stop the so-called Dubai Ports deal – the attempt on the part of DPWorld, a company owned by the government of Dubai, to acquire the Peninsular and Oriental Steam Navigation Company (P&O), domiciled in London, which was then the fourth largest port operator in the world, running major US port facilities in New York, New Jersey, Philadelphia, Baltimore, New Orleans, and Miami.

SWFs can be considered as important means of geo-economic strategies to improve power positions of states, disposing these funds, in the international system. An examination of the role of these funds, therefore, should take into account strategic, geopolitical and geo-economic perspectives.

9.2 SWFs: Definition, classification and sources

SWFs can generally be defined as state-owned or controlled financial assets in forms of special investment funds. Most of the savings of SWFs originate in accumulated foreign currency reserves. Usually, SWFs are distinct from the country's foreign exchange reserves.

SWFs can be classified into the following groups: (see table 9.1)

- *Stabilisation Funds* (designed to insulate the budget and the economy against commodity price swings)
- *Savings Funds for Future Generations* (to enable conversion of non-renewable assets into a more diversified portfolio of assets)
- *Reserve Investment Corporations* (these assets are still counted as reserve assets and are established to increase the return on reserves, though at a higher risk)
- *Development Funds* (designed to help fund socio-economic projects and infrastructure. These funds usually have a large domestic component)
- *Contingent Pension Reserve* (particularly to finance social security and health expenditures for rapidly ageing populations)

The sources of SWFs originate from the possession of important financial resources by countries that can be classified in two main categories: (1) States exporting natural resources mainly oil and gas (for instance, Russia, Kuwait, UAE, among others); (2) Emerging powers in which

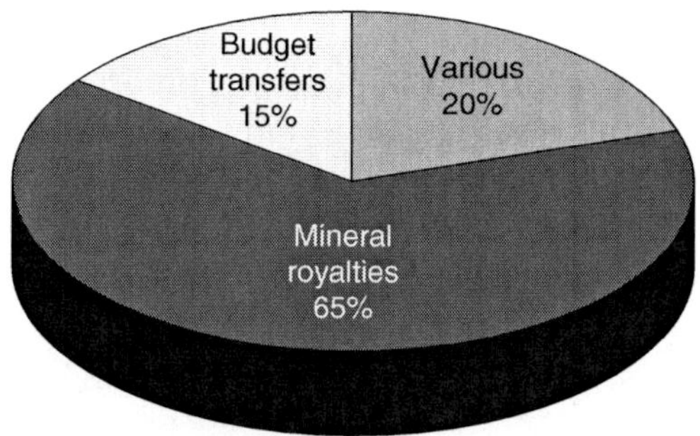

Chart 9.1   Primary source of funds for SWFs.
Source: International Working Group of Sovereign Wealth Funds[2].

industrial production has been growing rapidly and their products are exported to world markets (China and India for instance). These countries have competitive advantage due to undervalued national currency and relatively cheap and abundant work force.

The majority of SWFs are funded out of mineral royalties (principally oil), while the remainder are funded from fiscal surpluses, as well as other sources including foreign exchange reserves and returns on fund investments (see Chart 9.1).

It is important to note that most important SWFs are controlled by countries that are not part of Europe and North America, commonly called the Western hemisphere. Asian countries dispose about one third and the Middle Eastern states almost half of total funds (see Chart 9.2). This fact illustrates the increasing importance of emerging powers and represents to a certain extent the gradual shift of the geopolitical and geo-economic gravity of the world system, from the Euro-Atlantic zone towards the emerging powers and in particular towards Asia, in the next decades. In 2025, China, Japan and other countries of Asia will represent an economic zone in which industrial production will be the double that of the Euro-Atlantic zone. The population of Asia will be four times larger than that of the Euro-Atlantic zone. By 2050, three of the four largest economies will be Asian in the following order: China, United States, India and Japan.[3] The growth of SFWs reflects a redistribution of international wealth from traditional industrial countries, such as the US and Western European states, to the emerging powers that historically have had very little role in shaping practices, norms and regulations of the international financial system.[4]

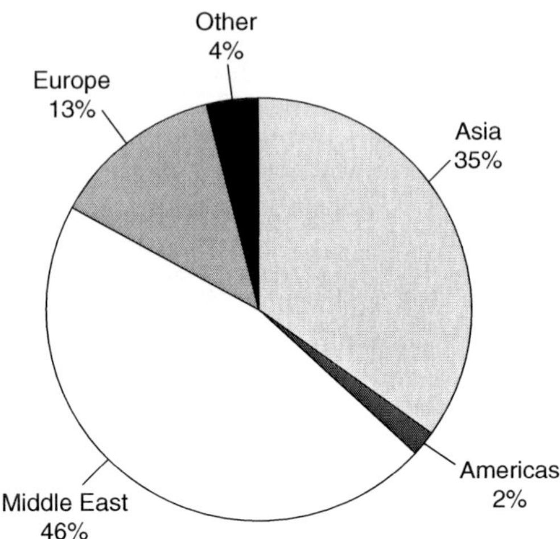

Chart 9.2   SWFs by region.

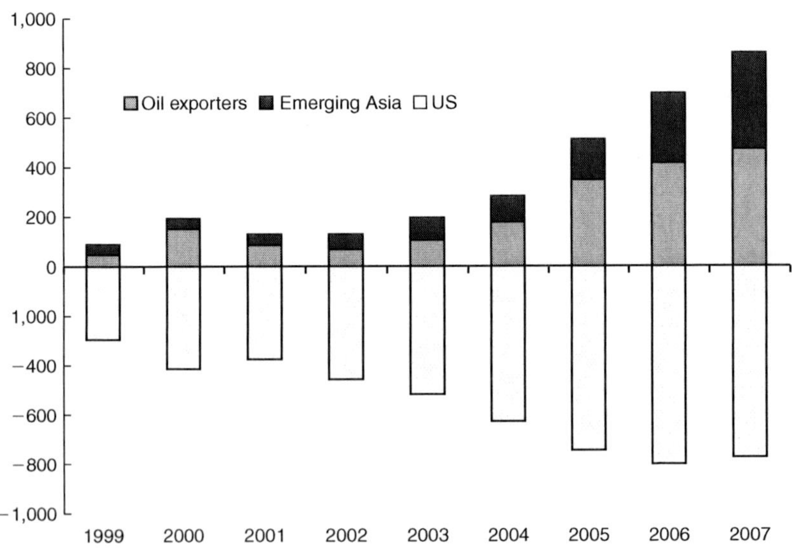

Figure 9.1   Current account balances in US$.
Source: JP Morgan[5].

The accumulation of important currency surpluses that were used for the creation of SFWs reflects the evolution of trade relations in recent decades between the United States and emerging powers, in particular China, on one hand, and the United States and oil exporter countries, mainly in the Middle East, on the other (see figure 9.1). As a result of considerable trade imbalance, the US commercial deficit has been growing considerably in the last decades, while China and the oil exporter countries gained important US dollar reserves. The biggest currency reserves and capitals are controlled by Asia and the Gulf states, illustrating the weakening of economic power of the United States and Western Europe.

9.3   The 'strategic state', geo-economics and power projection

Geo-economics as a concept and approach to analyse economic power rivalries of states in the international system, was introduced at the end of the Cold War mainly by the American strategist Edward Luttwak.[6] According to Luttwak, Cold War ideological rivalries were replaced by worldwide economic competition, in which trade and finance overshadow military power.[7] Although the concept of geo-economics appeared at the end of the Cold War, the interrelations between state power, economy and international trade had been taken into consideration throughout history. Mercantilism, closely associated with the rise of the nation-state in Europe during the fifteenth and eighteenth century, advocated state intervention in the economy for the sake of the security of the state.[8] Protectionist trade and monetary policies were applied to achieve trade surplus that increased the wealth and power of the state. The German economist, Friedrich List (1789–1846), advocated economic nationalism to support state policies to help industrialisation and, in general, to build a domestic economic power in order to gain security and independence.

The influence of globalisation combined with the impact of information and communication technologies on politics, the growing competition and interdependence in international economic relations and the declining demography of several major Western powers have led to the transformation of the concept of power in international relations. Living standards, job security depend more and more on external factors, as globalisation has diminished the frontiers between domestic and international economies. Direct control of a given geographic zone, for instance by military occupation, is not always advantageous and can lead to situations that are difficult to manage by the occupying power, as the current Iraq situation illustrates. The indirect control of a geographic zone can be more efficient; to achieve this objective, a given power can use economic, financial, political and cultural means. For instance, the rapidly increasing German geopolitical influence since the end of the Cold War in Central Europe, a traditional sphere of interest of Germany, has been achieved with the use of financial, economic and cultural power.

The objective of a state's geo-economics strategy is to attain and preserve a privileged position in the world economy. In geo-economics, states seek to protect their national economic system, to obtain and master important technologies, to penetrate new markets and to maintain a predominant power position in traditional markets. To achieve geo-economic objectives, states use mainly soft power and indirect strategies.

The nation-state has a strategic role to play in the creation of a successful geo-economic framework that can enhance public private cooperation to improve the power position of a given state in international economic relations. This does not mean a return to a collectivist economic model that failed in the former communist countries. This notion of the 'strategic state' also questions the so-called neo-liberal approaches and Washington Consensus theories and practices, advocated by certain economists and some international organisations such as the IMF (International Monetary Fund). The notion of the strategic state is influenced by cultural, historical, geopolitical factors and shared perceptions by various actors of public and private sectors on the role of geo-economics in economic security and development.

The so-called Asian model that was successfully applied by Japan, South Korea and Singapore among others, and has been gradually applied by China since the introduction of economic reforms by Deng Xiaoping in 1979,[9] illustrates well the role of the strategic state in developing geo-economic dispositions. In the case of Japan, the following cultural, historical and geopolitical factors exercised considerable influence in developing a different geo-economic disposition. The relatively small size of Japanese territory combined with high population density, the lack of natural resources, a consensus-based society in which authority, discipline, collectivism are important values, and the country's defeat in the Second World War, impacted Japanese strategic thinking after the Second World War to create a strong national geo-economic disposition. The Ministry of International Trade and Industry (MITI) played an important role in the strategic coordination between the public and the private sector. Training and other activities in fields related to the elaboration of geo-economic strategies, were organised and a network called 'Keiretsu' between industrial groups was created to develop a culture of competitive intelligence.[10] In particular from the 1970s, the strategy of major Japanese companies in different parts of the world has been to focus strategic investments on areas pegged for expansion or traditional strongholds of economic penetration.[11] Since the beginning of the 1990s, Japanese enterprises have been very actively penetrating Mexico even though, from a strictly economic point of view, the profits generated in this country by these companies were not very significant. However, this implementation should be analysed within the framework of a Japanese geo-economic strategy that considered the pacific coast of Mexico as a strategic zone for future market penetration in California. This objective is facilitated by the NAFTA agreement.

The possession of important financial resources, including SWFs, and using these in a coordinated strategic framework between private and public actors of a given country to enhance its geopolitical and geo-economic position in the international system, should not be analysed only from a pure market theory. Classical economic theories on international exchanges do not reflect all aspects of international economic relations in which economic decisions are often fashioned along the tactics and strategies advocated by Sun Tzu and Machiavelli. Some of the so-called non-market factors that influence contemporary international economic relations are information strategies, lobbying, strategies of influence, state support to private business by various means, hostile acquisition of companies of strategic importance, hidden protectionist measures and the devaluation of national currency to make exports cheaper to other countries while imports from abroad become more expensive.

9.4   SWFs and geo-economic strategies

SWFs can be used as geo-economic instruments of the state to invest in strategic industries, to gain relevant business or technological expertise and to develop geopolitical influence in regions of strategic interests. Countries exporting natural resources, mainly oil and gas, and with SWFs at their disposal, seek to reduce their dependence on a natural resource-based economy by developing other sectors of the economy, the education system and by penetrating different segments of economic sectors of foreign countries. The objective is to prepare successfully for a period in which the oil and gas reserves of these states will be reduced or exhausted. For instance, the Gulf states, with large SWFs at their disposal, invested in the financial and industrial sectors of Western economies. The Abu Dhabi Investment Authority (ADIA), with a fund of US$875 billion at its disposal, acquired 7.5 per cent of the Carlyle Group for US$1.35 billion and five per cent of Citigroup for US$7.5 billion. It has also bought an undisclosed stake in SONY. The Kuwait Investment Authority (KIA), which took a stake of US$14.5 billion in the Citigroup, along with Saudi Prince Alwaleed bin Talal and Singapore's Temasek. Dubai Sovereign Funds have snapped up shares in big names such as MGM Mirage casinos, aerospace giant EADS and the Barneys department stores. Qatar Holding and Dubai Borse have bought 24 per cent and 28 per cent respectively of the London Stock Exchange. Dubai has formed an alliance with NASDAQ, of which it already owns about 20 per cent. One of the geo-economic objectives of the Gulf states is to enhance their power position in international banking and finance. These states can take advantage of their geographic location, between Europe, Asia and Africa, to become an important centre of finance, trade and transport between these continents. In the past, Arab-Islamic civilisations were able to enhance their economic development considerably by using their advantageous geographic position along important trade routes such as the Silk Road. However their power position started to decline, with the opening of oceanic trade routes by European powers from the sixteenth century that allowed the Europeans to bypass the land trade routes going through the Middle East and connecting Europe with Asia.[12] With the rising power of Asia, the Middle East can again become an important connecting region between Europe, Asia and Africa in the twenty-first century.

It is interesting to examine the Russian case. Russia has at its disposal an estimated US$225 billion in SWF.[13] The use of the Fund is integrated in Russian geopolitical and geo-economic strategies having both internal and external objectives. Some references to these objectives were presented in an article written by Vladimir Putin.[14] According to Putin, the state should use the financial sources, obtained from the export of natural resources, mainly oil and gas, to enhance socio-economic development in Russia. The state should maintain a strong influence on the natural resource sector to ensure stable raw material supply for the Russian economy and to contribute significantly to the Russian budget. Financial means should also be used to develop extractive and processing infrastructure and scientific-technical potential in the natural resource sector. The state with its financial resources should support the creation and development of Russian financial and industrial groups that are capable of competing with Western multinationals and of developing strategic segments of the Russian economy such as the aviation industry and high tech sectors to improve the export potential of the country. This process can reduce Russia's dependence on the natural resource sector and can enhance other sectors in the real economy. The Russian geo-economic strategy, advocated by Putin, and gradually applied in the last ten years, meant the abandon of the so-called neo-liberal model and illustrated the important role of the strategic state.

The external objective of Russian geo-economic strategy is to regain geopolitical influence in strategic zones that Moscow considers as its spheres of interests 'near abroad', mainly the Caucasus, Central Asia and Eastern Europe. Russia wants to become a dominant player in energy geopolitics in Eurasia. Russian funds are used to penetrate the energy sectors of different countries and to influence pipe lines routes projects according to the geopolitical interests of Russia. Gazprom, a major Russian energy company, in which the majority ownership belongs to the Russian state, seeks to gain a quasi-monopoly position in the gas supply to the European Union (EU) and also to Southeast Europe. Gazprom also wants to penetrate the domestic distribution networks in Europe, in particular England, Germany, Italy and Greece.

Concerning the use of SWFs by China, the following objectives can be put forward: to look for higher returns for her huge foreign currency reserve, to reduce her excessive domestic savings and liquidity, to relieve international pressure on the national currency to appreciate too fast, to facilitate the globalisation of China's financial services, to sharpen her international financial expertise and to gain international strategic leverage, to obtain technology transfer, to increase geopolitical influence, in particular in areas disposing natural resources. It is important to take into consideration that all of China's major multinationals are controlled by the state. Their funds and investments are therefore considered in the category of SWFs. The following actions illustrate the aspirations of China to use its huge state-controlled financial assets to improve its geo-economic posture and geopolitical influence. A takeover of IBM's personal computer business by China's Lenovo Group took place in 2004 for US$1.75 billion. This investment led to technology and knowledge transfer and helped Lenovo to become an important player in the laptop computer business. To gain more knowledge and enhance the development of its international position in finance, the China Development Bank invested US$3 billion in 2007 in Barclays. The China Investment Corporation (CIC) has been set up to manage US$200 billion of China's US$1.4 trillion foreign currency reserve. It acquired a 9.9 per cent stake for US$5 billion in Morgan Stanley, following an earlier ten per cent stake for US$3 billion in Blackstone. The Industrial and Commercial

Bank of China (ICBC), the world's largest bank by market capitalisation, has taken a 20 per cent stake (US$5.6 billion) in Standard Bank, the largest bank in South Africa. This was one of the largest single foreign direct investments in Africa in recent decades. This followed China Development Bank's acquisition of a 2.6 per cent stake for US$3 billion in Barclays Bank and Citic Securities' 6.6 per cent stake for US$1 billion in Bear Stearns. China has spent an estimated US$29.2 billion in acquiring overseas assets. As of 2007, China accumulated an estimated US$1.8 trillion in foreign assets in order to prevent the Chinese currency from appreciating too rapidly, which would negatively affect Chinese exports in particular towards the United States and Europe.[15]

China has growing needs of natural resources due to its economic development and the evolving consumption patterns of its increasing middle class population, an estimated 300 million people. Car sales in China already exceed the number of cars sold in Japan and between 2015 and 2020 more automobiles will be sold in China than in the United States.[16] In 2010, China will consume more energy than the United States and will become the world's largest consumer of energy. By 2035 the Chinese economy could become more important than the US economy. For these reasons, energy security and the supply of raw materials is a fundamental question in the foreign policy of China. China therefore uses its state-controlled funds to invest and gain geo-political influence in geographic areas rich in natural resources. One of the most important targets for Beijing in this context is Africa. The importance of Africa in Chinese foreign policy was illustrated by the organisation of the China–Africa Summit, held in Bejing in November 2006, in which 48 African countries participated. China has become an important aid provider for African countries in recent years. Through its aid programs, provided without any political conditionality and interference in the internal affairs of African countries, and through foreign direct investments, China has gained considerable geopolitical influence in resource-rich African countries. The use of state-controlled funds has played an essential role in this strategy. The Chinese oil company SINOPEC acquired significant shares in off-shore oil exploration in Angola after Beijing awarded an interest-free loan of US$2 billion to the government of this country. Since 2004 SINOPEC has also penetrated significantly into the Nigerian energy sector. Chinese energy companies are also active in Chad, Equatorial Guinea, Sudan, Algeria and Libya.[17]

Chinese SWFs can also play an important role in the near future in the establishment of an 'Asian Co-Prosperity Zone'. The international financial crisis and economic recession started in 2008 can accelerate this process. China is perceived by several Asian countries, since the 1997 Asian crisis, as a factor of regional economic stability due to its constructive role during this crisis. China has launched its initiative to establish the China-ASEAN Free Trade Area in the upcoming years. This process will create the world's largest free trade zone in terms of population (1.7 billion) with a total GDP of US$2 trillion and trade volume of US$1.2 trillion. This free trade area is to be extended to Japan and Korea. China has been also exploring with Japan and South Korea the creation of a three-nation free trade zone, which will be a zone with a total GDP of US$7 trillion and total trade volume of US$3 trillion. A compromise can take place between Japan and China about the definition of their respective spheres of geopolitical influences in Asia and this could facilitate the process to create an Asian regional currency. With the growing concerns of China and other Asian countries about the role of US dollar as an international reserve currency, the establishment of an Asian regional currency is perceived as a positive step for greater economic stability in the region. China also calls for the creation of an international reserve currency that is disconnected from individual nations and is able to remain stable in the long run, thus removing the inherent deficiencies caused by using credit-based national currencies.[18]

9.5   Policy responses

If others practice geo-economics, abstention may mean economic defeat.[19] With the rising influence of SWFs, Western countries have to re-evaluate the links between national security considerations, foreign investments and open trade relations. As a result of the severe 2009 economic recession, several countries could opt for the introduction of some protectionist measures including against SWF investments. However, protectionism can also hurt these countries as other states may opt for retaliatory measures. SFWs should be also perceived as a useful source of capital for different economic sectors in Western Europe and North America in a rather difficult financial and economic situation. This was illustrated by SWFs investments in different financial institutions in the United States, Western Europe and other parts of the world. Therefore, the potential positive role of SFWs should also be emphasised. However, in case of hostile takeovers of strategic segments of economies, states should use protectionist measures to block these actions. In the United States there is an inter-agency called 'Committee on Foreign Investments in the United States' (CFIUS) that examines the potential security threat of foreign takeovers and can recommend blocking an eventual takeover by a foreign investor.

The creation of SWFs by European countries to enhance their geo-economic position can take place in the near future. President of France, Mr. Sarkozy, declared in October 2008 that European countries should create SWFs to defend their economic interests and security. At the end of 2008, France established its own SFW. The German government, for its part, is considering establishing an investment fund of its own, which could serve as a strategic investor for selected German companies and protect them against undesired foreign investment.

Some EU countries has been arguing for an effective coordination at EU level of European SWFs in order to avoid a patchwork of national rules and a potential negative impact on the internal market. European countries also call for reciprocity in terms of market access and investments. For instance, the Russian government takes a rather protectionist stance on foreign investments, while Moscow is operating important state-controlled funds to penetrate strategic sectors of foreign economies. Following recent legislation, the Russian national intelligence agency, the Federal Security Service (FSB), is actively involved in decisions regarding foreign ownership of 39 key industries, such as nuclear energy, aerospace, natural resources and the arms industry.

In terms of regulation, on 27 February 2008 the European Commission called on state-run investment funds to sign a voluntary code of conduct.[20] The Commission called for a clear allocation and separation of responsibilities (presumably, between the government and the SWF), an investment policy that defines SWFs' overall objectives, operational autonomy to achieve those objectives, public disclosure of the principles governing the relationship between the SWF and its governmental authorities and disclosure of principles of internal governance providing assurances of integrity.[21] On the issue of transparency, the EU Commission called for annual disclosure of investment positions and asset allocations, exercise of ownership rights, the currency composition of assets, and the size and source of the fund's resources; and disclosure of the home country's regulation and oversight governing the SWF. The Commission also advocated the importance of reciprocity and called for the opening of markets of countries using SWFs for European investors.

On a multilateral level, the IMF called for a 'code of conduct' for SWFs. Within this framework, issues of public governance, transparency, and accountability principles in the set of voluntary best practices would be covered.[22] IMF established an International Working Group (IWG) of SFWs that comprises 26 IMF member countries with SWFs. The IWG met on several occasions to identify and draft a set of generally accepted principles and practices (GAPP) that properly reflects their investment practices and objectives, and agreed on the Santiago Principles, which represent generally accepted principles and practices that properly reflect SWFs investment practices and objectives. The Principles are voluntary, which the members of the IWG support, and which they either have implemented or aspire to implement. The following key areas are covered in the Principles: legal framework, objectives, and coordination with macroeconomic policies, institutional framework and governance structure, investment and risk management framework. The guiding purpose of these Principles is to have in place a transparent and sound governance structure that provides for adequate operational controls, risk management and accountability to ensure compliance with applicable regulatory and disclosure requirements in the countries in which SWFs invest, to ensure SWFs invest on the basis of economic and financial risk and return-related considerations, and to help maintain a stable global financial system and free flow of capital and investment.

The OECD also discussed the SWF issue. The OECD Investment Committee and its non-OECD partners have agreed that they will follow a two-track approach:[23] Dialogue among governments, SWFs and the private sector in order to improve understanding of both home and host country approaches to foreign investment and exchange experiences in relation to national security protection and develop shared views on investment policies that observe the principles of proportionality, transparency and predictability, and accountability and avoid unnecessary restrictions to international investment, including by SWFs.

The debate is far from over and doubts were raised by financial analysts and policy makers about the possibility of developing efficient governance structure, increased transparency and a code of conduct in order to better control SWF operations. Russia and China in particular expressed their skepticism about the establishment of code of conducts and best practices by multilateral organisations. It should also be noted that Western countries heavily invested in strategic industries and other segments of economies in different areas in the world in the past. For instance, Spain gained significant influence in economies of Latin American countries in the 1990s. Moreover, it is important to note that there are transparent SFWs. This is the case with the SFW of Norway for instance. In general, there is a correlation between SFW transparency and the political and democratic accountability and the quality of the legal system in a given country.[24]

9.6   Concluding remarks

The role of the rapidly increasing financial leverage power of SWFs has to be considered beyond classical theories of macroeconomics and economic exchanges. In order to fully understand the strategic motivations of states controlling these funds and investing in strategic sectors of foreign economies, geopolitical and geo-economic perspectives also should be taken into consideration.

SFW investments can have a significant impact on different economic and financial sectors. Due to the fact that most often state interests guide SWF investments, and the majority of these funds are not transparent, their operations should be monitored and regulated. On the other hand, the use of protectionist measures should be limited, as SWFs can also contribute positively to economic development in countries where these funds are invested.

Access to markets for SWFs should be kept open, with the following considerations: reciprocity in openness of market access, political intervention in case of investments that can impact national security and decision making based on pre-defined principles. Within the EU, the design of measures and instruments concerning the operations SWFs should be coordinated. Greater transparency of SWFs should be achieved through internationally agreed codes of conduct and best practices established by multilateral and regional organisations.

Annex

Table 9.1   SWFs ranking

Country	Fund Name	Assets $ Billion	Inception	Origin	SWF to Foreign Exchange Reserve Ratio
UAE – Abu Dhabi	Abu Dhabi Investment Authority	$875	1976	Oil	29.5
US – Alabama	Alabama Trust Fund	$3.1	1986	Gas	Nil
US – Alaska	Alaska Permanent Fund	$29	1976	Oil	0.5
Canada	Alberta's Heritage Fund	$14.9	1976	Oil	0.4
Australia	Australian Future Fund	$43.8	2004	Non- Commodity	1.8
Brunei	Brunei Investment Agency	$30	1983	Oil	
China	China Investment Corporation	$200	2007	Non- Commodity	0.1
China	China – Africa Development Fund	$5	2007	Non - Commodity	Nil
Nigeria	Excess Crude Account	$11	2004	Oil	0.2
Venezuela	FIEM	$0.8	1998	Oil	Nil
Indonesia	Government Investment Unit	$0.3	2006	Non- Commodity	X
Norway	Government Pension Fund – Global	$301	1990	Oil	7.1
Singapore	Government of Singapore Investment Corporation	$330	1981	Non- Commodity	1.9
Trinidad & Tobago	Heritage and Stabilization Fund	$2.9	2000	Oil	n/a
China – Hong Kong	Hong Kong Monetary Authority Investment Portfolio	$173	1998	Non- Commodity	1.0
UAE – Dubai	Investment Corporation of Dubai	$82	2006	Oil	2.8
Kazakhstan	Kazakhstan National Fund	$38	2000	Oil	1.1
Malaysia	Khazanah Nasional	$25.7	1993	Non- Commodity	0.3

(*Continued*)

Table 9.1   (Continued)

Country	Fund Name	Assets $ Billion	Inception	Origin	SWF to Foreign Exchange Reserve Ratio
South Korea	Korea Investment Corporation	$30	2005	Non- Commodity	0.1
Kuwait	Kuwait Investment Authority	$202.8	1953	Oil	12.7
Libya	Libyan Investment Authority	$65	2006	Oil	0.8
UAE – Abu Dhabi	Mubadala Development Company	$10	2002	Oil	0.3
Bahrain	Mumtalakat Holding Company	$14	2006	Oil	2.9
Mauritania	National Fund for Hydrocarbon Reserves	$0.3	2006	Oil & gas	X
Ireland	National Pensions Reserve Fund	$22.8	2001	Non- Commodity	36.6
China	National Social Security Fund	$74	2000	Non- Commodity	Nil
Russia	National Welfare Fund	$225.1*	2008	Oil	0.4
US – New Mexico	New Mexico State Investment Office Trust	$16	1958	Non- Commodity	0.2
New Zealand	New Zealand Superannuation Fund	$9.1	2003	Non- Commodity	0.8
Iran	Oil Stabilization Fund	$12.9	1999	Oil	0.2
US – Wyoming	Permanent Wyoming Mineral Trust Fund	$3.9	1974	Minerals	Nil
Saudi Arabia	Public Investment Fund	$5.3	2008	Oil	Nil
Botswana	Pula Fund	$6.9	1966	Diamonds & Minerals	0.7
Qatar	Qatar Investment Authority	$60	2003	Oil	8.6
UAE – Ras al Khaiman	RAK Investment Authority	$1.2	2005	Oil	X
Kiribati	Revenue Equalization Reserve Fund	$0.4	1956	Phosphates	n/a
Algeria	Revenue Regulation Fund	$47	2000	Oil	0.3
China	SAFE Investent Company	$347.1**	n/a	Non- Commodity	0.2
Saudi Arabia	SAMA Foreign Holdings	$433	n/a	Oil	12.7
Chile	Social and Economic Stabilization Fund	$21.3	1985	Copper	0.9
Brazil	Sovereign Fund of Brazil	$5.9	2009	Non- Commodity	Nil

Vietnam	State Capital Investment Corporation	$2.1	2006	Non- Commodity	0.1
Oman	State General Reserve Fund	$8.2	1980	Oil & gas	0.3
Azerbaijan	State Oil Fund	$10.2	1999	Oil	0.6
France	Strategic Investment Fund	$28	2008	Non- Commodity	0.2
Singapore	Temasek Holdings	$85	1974	Non- Commodity	0.8
Malaysia	Terengganu Investment Authority	$2.8	2008	Oil	New
East Timor	Timor-Leste Petroleum Fund	$3.2	2005	Oil & gas	n/a
Total oil & gas related		$2,485			
Total other		$1,431			
Total		$3,916			

*This includes the oil stabilization fund of Russia.

**This number is a best guess estimation.

***All figures quoted are from official sources, or, where the institutions concerned do not issue statistics of their assets, from other publicly available sources. Some of these figures are best estimates as market values change day to day.

Source: Sovereign Wealth Fund Institute, January 2009. http://www.swfinstitute.org

Notes

1. Sovereign Wealth Fund Institute, January 2009. http://www.swfinstitute.org
2. The IWG (International Working Group) of SWFs comprises 26 IMF member countries with SWFs. The IWG met several occasions to identify and draft a set of generally accepted principles and practices (GAPP) that properly reflects their investment practices and objectives, and agreed on the Santiago Principles at its third meeting. A subgroup of the IWG – chaired by David Murray, Chairman of the Australian Future Fund Board of Guardians – was also formed to carry forward the technical drafting work.
3. An interesting analysis on the rising power of Asia is provided by Kishore Mahbubani in his recent book, *The New Asian Hemisphere, The Irressistable Shift of Global Power to the East*, Public Affairs, New York, 2008.
4. Edwin M. Truman, *A Blueprint for Sovereign Fund Best Practices*, Peterson Instiute for International Economics, Washington, April, 2008, p. 3.
5. Bernhard Eschweiler and David G. Fernandez, *Sovereign Wealth Funds: A Bottom-up Primer*, JP Morgan Research N.A., Singapore Branch, May 2008.
6. Luttwak, Edward N., et al. (1997) "PART 3: New World Order Geopolitics," Chapter 16, *From Geopolitics to Geo-Economics: Logic of Conflict, Grammar of Commerce*. Routledge, London, pp. 125–130.
7. Edward Lutwak, *The Logic The Endangered American Dream*, New York: Touchstone, 1994; *Turbocapitalism. Winners and Losers in the Global Economy* London: Weidenfeld & Nicolson, 1998.
8. David D. Balaam and Michael Veseth, 'International Trade' in Introduction to *International Political Economy*, Pearson, New Jersey, 2005, p. 28.
9. Deng Xiaoping was inspired to promote economic reforms in China, in particular, by the successful economic development of Singapur that he visited in 1978. Kishore Mahbubani, *The New Asian Hemisphere, The Irressistable Shift of Global Power to the East*, p. 76.
10. Competitive intelligence can be defined as the research, analysis and dissemination of information useful to different actors in the economy to support geo-economic strategies.
11. An interesting analysis on this issue can be found in Christian Harbulot, 'La Machine de Guerre Economique', *Economica*, Paris, 1992, p. 23–33.
12. Aymeric Chauprade, 'Chronique du Choc des Civilisations', *Editions Chronique*, Paris, 2009, p. 43.
13. Sovereign Wealth Fund Institute, January 2009. http://www.swfinstitute.org
14. Vladimir Putin, 'Mineral Natural Resources in the Strategy for Development of the Russian Economy', *Problems of Post-Communism*, vol. 53, no. 1, January/February 2006, pp. 48–54
15. Daniel W. Drezner, *Bric by Bric: The Emergent Regime for Sovereign Wealth Funds*, Fletcher Shool of Law and Diplomacy, Tufts University, August, 2008.
16. OECD, 'International Energy Agency', World Energy Outlook, 2006 report.
17. Michael T. Claire, *Rising Powers and Shrinking Planet, The New Geopolitics of Energy*, Metropolitian Books, New York, 2008, p. 169.
18. Zhou Xiaochuan, *Reform the International Monetary System*, People's Bank of China, 23 March, 2009. http://www.pbc.gov.cn/english/detail.asp?col=6500&id=178

19. Edward Lutwak, *Turbocapitalism. Winners and Losers in the Global Economy*, p.134.
20. 'EU calls for code of conduct for sovereign wealth funds', AFP, Feb. 27, 2008, Brussels.
21. *Sovereign Wealth Funds and Financial Stability – Guide*, European Commission, Brussels, 27 February 2008.
22. Robert M. Kimmitt, 'Public Footprints in Private Markets Sovereign Wealth Funds and the World Economy', *Foreign Affairs*, January/February 2008, pp.119–130.
23. OECD, Directorate for Financial and Enterprise Affairs, Investment Committee, Andrea Goldstein, *International Investment of Sovereign Wealth Funds*, October 2007, Newsletter based on DAF/INV/WD(2007)15/ADD1 submitted at Roundtable V on 'Freedom of Investment, National Security and "Strategic" Industries'.
24. Daniel W. Drezner, *Bric by Bric: The Emergent Regime for Sovereign Wealth Funds*.

10
The WTO's Doha Development Agenda: An Unclear Roadmap

Sergio Marchi

10.1   Introduction

In light of the current financial and economic crisis, the fate of the International Trading System has become an even more important and timely issue for individuals and the international community to consider. As a former Canadian Minister of International Trade and WTO Ambassador, the international trade dossier continues to animate and interest me. In this chapter, I will touch upon a few specific aspects of world trade; namely, the role of domestic politics, the influence of the United States, and the World Trade Organization (WTO) as an institution. I will then conclude by recounting my personal story and share my own perspective on the WTO.

Established in 1995, the WTO draws its roots from its predecessor, the General Agreement on Trade and Tariffs (GATT), which was created in 1948 by 23 founding countries. GATT was one of the key institutions to be built after World War II (WWII).

In pursuit of trade liberalization, the international trading system has successfully completed eight rounds of global trade negotiations to date. The cumulative impact of these efforts has contributed significantly to the economic growth and stability of the world economy. These initiatives have also served as a bridge between different people and various countries, helping to foster greater understanding between societies and lessening the risk of isolation.

When you consider how small the world is becoming and the tremendous growth of international trade within every corner of the globe, I believe that the best guarantee for continued access and fair play, by all countries big and small, rich and poor, is through clear, predictable international trade rules. And it is precisely at the WTO that the family of nations comes together to negotiate and implement those very rules. Beyond this central function, the WTO also monitors trade policies, offers technical assistance and training to developing countries, and coordinates its work and efforts with other major international bodies. In addition, as part of this trade governance, the WTO has a dispute settlement mechanism whereby differences between trading partners are decided by who is right and not necessarily by who has the might. This remains an important principle and cornerstone of the WTO architecture.

In short, the WTO is the main intersection for the multilateral trading system. Despite the complexities behind many different trade issues, a single rules-based regime is the most efficient way of exchanging products and services around the world. For some of our small and medium sized exporters, for instance, trying to navigate the maze of some 300 regional and bilateral free trade agreements (FTAs) can be quite a frustrating and costly adventure. As well, it is at the WTO, given its critical mass of members and issues, where the need for new rules and policies to meet the ever-changing economy can be best addressed.

10.2   The current context

Don't get me wrong, regional and bilateral FTAs have a valuable role to play. After all, when I was Trade Minister for my country, I pursued a few of them myself. However, it is at the international level, where all nations, developing and developed, that the private sector actually does the trading and investing to enjoy the best opportunity for effectively facilitating their global trade ambitions. Thus creating economic opportunities that, in the process, improve the standard of living for peoples the world over, which is the end game of the trading system. For these reasons, I believe that bilateral and regional FTAs should complement the WTO, and not seek to compete with it.

Secondly, let us consider the context of the current round of WTO trade negotiations, known as the Doha Development Agenda (DDA). In this regard, one really needs to go back to the 1999 Ministerial Meeting in Seattle, affectionately known as the "Battle of Seattle." That was my first meeting, as a WTO Ambassador, and it was a real dive into the deep end of the pool! As you may recall, that meeting failed miserably and cast a dark mood over the WTO. When we regained our confidence, all interested parties swore not to repeat the experience. Once was truly enough.

With some considerable determination, two years later, in Doha, Qatar, the DDA was launched. We had not only learned a few lessons from the Seattle debacle but the process was greatly facilitated by two dynamics that were instrumental in galvanizing the negotiating room.

One was the marked leadership of the Unite States. They came to play and backed it up by placing on the negotiating table two of their more sensitive issues: antidumping measures and pharmaceuticals. They acted in the opposite fashion to how trade negotiators traditionally practice their craft. Rather than keeping his cards close to his vest until one minute to midnight, the US Trade Representative led the process by making early and important concessions, in the hopes of challenging his colleagues to do the same; thereby creating the necessary engagement and momentum needed to produce a deal. The strategy worked.

For me, this was a pragmatic example of where the United States, using its significant economic leverage, exercised strong leadership in an assertive and constructive manner to bring about desirable outcomes for the international trading system. Quite simply, without this kind of political will, the DDA would not have been born.

The other dynamic at play in the negotiating room was the ever-lingering shadow of 9/11. As the meeting took place during the immediate aftermath of this tragic and destabilizing event, it was clearly on the minds of every participant. It pushed Ministers to find common ground and emerge united at the end of the day, sending a reassuring message to the nervous international community. Most Ministers believed that failure was not an option.

Given today's economic turbulence, it will be interesting to see how the global financial crisis impacts the DDA negotiations. Will leaders see the benefit, both economic and political, of trying, at this particular juncture, to invest some political capital and finally reach agreement on this trade deal? In completing the DDA, they would achieve some important objectives. It would give a much needed boost to the global economy and help push back the forces of protectionism that usually accompany turbulent economic times. Hopefully, it would begin to reverse the sluggish trade numbers of recent months and would deliver significant development dividends to developing countries. Finally, a successful round would revitalize the WTO as an institution.

In addition, from a process perspective, the G20 meetings could be the ideal venue to reach across the divide and find a political accommodation on the DDA, since the leading developed and developing countries will be sitting at the same table. In acting as a potent influence on the outcome in Doha, the issue of 9/11 may have inadvertently created false expectations. At the time, some had argued for a period of consolidation at the WTO, rather than embarking on another elaborative round. Nonetheless, the Ministers launched the DDA and gave it a three-year timeline for completion.

This was quite an unrealistic goal given the complexity and size of the DDA agenda. However, by setting a three-year window, Ministers wanted to avoid the almost eight years it took to complete the previous Uruguay Round. They argued that today's world was moving and changing at an unprecedented speed, and that the WTO could not afford such a leisurely pace. But, here we are, seven years later, and there is still no closure in sight. Many deadlines, senior officials' meetings, and ministerial sessions have come and gone, but success continues to elude the WTO.

10.3   Challenging times

Indeed, recent years have not been very kind to the WTO. In all fairness, the circumstances of our times have made it much more difficult to achieve a multilateral agreement, compared to years gone by. What are some of these circumstances? Let me mention a few:

- WTO membership has expanded rapidly in the intervening years, currently standing at 153 countries, which is a far cry from the 23 founding countries of GATT. This means that the political and economic agendas have multiplied tremendously, making it more difficult and time consuming to arrive at a multilateral consensus.
- The vast majority of WTO Members are developing nations, and they have become much more active, vocal and organized in asserting their interests. The old days, where a core group of countries, anchored by the United States and the EU, would set and drive the agenda, are now gone. And this should be seen as a positive development, if one believes in true multilateralism and in giving every member an equal stake. But, as a consequence, the process of constructing a balanced deal simply takes much more time and patience. In addition, developed countries, such as the United States, must display greater economic generosity vis-à-vis the many needs of developing countries, which are at different stages of development.
- Decision making is by consensus. This means that every country walks around with a veto in their back pocket, and proceedings therefore move as fast as the slowest member is capable or willing to go!
- Governments still operate on the principle that "all politics are local," and this is a formidable hindrance in formulating an international

consensus. It means that the political decisions required for a global trade deal are subservient to the parochial politics back home, and here I refer to all homes in developed and developing country capitals alike. All too often, countries that fear some political backlash back home refrain from making the necessary commitments on the international level. And with a membership of 153, some countries are always in the midst of an election campaign, which places them and the system in an even more volatile grip. In an increasingly globalized world, the challenges posed by this model of political governance puts an enormous strain on our international institutions, such as the WTO. Leaders urgently need to address this dysfunctional reality. Otherwise, global decision-making will lag far behind the many pressing needs that we currently face as an international community, especially as it relates to the development agenda.

- Compared to previous trade rounds, the business community has not been as active or involved in pressing its case, nor in mobilizing the political agenda of key governments at home and abroad.
- And finally, for much of the public and civil society, the WTO has become a poster child for everything that ails our globalized era. There are many unfair and disingenuous slogans thrown at the WTO, which unfortunately paints a very distorted and negative perception of the organization. This creates a difficult environment to operate in and weakens the resolve of many political leaders who, rather than try to lead their citizens to a greater understanding of the real issues involved, are often happy to follow local public opinion.

So one must ask: where is the DDA today? The DDA has a wide and ambitious agenda but, at its very core, there are three areas of market access that all Members have agreed to open further and liberalize. These are the agricultural, industrial, and service sectors. They constitute the central stage of DDA production and out of these three categories; agriculture is the leading political lady. Many members, especially from developing countries, take the firm stance that if agriculture is not seriously reformed then nothing else on the DDA agenda should progress. In part, one can see the rationale behind this passion.

Large levels of government support and subsidies currently distort the global playing field in agriculture. Approximately US$1 billion a day is spent by developed countries in backstopping their agricultural production. That is an incredible amount of largesse. To put this in measurable context, the previous figure represents roughly two thirds of Africa's GDP. Or, four times the annual aid and development provided by wealthy nations. In fact, the average cow in Europe receives $2 a day in government support and a Japanese cow lives even more richly. Yet some 3 billion people live on less than $2 a day!

The prevailing situation is morally and economically wrong. It is also unsustainable, given that an estimated 75 percent of our world's poor people live in rural areas, where agriculture is the main livelihood. But how are these farmers able to get their produce to the markets when they must compete with the significant subsidies that have been extended to their competitors from developed nations? Farmers should farm the land and not the mailbox. These subsidies clearly need to be eliminated. And it is this sentiment that represents the loudest and most emotional battle cry within the DDA talks.

Yet, any successful trade negotiation requires a healthy dose of give and take. A sense of balance and compromise between the competing agendas is a central ingredient, if white smoke is to eventually emerge from the WTO chapel. Moreover, in developed countries, while agriculture is an important sector and way of life, it only represents on average two to three per cent of GDP. Therefore, it stands to reason that the DDA cannot only focus on agriculture. There must also be progress made on the industrial and service fronts. In this regard, developing countries have a special role to play given the relatively high level of their average tariffs and barriers within these two areas.

While many feel that the DDA process is being hijacked by agriculture, the reality is that the membership must find its collective will to link together; otherwise this ongoing game of "chicken" will haunt the negotiations. The most recent high-level effort in trying to move the DDA talks forward took place last summer, when the WTO Director General, Pascal Lamy, brought Trade Ministers from around the world to Geneva and required them to attend endless meetings for a total of ten days. The objective of these meetings was to bridge the existing gaps and focus on priority areas, beginning with agriculture. Depending on whom you talk to, there was a considerable amount of progress made regarding several issues and hopeful signs indicated that a deal was likely to be made. However, the talks eventually collapsed, principally around the agriculture file and between the two chief combatants, the United States and India. To be sure, there were other issues to resolve beyond agriculture, but we will now never know if these goals would have been achievable, had the agricultural hurdle been overcome.

10.4   Moving forward?

Finally, where does the DDA go from here? Efforts are still underway today at the WTO, among Ambassadors and senior officials from capitals, to try and recapture the moment that was lost last year and during the drawn-out run of the US election campaign. The task continues to be an effort, to narrow the main differences so as to provide their Ministers with the conditions for another opportunity of reaching a breakthrough. There has been a considerable amount of shuttle diplomacy, by Lamy and other individuals, to keep participants engaged in discussion and to apply pressure on the system. However, the time meter is certainly running on the WTO, and its credibility is on the line.

Naturally, many have been waiting anxiously for the Obama Administration to fully pronounce itself on the future of the DDA. However, to date, the new US Trade Representative has been fairly general in his public statements, and the first annual trade report submitted during Obama's early watch seemed to pour cold water on efforts to restart the WTO round. In addition, during the Democratic primaries and election campaign, there was a strong trade protectionist sentiment coming from Obama and supported by the actions of the Democratic constituency. Analyzing early signs of action from the new US government, things do not look too promising for the prospects of the DDA, in finding early traction.

It will be important to see how the DDA fares vis-à-vis the global financial crisis. In other words:

- Will the crisis consume all the political attention and capital in the months ahead, and completely overshadow issues such as the DDA?
- Or, will the DDA receive a boost and pressure from enough world leaders to become an integral part of the recovery package to the current crisis?
- Will leaders respond to the crisis by practicing local politics and usher in their own forms of protectionism?
- Or, will they take the broader view and seek to further liberalize trade and push for more open markets, as part of a recipe for economic recovery?

If the last few months are an indication, then "local" seems to be the preferred political favor. Already Russia has jacked up import barriers on cars; the EU has reintroduced subsidies on dairy products; India and Brazil have raised tariffs on imported steel; and in the US stimulus bill, there is a "Buy America" provision. Furthermore, given that this trade round is actually entitled, the Doha Development Agenda, with the emphasis on *development*, leaders cannot easily dismiss the expectations of this round from the part of the developing world, especially while their countries are being hit hard by the current crisis.

Until the financial crisis hit, many developing countries were enjoying solid economic performances. In fact, they had been largely responsible for the world's economic growth in recent years, as the emerging economies of China, India, Russia, South Africa, Indonesia; Mexico and others compensated for the sluggish economies of the North. As developing countries became more integrated into the world economy, their trade, foreign investment, and private capital flows grew at impressive rates. However, today's financial crisis stands to potentially and dramatically undermine these significant gains. The world economy is expected to shrink this year for the first time since WWII, and because consumption is drying up, trade is declining sharply. For developing countries that rely on their export sector to sustain their national economies this is bad news.

Regrettably, we have already begun to witness the repercussions:

- China's exports globally, are down 17 percent as of January this year
- South Korea is down 29 percent
- In India, where shipments were growing at an annual rate of 50 percent, this year they are down 18 percent
- The three biggest economies in South America – Argentina, Brazil, and Chile – are now down between 27 and 42 percent.

To top it all, falling commodity prices, declining foreign investment, and vanishing credit lines are all compounding the problem. Furthermore, despite the crisis having originated in the United States, during these volatile and uncertain times more and more investors are now buying US Treasury Bills, which means that there are fewer dollars available elsewhere around the world. As the global financial and economic crisis continues to take its toll, leaders cannot escape the difficult decisions that need to be made in the face of these challenges; this includes the future of the multilateral trading system. Members will need to weigh carefully the many intertwined economic implications when calculating the next steps to take in the DDA journey.

10.5   In closing

In conclusion, it would appear that the WTO journey has arrived at yet another fork in road. One path would see the DDA talks continue for an extended period of time, in Geneva, among only Ambassadors and trade officials, without senior political engagement. This would mean that discussions are unlikely to come to a conclusion any time soon. In effect, WTO Ambassadors will be on a stationary bicycle: there will be plenty of peddling, but no movement. The other path would have Members rethink the DDA impasse and what it means to the international community. And, at this time of economic crisis, agree to reengage at a senior political level, and find the political will, to finally bridge the gaps, that would give way to a compromise agreement.

The latter is not an easy task or roadmap to follow. The outstanding issues are numerous. The local politics, of many WTO players, are such that it might be easier for them to accept a minimal political cost and fail at the WTO, rather than make the difficult decisions required to foster a successful outcome and, therefore, run the risk of upsetting entrenched political interests at home.

The completion of the DDA would provide significant benefits to the world economy. It would be most unfortunate, especially at this time, if the fate of these far-reaching and desirable global outcomes were to be dictated by local and narrow political considerations. All 153 countries agreed to launch the DDA back in 2001 and since then all political leaders have talked a good talk globally. Let us now hope that at this hour of the WTO negotiations, they don't choose to walk locally.

11
The Multilateral Trading System: Special and Differential Treatment for Developing Countries in the WTO

Carlos Perez del Castillo

The economic argument for an open trading system is based on multilaterally agreed rules that rest largely on commercial common sense. Statistical data clearly shows a link between free trade and economic growth. The principle of "comparative advantage" has proven countries prosper by first taking advantage of their assets, in order to concentrate on what they can produce best, and then by trading these products for different products that other countries produce best.

In a post World War II scenario, the General Agreement on Tariffs and Trade (GATT), along with its rules, was created to reach objectives that were previously stipulated as measures to avoid chaos and anarchy. Nevertheless, protectionism was, and continues to be, applied by different members in order to safeguard specific subsectors. We are still far away from a world based on total free trade, but significant progress has been made through different negotiating rounds and demonstrates an unalterable trend toward liberalization. Undoubtedly, this process is taking much longer than originally planned and has encountered considerable setbacks. The World Trade Organization (WTO) is now in place and took over GATT's responsibilities in this field.

The position and view of developing countries has also changed. For many years they were not considered active players within the multilateral trading system. Benefits derived from trade did not have the same positive impact on their economies, as they did in the developed world. However, they are now becoming important players in the system; decisions and new agreements cannot be made without negotiating with them, and different agreements recognize their status and include special provisions specifically for them.

This paper will examine the topic at hand in two sections. First, it will examine the role played by developing countries, if any, in the multilateral trading system, as well as special provisions included in agreements for this special category of countries. Then, it will take a look at the new approach developed to mainstream trade as the core element in developmental strategies and the fight against poverty for developing nations.

In order to better understand the position of developing countries in the WTO, and the multilateral trading system, those propositions led me to formulate the following research question: "Do the WTO Agreements contemplate a degree of flexibility for developing countries?" and corresponding hypothesis: "Special and differential treatment are core issues in the development of underdevelopment."

11.1   Developing countries

Over three quarters of the current 153 WTO members are developing countries. During the Uruguay Round (UR), they were highly active and influential, much more than in previous rounds. This trend has also been reinforced in the current round of negotiations (Doha Development Agenda, DDA). They are playing an increasingly important and active role in the WTO, not only because of their increasing numbers, but also because they are becoming more important in the global economy. They are now starting to realize and consider trade as a vital tool in their development efforts and strategies. Nevertheless, developing countries remain a highly diverse group with very different views and concerns.

Assisting developing countries in participating more fully in the global trading system is one of the WTO's most important activities. Empirical data states that developing countries that trade successfully tend to be those that have made the most progress in alleviating poverty and raising living standards at home. But many endogenous as well as exogenous constraints impede this trend.

Many countries do not have the human, institutional, or infrastructural capacity to participate effectively in international trade (see Table 11.1). Without these components, countries are not able to expand the quality and quantity of goods and services they can supply to world markets at a competitive price. It is internationally recognized that most natural and nutritious fruits come from Africa. Nevertheless, a limited stock is available in Northern markets, mainly due to issues in transport logistics (i.e., no adequate means of transport and cooling capacity, and customs bureaucracies). That is why building trade capacity is so important. WTO members have recognized that the multilateral trading system needs to be accompanied by improvements in trade capacity.

Table 11.1 Trade capacity.

	Main characteristics
Human capacity	Refers to the professionals governments rely on for advice on WTO matters (economist, skilled negotiators, trade lawyers). A country that lacks these professionals is clearly at a disadvantage when trying to implement existing trade agreements, or negotiate new ones, and when handling trade disputes.
Institutional capacity	Refers to the institutions and businesses that governments rely upon for trade (i.e., customs, national standards authorities, and the delegation representing the country at the WTO and the UN). Nonetheless trade suffers if these institutions are inadequate.
Infrastructure	Refers to the physical setup required for trade to happen (road, ports, airports, banking and insurance sector, and telecommunications). Again, countries lacking infrastructure will find it difficult to develop trade.

How the WTO deals with the special needs of an increasingly important group is through:

11.1.1 Special and differential treatment

At the end of the UR, developing countries were prepared to take on most of the required obligations. But the agreements did give them periods of transition to adjust to the more unfamiliar, and perhaps difficult, WTO provisions. A ministerial decision was adopted at the end of the UR that established: "better-off countries should accelerate implementing access commitments on goods exported by LDCs" and it sought to increase technical assistance for them. More recently, developed countries have started to allow duty-free and quota-free imports for almost all products from Least Developed Countries (LDCs).[1] In other words, products originating from these countries do not pay, in principle, any duties or tariffs when entering the markets of developed economies.

The WTO agreements include numerous provisions giving developing nations and LDCs special rights or extra flexibility. Among these are provisions that allow developed countries to treat developing countries more favorably than other WTO members, without violating the Most-Favored

Nation (MFN) principle. GATT has a special section (part 4) on trade and development that includes provisions on the concept of non-reciprocity in trade negotiations between developed and developing countries. When developed countries grant trade concessions to a developing country, they should not expect developing countries to make matching offers in return. The WTO Secretariat has special legal advisers for assisting them in any WTO dispute and for providing legal counsel.[2]

Other measures concerning this special and differential treatment include: (i) extra time to fulfill their commitments; (ii) provisions designed to increase countries' trading opportunities through greater market access; (iii) provisions requiring WTO members to safeguard the interests of developing countries when adopting some domestic or international measures; and (iv) provisions for various means of helping developing countries.[3]

As noted, there are a variety of ways in which the WTO provides assistance in building trade capacity. However, guiding and instructing delegates from developing countries, on acquiring positive gains through the trading system, is the central focus of Secretariat efforts. The vast bulk of WTO's technical assistance spending is dedicated to helping officials better understand the complex WTO rules, so they can implement WTO agreements in ways that will bolster trading regimes and negotiate more effectively with their trading partners.

But there are countries, including a large number of LDCs, where trade is failing to make the contribution that it should to economic growth and poverty reduction. That is why, in the following sections, we are dedicating a special part of this study to this specific category of countries, and analyzing a special instrument developed to help them in this arena.

11.1.2   Least Developed Countries (LDCs)

Due to their special needs, LDCs receive extra attention in the WTO. All of the WTO agreements recognize that they must benefit from the greatest possible flexibility, and better-off members must make an extra effort to lower import barriers to LDCs exports. It sounds very nice and lovable, but the reality of the world is far away from this theory. In 1996, a plan of action for LDCs was agreed upon. It included technical assistance to enable them to participate more effectively in the multilateral trading system and a pledge from developed countries to improve market access for LDCs' products.

In 2002, the WTO adopted a work program for LDCs. It contained several broad elements: improved market access; more technical assistance;

support for agencies working on the diversification of LDC economies; help in following the work of the WTO; and a speedier membership process for LDCs negotiating to join the WTO. Having a permanent mission in Geneva to deal with WTO matters can be very expensive, even more if we consider the profile of the LDCs.[4] As a result of the negotiations to locate the WTO headquarters in Geneva; the Swiss authorities agreed to provide subsidized office space. A number of WTO members also provide financial support for ministers and their delegation to assist in helping them attend WTO ministerial conferences.[5]

11.1.3   Working together

Assisting the integration of LDCs into the multilateral trading system and the global economy will contribute to the poverty reduction goal. Trade liberalization and reform are indispensable key elements that contribute to the "integration objectives" of faster growth, increased earnings and reduced poverty. However, frequently trade priorities, including the implementation of WTO obligations and commitments, are integral neither to overall development plans, nor to strategies for poverty reduction (Poverty Reduction Strategy Paper, PRSP). Furthermore, in many instances, trade priorities are not taken into account by finance and planning ministries. Thus, although openness to trade is strongly associated with economic growth and poverty reduction, trade as a growth strategy is yet to be mainstreamed into development plans and PRSPs of many of the LDCs and developing countries as well.

It is clear that WTO members are at different stages of development. Although there have been some gains, LDCs are not benefiting as much as had been hoped from the expansion of international trade and from the multilateral trading system. Most formidable of the obstacles faced by developing partners, and specifically LDCs, are their own domestic political administration, and institutional problems. This reality is being further deteriorated by the approach visualized by development agencies in the delivering of aid and technical assistance. LDCs not only trade one or, at the utmost, two commodities, but also their institutions (mainly government) are scarce, and sometime inexistent. Human and material resources are not a luxury they can afford.

Until very recently, coordination among agencies was quite ineffective. Beginning with the fact that it was not a country-driven process, one agency/organization would approach the country with a battery of recommendations and policies to be adopted and implemented immediately. The other organizations would use a similar approach, or, even worse, sometimes they would simultaneously disembark in the country, each with their own recipe to fight poverty and promote development. Not only was it assumed that the objectives of the agencies were going to help and not create further burdens to the already weak patient, but also in many situations the remedies prescribed by each institution were in direct conflict (i.e., reducing government spending in order to control inflation, but affecting social basic expenditures), and created more chaos and misery.

There is a need to enhance coordination and improve interface between multilateral and bilateral donors, in the delivery of trade-related technical assistance to LDCs, within the framework of development vehicles. Coherence in the activities of multilateral agencies with respect to LDCs is essential. The Integrated Framework (IF) incorporates the program of six organizations. An increasing recognition of these problems and political will to act exists among these agencies and there is an urgent need to improve coordination among them.

On the other hand, LDCs have expressed their frustration with the multiplicity of vertical initiatives but the little horizontal coordination. There is an outstanding need to combine efforts, not only from the agencies/donors side, but also and primordially from the recipient of this aide, the government country. It is necessary to find a more effective response to the variety of trade development needs related to LDCs, so that they can become active players and beneficiaries of the multilateral trading system, if ever an IF initiative was to be developed.

The realities of this century demand a new agenda for global cooperation. The challenges facing LDCs are of such a magnitude that the WTO alone, or any other agency, cannot address them in their entirety. The extent of the challenge has exceeded the initial core responsibilities, expertise and resources of the WTO. Redistribution of different functions among agencies is vital in order to tackle this pandemic effectively. Problems are complex and collective action at all levels is required.

A more pragmatic, country-by-country approach was designed by the agencies, and it has taken the form of the IF.

11.2   The revamped Integrated Framework (IF)

The Integrated Framework, an incorporated approach, was originally launched in October 1997 at the High-Level Meeting on LDCs' Trade Development, organized by the WTO, in recognition of the supply-side constraints facing LDCs. The IF is a unique instrument of coherence intended to ensure the maximum use of scarce resources to support and enable LDCs in becoming full and active players of the multilateral trading system.[6] It is a valuable mechanism, applicable only to LDCs, for coordinating the delivery of trade-related technical assistance to LDCs and "mainstreaming" trade integration strategy chapters into development plans. The aim is to "make trade work for development." The IF was defined by former WTO Director, General M. Moore, as "the first-ever attempt at institutionalizing inter-agency cooperation, and as a test of the institutions themselves."[7]

The main idea behind the IF, and close cooperation between the agencies/donors and an eligible country, is that trade is a key factor for economic growth, and can alleviate chronic poverty. While trade is not an end in itself, it can (i) enhance a country's access to a wider range of goods and services, technologies and knowledge; (ii) stimulate the entrepreneurial activities of the private sector; (iii) create jobs; (iv) attract private capital and foreign direct investments; (v) increase foreign exchanges earnings; and (vi) generate the resources needed for sustainable development and the alleviation of poverty.[8]

One of the main pillars for trade to have a positive and long-range impact on poverty reduction is that it needs to be an integral part of a country's development strategy. Although led by the government, it requires awareness raising and active engagement by a wide range of stakeholders from different parts: (i) nationally, all stakeholders, both within the government (i.e., ministries of trade, finance and planning) and outside the government, need to come together to build consensus on the way forward; (ii) from the outset, the government must reach out to the international development community to support its plan for integrating trade into overall national development plans; and (iii) international partners must engage with the government for coordinated delivery of trade-related assistance and capacity building.[9]

The IF enables LDCs to work with the agencies, as well as with other development partners and the donor community, to ensure that national trade policies are integrated into their respective development strategies (PRSPs). The IF will need to facilitate the coordinated responses provided by various agencies and development partners (each in their own area of expertise/competence) to the trade-related assistance and capacity-building needs identified by each LDC government and other national stakeholders. However, LDCs should be aware that this process will require a long-term commitment by all stakeholders, particularly since it involves systemic changes.

The four-part process involved in the IF is: (i) awareness building about the importance of trade for development; (ii) Diagnostic Trade Integration Study (DTIS), a strategy to identify constraints to traders, sectors of greatest export potential, and a plan of action for integrating into the global trading system; (iii) integration of the plan of action into the national development plan, such as the PRSP; and (iv) implementation of a plan of action in partnership with the development cooperation community. The IF is a process, using existing channels, to ensure that the trade-related assistance needs of each LDC are included in the dialogue between governments and their development partners on the overall development policy to be implemented in each country. It aims to achieve the incorporation of trade policy into the heart of the LDCs.

The IF was established to support LDC governments in trade capacity building and integrating trade issues into overall national development strategies. The IF is an international initiative through which the IMF, International Trade Centre (ITC), United Nations Conference on Trade And Development (UNCTAD,) United Nations Developing Programme (UNDP), World Bank, and WTO combine their efforts with those of LDCs and donors in order to respond better to the trade development needs of LDCs. National development plans, including components aimed at reducing poverty within the developing country, are used to assist in the coordination and delivery of the trade-related assistance provided by each of the core agencies in their specific field of competence and by other development partners.

The IF is an instrument specially designed for LDCs and all are eligible, if they fulfill the following conditions. First, to be considered for the program they must apply to the IF Secretariat, based in the WTO. The following selection criteria are then applied with a view to achieving maximum effectiveness: (i) demonstrate strong government commitment to integrate trade into its national development strategies; (ii) show that the country is at the preparatory stage in the development of its overall poverty reduction strategy; (iii) prove that the country has created an environment that helps the integration of trade in its plan for economic growth and development. This should include providing an institutional arrangement, implementing domestic reforms that favor trade, and engaging donors; and (iv) show a conducive operational country environment, sufficient agency/donor activity in the country to be able to ensure a good DTIS and follow up.[10]

In order to be prepared to receive and implement the IF, a government needs to identify: (i) local expertise; (ii) main stakeholders (governments departments, academia, private sector associations, civil society, NGOs); (iii) current research and analysis available; (iv) development partners (bilateral and multilateral); and (v) existing country trade-related assistance, capacity building and training programs.[11]

After the preparatory stage and upon acceptance into the IF, the following phases will be initiated: (i) establish a national implementation structure (involving all the institutions with responsibilities in this project); (ii) select a "Facilitator" (lead donor) to assist and support the government in managing the process; (iii) agree on the terms of reference and timing for the DTIS; (iv) develop the DTIS in order to identify sectors of export potential, supply-side constraints to trade, human and institutional capacity constraints, measures to be taken to implement and apply international and regional agreements, implications of analysis and recommendations on growth and poverty reduction; (v) establish, as part of the DTIS, an action plan (Action Matrix) including policy reform measures, sectoral plans, and trade-related assistance needs; (vi) convene a National Workshop to discuss, prioritize and approve the DTIS and its Action Matrix with stakeholders, and to define the way forward; and (vii) link trade with development, incorporating the Action Matrix into the country's national development plan.[12]

The IF is a process that uses existing channels to ensure that the trade-related assistance needs of each LDC are included in the dialogue between governments and their development partners on the overall development policy to be implemented in each country. The funding for the IF process is based on the following: (i) Window I finances the preparation of the DTIS; and (ii) Window II bridges money for small assistance or capacity-building activities that are part of the DTIS Action Matrix. The supply of these funds comes primarily from bilateral donors as part of the overall response to national reduction strategies.

Finally, one of the main criticisms of the existing multilateral trading system is that rich countries use their political power, through international organizations, to make it difficult for developing countries to challenge them. As J. Stiglitz noted, "the rules set by international organizations all too often serve the interests of the more advanced industrialized countries, rather than that of those in the developing world."[13]

Since the last century, developed countries have preached and forced their industries and products into the markets of developing countries. But, at the same time, kept their own markets relatively closed to products from the developing world, especially in the agriculture sector. The aim of the Rounds is to try and redress this current imbalance, with a sincere hope of eliminating them in the future.

But the history of GATT and the WTO has clearly shown that it will not be an easy process. The developing world needs to be prepared, in order to attain a "dominant position" in negotiations, and leverage the balance in its favor. Given LDCs' weak resources this task can be perceived as impossible. This is where the WTO Secretariat alliance can make a difference by creating capacity building and strengthening their negotiating position.

To conclude, the special and differential treatments were included in the agreements to provide poorer members with considerable freedom to design and develop strategies related to their own circumstances within the framework of the multilateral trading system. At the same time, it is becoming extremely complicated for developed members to make decisions unilaterally, without consulting or taking into consideration the needs and claims of the "poor.

Notes

1. The EC initiative name is "Everything But Arms" (EBA), and in the US the "African Growth And Opportunity Act" (AGOA.) The UN Generalised System of Preferences (GSP) also plays an important role.
2. World Trade Organization, "Understanding the WTO," 2003 Geneva.
3. Ibid.s
4. Only about one third of the 30 LDCs members in the WTO have permanent offices in Geneva.
5. The minister and two of its delegates are financed through these funds. It includes air tickets plus per diems.
6. As June 2008, 46 LDCs (of a total of 50) have become beneficiaries under the IF. Of the 46, 30 have completed the DTIS and are now implementing the Action Matrix.
7. World Trade Organization, "The Policy Relevance of Mainstreaming Trade into Country Development Strategies: Perspectives of Least Developed Countries," April 2001, Geneva, p. 9.
8. World Trade Organization, "The Policy Relevance of Mainstreaming Trade into Country Development Strategies."
9. World Trade Organization, "The Integrated Framework Explained," (undated) Geneva.
10. World Trade Organization, "The Integrated Framework Explained."
11. Ibid.
12. Ibid.
13. J. Stiglitz, *The Way Ahead, Essential Reading in World Politics*, 2nd edition, 2004, New York, p. 454.

12

Swiss Financial Self-Regulation Mechanisms in the Fight Against Money Laundering and Terrorist Financing

Norberto Birchler

12.1 Introduction

The role that self-regulation plays in the Swiss financial sector has proven its efficiency, since the legislation supports and encourages its developments as an alternative form of regulation. Contrary to state regulation, self-regulation brings a bottom-up approach, granting all financial actors the possibility to be heard and to participate in the regulatory process, which makes the Swiss system so unique in the financial world. As the cornerstone of Switzerland's financial market architecture, self-regulation plays an important part in the fight against money laundering and terrorist financing. In spite of old criticisms formulated by the Financial Action Task Force (FATF) towards the Swiss complex self-regulation system, self-regulatory norms are now given greater legitimacy, effectiveness and credibility to coexist with state regulations in the international combat against money laundering and terrorist financing, particularly in the perspective of both globalisation and bank reform.

12.2 Overview of the legislation

12.2.1 Combating money laundering and terrorist financing

Combating money laundering is an important part of the overall fight against international drug traffickers, transnational organised crime and, for a number of years, also against terrorist financing. The extensive measures taken for the purpose of combating money laundering has proven useful for investigations into terrorist activities. For this reason, the original regulations governing the fight against money laundering are also applied today, in a slightly adapted form, to countering terrorist financing.

As the laundering of money most often takes place in a country other than where the predicate offence was committed, it is important that the fight against money laundering is internationally coordinated. This requires national regulations that are comparable and consistent with each other. In order to achieve this, international and multilateral standards have been drawn up to provide the foundation for national regulations.

12.2.2   International standards

The FATF is an inter-governmental body whose purpose is the development and promotion of national and international policies to combat money laundering and terrorist financing. Since its creation in 1989, the FATF has established a series of international standards, regularly revised, which set out the basic framework for anti-money laundering efforts and are intended to be applicable universally:

- The 40 Recommendations on Money Laundering(April 1990, revised in 1996 and in 2003)
- The nine Special Recommendations on Terrorist Financing(October 2001, revised in 2004)

As a member of the FATF, Switzerland has made a commitment to comply with the 49 Recommendations and thus the Swiss system for combating money laundering and terrorist financing has been influenced by these standards.

Switzerland also signed the most important international conventions about fighting terrorism and its financing. Yet it has not signed nor ratified the Council of Europe Convention on Laundering, Search, Seizure and Confiscation of the Proceeds from Crime and on the Financing of Terrorism (16 May 2005).

12.2.3   The Swiss legislation

The Swiss legal basis of the prevention and fight against money laundering is formed by the Federal Act on Combating Money Laundering in the Financial Sector – Anti-Money Laundering Act (AMLA). The AMLA implements the fundamental principles of the obligations of financial intermediaries and governs the supervisory system of the Swiss financial markets.

The Swiss Criminal Code (SCC) is the framework of criminal prosecution of money laundering and terrorist financing, most relevantly through the following provisions:

- Art. 102 SCC : Corporate Criminal Responsibility
- Art. 260ter SCC : Criminal Organisations
- Art. 260quinquies SCC : Financing Terrorism
- Art. 305bis SCC : Money Laundering
- Art. 305ter SCC : Insufficient Diligence in Financial Transactions and Right to Report

The fundamental principles of the AMLA are implemented in more detailed rules by additional regulations, which are issued by the supervisory authority of each financial sector. The special laws relating to financial markets are the Banking Act, the Stock Exchange Act, the Collective Investments Act, the Insurance Supervision Act and the Gaming Act.

Implemented by the AMLA, the due diligence obligations to be respected by all financial intermediaries are:

- Verification of the identity of the customer
- Identification of the beneficial owner of funds
- Further verification of the identity of the customer or further identification of the beneficial owner
- Special obligation of clarification
- Obligation to draw up and retain documents for up to 10 years
- Organisational measures
- Reporting obligation
- Freezing of assets
- In case of reporting, exclusion of criminal and civil liability (if certain conditions are fulfilled).

12.3   Terrorist financing

12.3.1   Definitions

Due to the implementation of the FATF 49 Recommendations, Switzerland enacted Art. 260quinquies SCC, introducing terrorist financing as a criminal offence in October 2003.

Art. 260quinquies Financing terrorism [*unofficial translation*]

1. Whoever collects or provides funds with a view to financing a violent crime that is intended to intimidate the public or to coerce a state or international organisation into carrying out or failing to carry out an act is liable to a custodial sentence of up to five years or to a monetary penalty.

2. If the person merely acknowledges the possibility that the funds may be used to finance terrorism, he does not commit an offence under this Article.
3. The act does not constitute the financing of a terrorist offence if it is carried out with a view to establishing or re-establishing a democratic regime or a state governed by the rule of law or with a view to exercising or safeguarding human rights.
4. Paragraph 1 does not apply if the financing is intended to support acts that do not violate the rules of international law on the conduct of armed conflicts.

The identification of terrorist financing in the sense of Art. 260[quinquies] SCC is subject to discussions among experts. Under international public law, there is no uniform classification or definition in this issue. How can terror be distinguished from the struggle for freedom? Swiss legislation stipulates that the struggle for freedom serves the purpose of establishing or re-establishing democratic or constitutional circumstances; however, it is not established who may refer to this and which activities are therefore included and excluded. In consideration of paragraph 4 of Art. 260[quinquies] SCC, donating to charitable organisations, which have terror financing activities, is therefore not punishable?

12.3.2   Scheme of terrorist financing

Although linked in legislation and regulation, terrorist financing and money laundering are conceptual opposites. Money laundering is the process by which cash raised from criminal activities is made to look legitimate for re-integration into the financial system, whereas terrorist financing cares little about the source of the funds, but it is what the funds are to be used for that defines its scope.

12.3.3   International measures

The international fight against terrorist financing is based on several resolutions of the UN Security Council. Worldwide, the implementation of these resolutions occurs through comprehensive economic and trade sanctions or other targeted measures such as arms embargoes, travel bans, financial or diplomatic restrictions. Since 1990, Switzerland also applies such sanctions.

Certain states and organisations, mainly the United States and the European Union (EU), produce their own lists of persons and entities linked to terrorist activities ('Bush list', 'UN sanctions list') to take measures against them on the basis of the relevant UN resolutions.

12.4   Supervisory system of the Swiss financial markets

[Subject to change as of 1 January 2009. See chapter 4.5, FINMA]
The AMLA allocates the task of supervision to specific authorities in the particular financial market they regulate:

- the Swiss Federal Banking Commission (SFBC)
- the Swiss Anti-Money Laundering Control Authority (AMLCA)
- the Federal Office of Private Insurance (FOPI)
- the Swiss Federal Gaming Board (SFGB)

Globally, the SFBC supervises the banks and the AMLCA the non-banking sector, the FOPI exercises supervision over the insurance institutions and the SFGB towards casinos. Financial intermediaries are subordinated directly to one of these supervisory authorities. Only in the non-banking sector, can the financial intermediaries be subordinated directly or indirectly (through a self-regulatory organisation). (Figure 12.1).

Attached to the Federal Office of Police (fedpol), the Money Laundering Reporting Office of Switzerland (MROS) is responsible for receiving and analysing suspicious activity reports in connection with money laundering and terrorist financing and, if necessary, forwarding them to the law enforcement agencies.

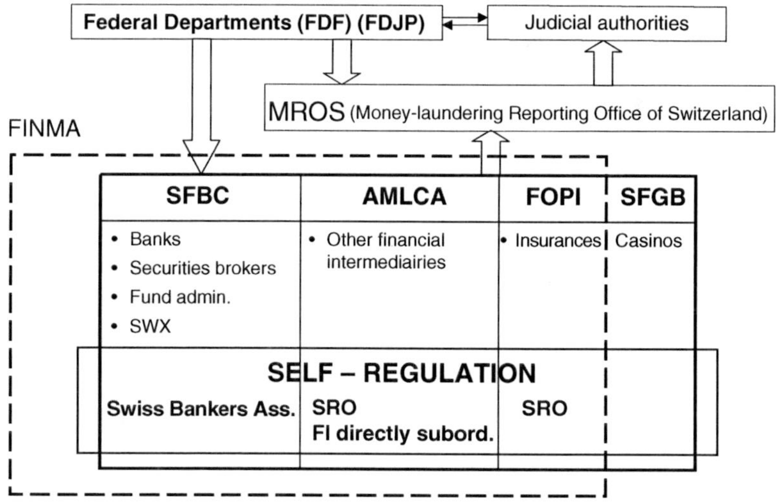

Figure 12.1   Bank regulation flow chart.

The MROS is a member of the Egmont Group (EG), which is an international association of 'Financial Intelligence Units' (FIUs) whose objective is to foster a safe, prompt and legally admissible exchange of information in order to combat money laundering and terrorist financing.

12.4.1 Supervisory system in the banking sector

The Swiss Federal Banking Commission (SFBC) is administratively integrated within the Federal Department of Finance, but is not a part of central government administration. The supervision of the banking sector over which it has authority is assumed on an independent basis.

In matters of money laundering, the SFBC assumes the supervision of banks, securities dealers, fund management companies, investment companies with variable capital, investment companies with fixed capital, limited partnerships for collective investments and asset managers of collective investments.

The SFBC issued an ordinance (SFBC Money Laundering Ordinance, MLO SFBC) to define the due diligence obligations under the AMLA for the financial intermediaries it supervises.

The SFBC can also recognise self-regulations as a minimum standard (for example self-regulatory norms of professional associations). For instance, the SFBC has recognised the Agreement on the Swiss banks' code of conduct with regard to the exercise of due diligence (CDB) issued by the Swiss Bankers Association as the minimum standard for banks and securities dealers.

Furthermore, the SFBC regularly opens consultation processes when elaborating new regulations or amendments. Comments and reports from the self-regulatory organisations can provide guidance to the SFBC projects and are published online for public consultation.

Currently the most important self-regulatory organisations of the banking sector are the Swiss Bankers Association, the Swiss Funds Association SFA, the SWX Swiss Exchange and the Swiss Chamber of Trustees and Auditors.

12.4.2 Supervisory system in the private insurance sector

Anti-money laundering measures also play a part in the supervision of insurance companies. Under the Federal Department of Finance, the FOPI monitors the steps taken by life insurers to prevent money laundering.

Life insurance companies have made use of the self-regulation option allowed by the AMLA. In 1998, the Swiss Insurance Association (SIA) set up a self-regulatory organisation: the SRO-SIA.

The SRO-SIA, the only such organisation in the private insurance sector, is recognised by the FOPI and comes under its supervision. The majority of life insurers who have their head office in Switzerland are members of the SRO-SIA. Only five companies have not joined this organisation. The FOPI carries out exclusive and direct supervision of insurance companies that are not members of the SRO-SIA.

12.4.3   Supervisory system in the non-banking sector

Attached to the Federal Department of Finance, the AMLCA is the supervisory authority for the financial intermediaries in the non-banking sector.

As an alternative to direct subordination to the AMLCA, the legislator introduced a self-regulation system for this sector, which allows financial intermediaries to affiliate themselves to a self-regulatory organisation (SRO), recognised and supervised by the AMLCA, which carries out supervision of their members with regard to compliance with the obligations contained in the AMLA.

Consequently, some professions have formed themselves into a specialised SRO in several fields: lawyers-notaries, asset managers, fiduciaries, etc. However, there are three multidisciplinary SROs which every financial intermediary can join regardless of their profession. The other self-regulatory bodies either have their origins in organisations such as the Post Office and the SBB Rail Transports or are linked to professional associations that only accept their own members.

There are currently 11 such SROs in the country.

In any case, the financial intermediary has the choice to affiliate itself to a SRO or to request authorisation directly from the Federal supervisory authority. A financial intermediary that joins a SRO, will be supervised exclusively by the SRO for its compliance with its obligations in relation to the AMLA and the applicable implementing regulations.

12.4.4   Self-regulation mechanism

Self-regulation looks back on a long tradition in Switzerland and fulfils an important task for the financial centre.

The AMLA allows for the development of self-regulation and the system is currently used in most of the Swiss financial markets to combat money laundering.

There are different types of self-regulation. A distinction is drawn between voluntary or autonomous self-regulation, self-regulation that is recognised as a minimum standard, and compulsory self-regulation that is based on a mandate by the legislator to self-regulate.

Voluntary or autonomous self-regulation is based on private autonomy and is generally established without government agencies being involved. (See chapter 4.1, Supervisory system in the banking sector.)

In contrast, we speak of compulsory or led self-regulation when the Federal authority grants recognition to a self-regulatory organisation to fulfil a surveillance function. Consequently, a self-regulatory organisation can exercice either a direct or indirect role in markets supervision. (See chapter 4.2, Supervisory system in the private insurance sector and chapter 4.3, Supervisory system in the non-banking sector.)

12.4.5 The Federal Financial Market Supervisory Authority (FINMA)

As of 1 January 2009, state supervision of banks, insurance companies and other financial intermediaries was consolidated into a single Federal Financial Market Supervisory Authority (FINMA). All the supervisory authorities, except for the SFGB, are integrated into this new authority.

However, the legally defined task of the supervisory authority remains the same and the particularities of the different supervisory sectors have been taken into account. Thus the banks still have to fulfil the requirements of the Banking Act, insurance companies have to fulfil those of the Insurance Supervision Act, the investment funds those of the Investment Fund Act, etc. Even the system of self-regulation in accordance with the Anti-Money Laundering Act and the Stock Exchange Act is retained.

The aim of the financial market supervisory authority is to protect creditors, investors, insured persons and to ensure the general functioning of the financial markets in accordance with financial market legislation. It thus helps reinforce Switzerland's image and competitiveness as a financial centre (Art. 5, FINMASA).

With the establishment of this institutional structure, an organisational reorientation is underway to strengthen Swiss financial market supervision and to give it greater weight as a representative at the international level.

FIMNA is being organised as an establishment under public law, with functional, institutional, and financial independence.

The FINMA Act (FINMASA) contains the fundamentals of financial market regulation, liability rules and harmonised supervisory instruments and sanctions. It serves as an umbrella law for the other laws governing the content of financial market supervision. These subordinate laws remain unchanged (or with minimal modifications).

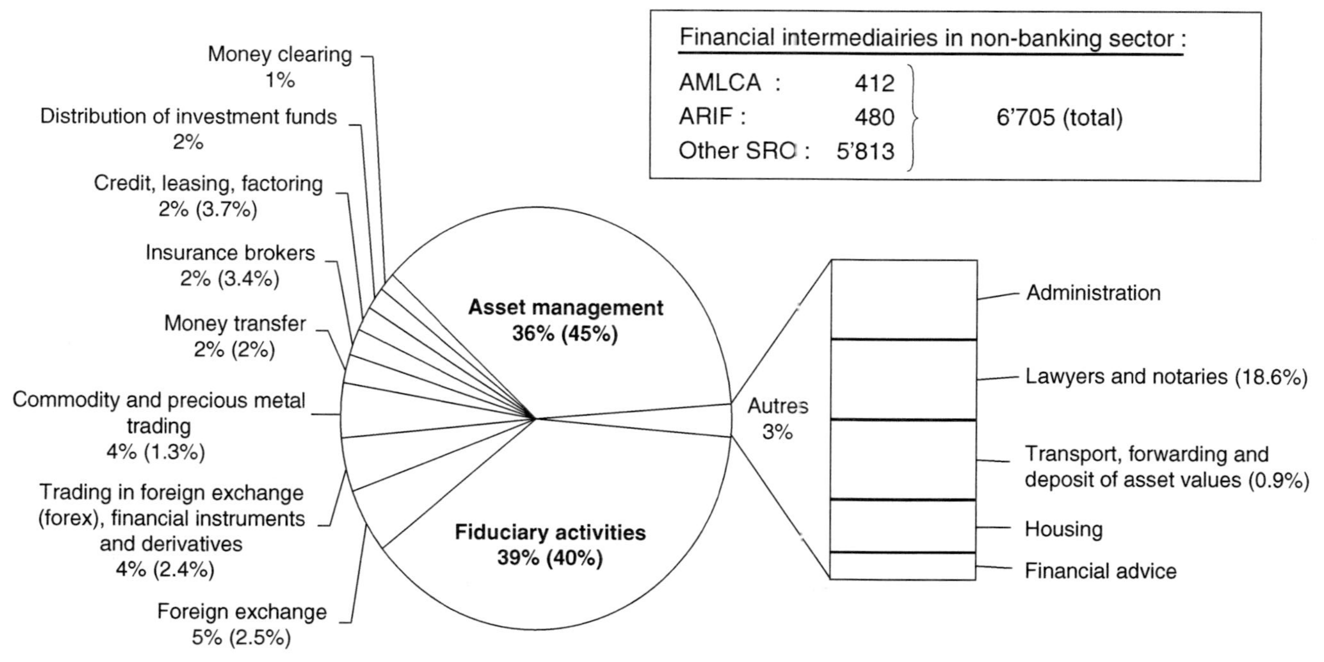

Chart 12.1 Types of financial intermediary members of ARIF.

12.5   The SRO ARIF

The Association Romande des Intermédiaires Financiers (ARIF, http://www.arif.ch) is an association founded in Geneva on 15 March 1999, initiated by a group of finance professionals.

On 24 December 1999, the Federal supervisory authority granted the ARIF recognition as a self-regulatory body.

ARIF is a private non-profit organisation, based on civil law, independent from any professional association or political group, whose purpose is to promote the prevention of and the fight against money laundering, as well as to apply and enforce amongst its members the Federal Act on Combating Money Laundering in the Financial Sector (AMLA).

ARIF is the only multidisciplinary SRO based in the French-speaking part of Switzerland and is therefore open to any non-banking financial intermediary exercising an activity in Switzerland. The association currently has more than 480 members, mainly from asset management and fiduciary activities.

As a non-specialised SRO, ARIF may accept as a member any financial intermediary in the following areas: asset management, foreign exchange, money transfer, company administration, trusts, payment services, credit-leasing and factoring, lawyers and notaries, insurance brokerage, and more. (See Chart 12.1).

12.6   Conclusion

The Swiss supervisory system of financial markets to fight against money laundering and terrorist financing is characterised by the self-regulation system. However, we speak of 'led self-regulation' as the freedom to act for the SRO is strictly limited to its subordination to the Federal authority. On the other hand, the system allows the simultaneous existence of 12 implementing texts of the AMLA, established by every SRO and the AMLCA itself.

With the merge into the FINMA on 1 January 2009, we can foresee that this regulation system will continue working but with great efforts made to harmonise the multiple existing regulations.

This has to be set in parallel with the recommendations issued by the FATF, following its evaluation of the Swiss anti-money laundering legal system (in 2005), and the entering in force on 1 February 2009 of the revised AMLA, whose amendments will need to be translated and implemented into the subordinated regulations. Through its evaluation report, the FATF now recognises that self-regulation has proven its worth as an alternative form of regulation against money laundering and terrorist financing, despite the complexity due to, on the one hand, a large number of regulatory bodies and multiple regulations and, on the other, the coexistence of supervisory authorities and self-regulatory organisations.

With the FINMA, an organisational reorientation is also underway to boost financial market supervision in Switzerland and considerably strengthen its position internationally.

(*Sources*: Anti-Money Laundering Control Authority / Financial Action Task Force / Money Laundering Reporting Office Switzerland / Swiss Federal Banking Commission / Federal Office of Private Insurance / Dr. iur. Josef Bollag / Alain Saint-Sulpice)

List of Abbreviations

AMLA	Swiss Anti-Money Laundering Act
AMLCA	Swiss Anti-Money Laundering Control Authority
ARIF	Association Romande des Intermédiaires Financiers
CDB	Swiss banks' code of conduct with regard to the exercise of due diligence (*Convention de Diligence des Banques*)
DUFI	Financial intermediaries directly subordinated (*direkt unterstellten Finanzintermediäre*)
EG	Egmont Group
FATF	Financial Action Task Force
FDF	Swiss Federal Department of Finance
FDJP	Swiss Federal Department of Justice and Police
FINMA	Swiss Federal Financial Market Supervisory Authority (*Finanzmarktaufsicht*)
FINMASA	Swiss Financial Market Supervision Act
FIU	Financial Intelligence Units
FOPI	Swiss Federal Office of Private Insurance
MLO SFBC	SFBC Money Laundering Ordinance
MROS	Money laundering Reporting Office Switzerland
OAR	Organisme d'Auto-Régulation (=SRO)
SBA	Swiss Bankers Association (Swissbanking)
SCC	Swiss Criminal Code
SFA	Swiss Funds Association
SFBC	Swiss Federal Banking Commission
SFGB	Swiss Federal Gaming Board
SRO	Self-Regulatory Organisation
SIA	Swiss Insurance Association
SWX	Swiss Exchange

13
An Epidemiologic Approach of Financial Markets

Christian Viladent

The current financial crisis is comparable to a pandemic (an epidemic which has spread to the entire world). Diamond and Rajan warned that local bank failures could lead to a "contagion" (domino effect or knock-on defaults) and financial crisis showing astonishing resemblances to disease propagating like an epidemic.[1] Both disease contagions and financial contagions are induced by one or a limited number of "infected" entities.[2] In the case of disease contagions, the infected entity is an individual incubating a micro-organism (e.g., a virus or bacteria) who eventually spreads the infection to the community the individual is connected to. The entity, in the case of financial crisis, is a financial institution committing fraud, internal irregularities or facing losses due to risky loans and investments.[3] The consequences of either an infectious disease pandemic or a financial crisis are dramatic, the former potentially leading to millions of deaths. The flu pandemic in 1918 was estimated to have killed between 50 and 100 million people in about six months, while the latter eventually resulted in millions of ruined shareholders and job losses.[4] An additional consequence of both disease and financial epidemics is that the remaining sensitive individuals (non-infected) become suspicious toward other individuals, considering them as infected and refusing to enter relationships with them. Allen and Gale focused their work on claim emissions that occurred against suspected institutions or regions, with the consequence of value loss of this claim, potentially leading to contagion.[5]

The first section of this article describes the global epidemic disease surveillance system; the second section provides details on network models and connectivity. In the discussion section, I will make recommendations for an integrated surveillance system of financial institutions (FIs).

13.1   The international epidemic and outbreak surveillance

Global centralized systems, to detect outbreaks, were developed and managed by the World Health Organization (WHO) since the 1950s. The two pillars of this system are the WHO Epidemic and Pandemic Alert and Response (EPR), which centralizes data collected worldwide, and the Global Outbreak Alert and Response Network (GOARN), which helps to identify outbreaks and provide appropriate interventions.

The surveillance systems are based on indicators, such as the number of new cases of specific diseases per unit of time, and events, such as unofficial local reports or news. Data is collected at the local level; in the case of EPR, data is collected by 100 regional centers worldwide and transmitted to the Collaborating Centres such as the Centre for Diseases Control and Prevention (CDC) based in Atlanta, United States or the European Centre for Diseases Prevention and Control (ECDC) based in Stockholm, Sweden.

The Collaborating Centres analyze the data and communicate the outputs to the World Health Organization (WHO), which in turn diffuses reports to governmental agencies and other private institutions for appropriate actions. In the case of the flu epidemic, the Collaborating Centres help to identify the flu strain on a yearly basis and organize the production of an appropriate vaccine.

Another role of the surveillance system is to search for cases of infectious disease that will potentially lead to an epidemic (human flu, avian flu, SARS). These cases are the epidemic sources. After the identification of these epidemic sources, they are followed up by targeted interventions, such as the destruction of the poultry in the case of avian flu or quarantine or containment of the infected individuals in the case of human flu. These measures are being utilized to curb or eliminate the risk of epidemic spread. Supranational coordination using appropriate indicators have been claimed to improve local policy.[6, 7]

In the case of financial markets, signals of contamination by risky assets or wrongful practices must be detected in the early stages (low signals), before they spread to large communities (strong signals) and eventually lead to financial panic and market collapse. These low signals can be associated with disease outbreak. Low signals of financial distress, confined to one financial entity, are not usually detected by the agents or dissimulated in cases of fraud. Neural networks, a concept that was originally used in the nineteenth century to describe the functioning of the human brain, are a powerful tool to detect the low signals of distress or fraud within financial institutions. Authors have described neural networks, also called expert systems, to extract information from accounting reports.[8] However, to provide an efficient support to financial institution surveillance systems, the expert systems should incorporate appropriate indicators and thresholds. These two elements have been pinpointed as critical components of financial systems surveillance.[9]

As a result of surveillance, FIs can be found in three statuses: non-infected (e.g., FIs possessing no or a minimal amount of risky assets), infected (e.g., possessing large quantities of risky assets, having committed fraud) or immune. We assume that a FI's "immunity" is based on three factors: their liquidity level, risk management system, and ethics. It is important to note that free riders exist in both human communities (e.g., individuals refusing vaccination) as well as in financial communities, where, in bank conglomerates, free riders take risks as they feel sheltered within the conglomerates.

13.2   Epidemic models

Having defined the three types of status that classify individual entities within a population, it is now essential to describe the various types of models that allow a representation of the epidemic. Several models have been developed to describe epidemic transmission. Models are either population based or individual based. Deterministic compartmental models fall in the former category while network models are part of the latter.

Deterministic models allow for determining R_0, which is defined as the number of people in a given population that a single infected individual can contaminate.[10] R_0 can be seen as a global measure of contamination, as it depends on the infected individual's network: the more connected an individual, the more individuals will be contaminated. When $R_0 > 1$, the epidemic develops; the epidemic usually stops when $R_0 < 1$. As a bank "population" is not homogenous, bank surveillance cannot be performed using only a general parameter such as R_0 but also needs network modeling, as explained further. While deterministic models are appropriate for assessing the impact of interventions against epidemics at a global level, under the assumption that populations are homogenous, these models are not appropriate for capturing the complexity of relations between-individuals.

Network models were described as the system of choice to capture the complexity of disease epidemics[11] in the early 2000s. Network models were developed to represent inter-bank connections.[12] This model uses homogenous connections where each bank is connected to the same number of banks. Later, network models were developed that better reflect the complex nature of inter-bank relations.[13]

Network models include nodes (e.g., individual banks) and inter-nodal links. As stated earlier, a node is either classified within one of the following three statuses: infected, non-infected/non-immune or immune (a representation of these three statuses for financial institutions is given below (see Figure 13.1)). According to its activities, the entity can evolve from one status to another.

In Figure 13.1, FIs are represented by nodes. A node is assumed to be, at a certain point of time, infected, non-infected or immune.

We assume that FIs' immunity status is only transitory. Depending on their activities, this "immune system" can be overflowed (e.g., when the institution does not possess enough liquidity to cover the risk). If this happens, the FI (or its partners) can take the necessary action, such as a capital raise, debt discharge or a bailout, which will bring the infected institution back to its immune status.

In banking networks, nodes are not connected in a homogenous way or equivalent in size. Each entity is connected to various and different types of institution (Figure 13.2). Network models should first help in identifying nodes that are statistically significant (connected with a large number of nodes and having a large number of risky assets/practices) and, second, support the decision for the most appropriate intervention or immunization strategy to avoid further contamination.

In Figure 13.2 each node develops a complex, connected network and includes cross-border and cross-sector connections (banking, insurance, security trading).

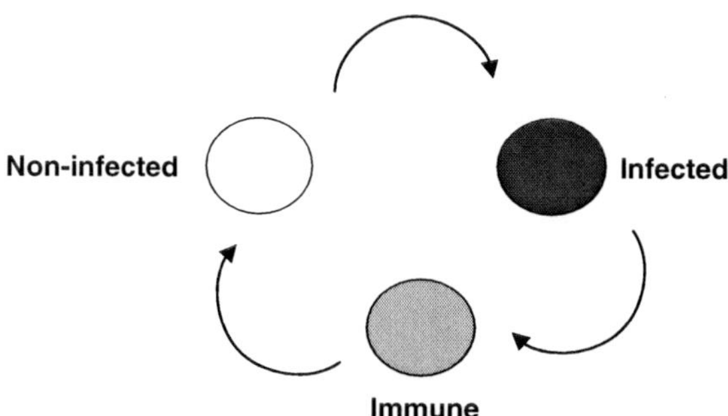

Figure 13.1   Element of a network: Node. Each network node can be in three possible statuses.

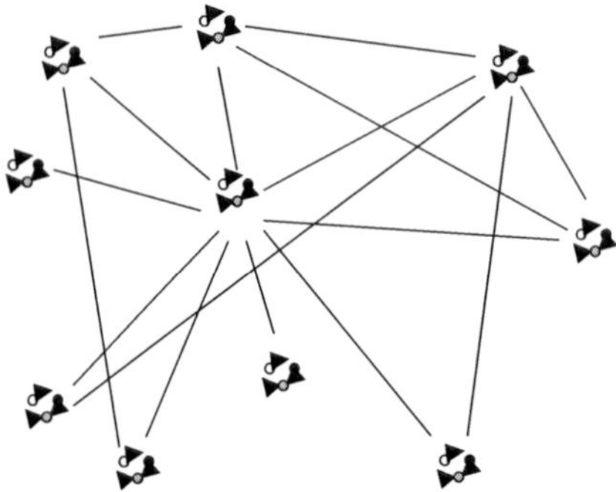

Figure 13.2   Node inter-connection.

13.3   The need for a macro-prudential approach in risk assessment

Influenced by the 1988 Basel Capital Accord, models used by FIs are mainly focused on assessing their own operational risk and are prone to bias.[14] A macro-prudential approach of risk is desirable in a sense that it leads to limit the risk of financial distresses and avoid spreading to the global community.[15] This directly relates to the argument that when each FI takes an aggressive position and mitigates their risk vis-à-vis other FIs, the global situation may worsen. In an attempt to analyze the relationship between supervision, regulation, and financial stability, Mitchener observed the difference in a number of bank failures and variations in prudential supervision and regulation within various states in the United States during the Great Depression.[16] He found that higher reserve requirements could lead banks to acquire riskier assets in order to increase return. Similarly, in a recent study, Nier et al. found that capital requirements alone may not suffice to protect bank networks from knock-on defaults.[13]

13.4   Discussion

We have exposed the WHO epidemic and pandemic surveillance systems as a comprehensive organization capable of detecting outbreaks and preventing a generalized epidemic. We believe that an efficient supervision system of financial markets should be developed beyond the Global Bank Insolvency Initiative (GBII) and mirror the system currently supervised by the WHO[1]. The body supervising financial markets should have the power to act in conjunction with state authorities to terminate fraudulent operators and reduce or stop the flow of risky operations in a timely manner. This body should also oversee the ratings of various FIs and help identify the riskiest ones. One of the problems affecting today's supervisory system is that each FI uses its own model to assess operating risks.[17] Global macro-prudential supervisory models should supersede micro-prudential models. In my opinion, FIs must be monitored by regional entities (e.g., central banks) that analyze the risks at a network (or conglomerate) level and the regional agencies must transmit their finding to a central international body.

The central body should, in turn, work with various local authorities to put intervention plans in place and work at reducing and stopping propagation. The supervision system must be developed in collaboration with FIs by determining the proper indicators and thresholds that need to be observed and applied in order to identify the riskiest practices and develop the most appropriate intervention mix.

Kanas demonstrated that the contagion effect might take place globally in conjunction with various effects on the supervision systems in various countries.[18] His work was based on the failure of a major international financial institution (BCCI) that occurred in 1990. Since that time the integration of the financial market has considerably developed. Nier et al. showed, with their network model, that when a network has a low degree of connectivity, an increase in connectivity increases the risk of knock-on defaults inversely – when a network is highly connected, a further increase tends to help dissipate losses. Similarly Leitner assumes that, among FI networks, large institutions have a tendency to bail out smaller institutions within the same network out of fear of contagion.[19] These findings confirm, de facto, the ambiguities in relation to FI connectivity and systemic shock within the FI networks. This conclusion leads me to assume that high connectivity between entities of various size and ethical codes increases the complexity of intra- and extra-network exchange, leading to free-rider problems and an overall increase in systemic risk.

However, FI supervision does have its limitations. Mitchener, in his observation of supervising activities during the Great Depression, did not find a significant relationship between supervisory activities and bank suspension rates. In a recent report, the Financial Stability Forum pointed out several weaknesses in the current prudential supervision system, in particular the definition of appropriate indicators and thresholds related to the scope and magnitude of public disclosures of on- and off-balance sheet exposures.[20]

13.5   Conclusion

In a global society, access to credit is a necessity for financial institutions, entrepreneurs, and consumers. Strengthening regulation seems to be the mainstream point of view among politicians. Considering that a wave of regulation will, a priori, consist of a set of measures to prevent wrongful practices, induce law infringement, strengthen tax havens, and ultimately lead, at a later stage, to a deregulation wave, we must aim for increased coordination between the surveillance agencies and for the creation of a central supervisory body, combined with the use of accurate and realistic models consisting of a superior model.

As a consequence of the current crisis, several politicians express the need to alter capitalism. I must argue that this point of view arises mainly from popularity-seeking reasoning and has little to do with economic rationale. More pragmatically, it is necessary to define a new approach to financial market supervision, primarily based on a global surveillance system. We must assume this system will help, in the long run, to develop a strong, universal code of ethics in the financial business world and increase the number of "immune" institutions while significantly reducing the occurrence of generalized crisis.

Notes

1. Diamond and Rajan (2005), "Liquidity Shortage and Financial Crisis," *The Journal of Finance*, 60, pp. 615–46.
2. Kanas (2005), "Pure Contagion Effects in International Banking: The Case of BCCI's Failure," *Journal of Applied Economics*, 8, pp. 101–23.
3. Aharony and Swary (1983), "Contagion Effects of Bank Failures: Evidence from Capital Markets," *Journal of Business*, 56, pp. 305–22.
4. Barry (2006), "What the 1918 Flu Pandemic Teaches Us: Yesterday's Lessons Inform Today's Preparedness," MLO, September issue, pp. 26–8.
5. Allen and Gale (2000), "Financial Contagion," *Journal of Political Economy*, 108, pp. 1–33.
6. Fock et al. (2002), "Influenza Pandemic: Preparedness Planning in Germany," *Euro Surveillance*, 7, pp. 1–5.
7. Aull et al. (2007), "A Novel Influenza Surveillance System: Outcomes from the 2005–2006 Flu Season," *Southern Medical Journal*, 100, pp. 873–80.
8. Trigueiros and Taffler (1996), "Neural Networks and Empirical Research in Accounting," *Accounting and Business Research*, 26, pp. 347–356.
9. Weber & Menoud (2007), "Systemic Risk as a Topic of Financial Conglomerates' Financial Supervision," *Banking and Financial Law Review*, 22, pp. 377–403.
10. McDonald (1952), "The Analysis of Equilibrium in Malaria," *Tropical Diseases Bulletin*, 49, pp. 813–29.

11. Pearl, J. (1985), "Bayesian Networks: A Model of Self-Activated Memory for Evidential Reasoning," Proceedings of the 7th Conference of the Cognitive Science Society, University of California, Irvine, CA, pp. 329–34.
12. Allen and Gale (2000), "Financial Contagion," *Journal of Political Economy*, 108, pp. 1–33.
13. Nier et al. (2008), "Network Models and Financial Stability," working paper no. 346, *Quarterly Bulletin* Q2. pp. 184–93.
14. Jobst (2007), "The Treatment of Operational Risk under the New Basel Framework: Critical Issues," *Journal of banking regulation*, 4, pp. 316–52.

There are currently three types of FI supervision: the prudential supervision which observes the solvency and the business supervision which monitors the way FI manage their businesses and aim to ensure ethical and legal practices. The solvency supervision is currently performed on an institutional basis. A third type of supervision aims at maintaining an overall stability. Basel II aims at a more macroprudential approach.

15. Borio (2003), "Toward a Macroprudential Framework for Financial Supervision and Regulation?" *CESifo Economic Studies*, 49, pp. 181–205.
16. Mitchener (2005), "Bank Supervision, Regulation and Instability During the Great Depression," *The Journal of Economic History*, 65, pp. 152–85.
17. Butkiewicz (2004), "Prudential Supervision: What Works and What Doesn't," *Eastern Economic Journal*, 30: 141.
18. Kanas, A. (2005), "Pure contagion effects in international banking," Journal of Applied Economics, 8: 101–123.
19. Leitner, Y (2005), "Financial networks: Contagion, commitment and private sector bailouts," The Journal of finance, 9: 2925–2953.
20. Panitchpakde, Supachai (2008), "Towards a World Financial Organisation," World Economy & Development In Brief, Luxembourg, November 24.
20. Financial Stability Forum (2008), Report on Enhancing Market and Institutional Resilience, April 7.

Bibliography

AFP (2008), "EU Calls for Code of Conduct for Sovereign Wealth Funds, Feb 27, Brussels.

Aharony and Swary (1983), "Contagion Effects of Bank Failures: Evidence from Capital Markets," *Journal of Business*, 56, pp. 305–22.

Allen and Gale (2000), "Financial Contagion," *Journal of Political Economy*, 108, pp. 1–33.

Apel, Hans (1975), "From Bretton Woods to Jamaica," Sozialdemokratischer Pressedienst – Volkswirtschaft; 9 December.

Artus, Patrick (2007), *Les Incendiaires. Les Banques Centrales Dépassées par la Globalisation*, Perrin, Paris.

Attali, Jacques (2009), *La crise, et après?*, Fayard, Paris.

Aull et al. (2007), "A Novel Influenza Surveillance System: Outcomes from the 2005–2006 Flu Season," *Southern Medical Journal*, 100, pp. 873–80.

Aymeric, Chauprade, Chronique du Choc des Civilisations, Editions Chronique, Paris, 2009, p. 43.

Balaam, David and Veseth, Michael (2005), "International Trade," in *Introduction to International Political Economy*, Pearson, New Jersey, 2005. p. 28.

Baladi, André (1991), "The Growing Role of Pension Funds in Shaping International Corporate Governance," Benefits & Compensation International, London.

Baladi, André (1999), "Quo Vadis Corporate Governance?" *Références, Le Temps* publication, Geneva, April.

Baladi, André (2001), "How to Improve Corporate Governance," interview in *Nikkei Financial Times*, Tokyo, July 12.

Baladi, André (2004), "The French Corporate Governance Paradox," *Investor Responsibility Research Center/IRRC Bulletin*, Washington DC, February.

Baladi, André (2006), "The Swiss Voting Right Caps Saga," *International Corporate Governance Network/ICGN Yearbook*, London, July.

Baldassari, Mario (Editor) (1991) *Building the New Europe, Volume I. Single Market and Monetary Unification in the EEC Countries, Rivista di Politica Economica*, Roma, May.

Baldassari, Mario (Editor) (1991), *Building the New Europe, Volume II. Transition to Market of Eastern European Countries and Integration With Western Economies, Rivista di Politica Economica*, Roma, June.

Bank for International Settlements, (March 2009), *BIS Quarterly Review*, BIS, Basel, March.

Bank for International Settlements, Monetary and Economic Department (2008), "Statistical Commentary on Provisional, Locational and Consolidated Banking Statistics at End-June 2008," BIS, Basel, October.

Barry (2006), "What the 1918 Flu Pandemic Teaches Us: Yesterday's Lessons Inform Today's Preparedness," MLO, September issue, pp. 26–8.

Barth, James R., Caprio, Jr., Gerard, and Levine, Ross (2008), *Rethinking Banking Regulation. Till Angels Govern*, Cambridge University Press, Cambridge.

Barth, Marvin and Patricia Pollard (2006), *The Limits of Fiscal Policy in Current account Adjustment*, Occasional Paper no. 2, US Department of the Treasury, Office of International Affairs, Washington, D.C.

BCBS (2006), *International Convergence of Capital Measurement & Capital Standards; A Revised Framework Comprehensive Version*, BIS, Basel.

Behrman, Greg (2007), *The Most Noble Adventure, The Marshall Plan and the Time When America Helped Save the World*, Free Press, New York.

Bernanke, Ben (2008), Statement before the *New York Bank Association*, NY, October 14.

Bernanke, Ben S. (2004), "Remarks," at the *Cato Institute 22nd Annual Monetary Conference*, Washington, D.C., October 14.

Bernanke, Ben S. (2009), "Presentation of the Semiannual Monetary Policy Report to the Congress," Before the Committee on Banking, Housing and Urban Affairs, US Senate, Washington, D.C., February 24.

Bernanke, Ben S. (March 10, 2009), "Financial Reform to Address Systemic Risk," Speech at the Council on Foreign Relations, Washington, D.C., March 10, Federal Reserve Board.

Bernstein, Peter (1996), *Against the Gods: The Remarkable Story of Risks*, John Wiley & Sons, New York.

Bhagwati, Jagdish (2004), *In Defense of Globalization*, A Council on Foreign Relations Book, Oxford University Press, New York.

Bhagwati, Jagdish (2002), *The Wind of the Hundred Days, How Washington Mismanaged Globalization*, The MIT Press, Cambridge, Mass.

BIS (2008), Quarterly Review, December.

Bod, Péter Ákos (1998), "The Social and Economic Legacies of Direct Capital Inflows: The Case of Hungary," in J. Bastian (ed), *The Political Economy of Transition in Central and Eastern Europe*, Ashgate.

Bod, Péter Ákos (2005), "A Great Transformation? Banking and Capital Markets in 'Transition Countries'," MES –Schriftenreihe no 3, Europa-Universitat Viadrina.

Bordo, D. Michael and Barry Eichengreen (Editors) (1993), *A Retrospective on the Bretton Woods System. Lessons for International Monetary Reform*, A National Bureau of Economic Research Project Report, University of Chicago Press, Chicago.

Borio (2003), "Toward a Macroprudential Framework for Financial Supervision and Regulation?" *CESifo Economic Studies*, 49, pp. 181–205.

Boughton, James M. (2009), "A New Bretton Woods," in *Finance and Development*, International Monetary Fund, Washington, D.C., March 2009.

Boulanger, Eric (2004), *Le Nationalisme Economique Dans l'Oeillère Libérale: De l'Antithèse au Frère Illégitime*, Cahiers de Recherche, CEIM, Université de Québec, Montréal.

Bourg, D. and Erkman S, (Editors) (2003) Perspectives on Industrial Ecology, Sheffield: Greenleaf Publishing.

Brancato, Carolyn Kay (1997), *Institutional Investors and Corporate Governance*, McGraw Hill, Chicago.

Bray, Jeremy (1978), "The Making of Economic Policy," *The Times*, London, April 19.

Bright, Julia (1999), "André Baladi—Shareholder Advocate and Governance Entrepreneur," *Governance*, London, March.

Brooks, Stephen G. and William C. Wohlforth, (2009), "Reshaping the World Order, How Washington Should Reform International Institutions," *Foreign Affairs*, New York, March–April 2009, pp. 49–63.

Brunet, Geneviève (1999), "André Baladi—Le défenseur de l'épargne retraite," *L'Hebdo*, Lausanne, November 4.

Burgenmeier, B. (2008), *Politiques économiques du développement durable*, de Boeck, Bruxelles.

Burton, John (Editor) (1986), *Keynes's General Theory: Fifty Years On. Its Relevance and Irrelevance to Modern Times*, Hobart Paper 24, The Institute of Economic Affairs, London.

Butkiewicz (2004), "Prudential Supervision: What Works and What Doesn't," *Eastern Economic Journal*, 30, p. 141.

Cadbury, Sir Adrian (2002), *Corporate Governance Chairmanship: A Personal View*, Oxford University Press, Oxford.

Camenzind, Mathias (1994), "André Baladi: Weisser Ritter des Aktionäre," *Handelszeitung*, Zurich, May 11.

Charkham, Jonathan (2005), *Keeping Better Company—Corporate Governance Ten Years On*, Oxford University Press, Oxford.

Claassen, E. and P. Salin (Editors) (1976), *Recent Issues in International Monetary Economics*, North-Holland, Amsterdam.

Claire, Michael (2008), *Rising Powers and Shrinking Planet, The New Geopolitics of Energy*, Metropolitian Books, New York, p. 169.

Cobb, C. and Cobb, J. B. (1994), *The Green National Product*, Lanham, New York, London.

Cockett, Richard (1995), *Thinking the Unthinkable, Think-Tanks and the Economic Counter-Revolution, 1931–1983*, Harper Collins, London.

Cohen, Benjamin J. (2008), *International Political Economy, An Intellectual History*, Princeton University Press, Princeton.

Committee on Policy Optimisation (Chairman Professor R. J. Ball) (1978), *Report Presented by the Financial Secretary to the Treasury by Command of Her Majesty March 1978*, Her Majesty's Stationery Office, London, Cmnd 7148.

Coombs, Charles A. (1976), *The Arena of International Finance*, John Wiley and Sons, New York.

Cooper, George (2008), *The Origin of Financial Crises. Central Banks, Credit Bubbles and the Efficient Market Fallacy*, Vintage Books, New York.

Cornford, Andrew (2004), "Basel II; Vintage 2003," *Journal of Financial Regulations and Compliance*, 12 /1, February, pp. 22–35.

Cornford, Andrew (2006), "The Basel Committee's Proposal for Revised Capital Standards," G24 Discussion Paper Series, no. 3.

Cornford, Andrew (2005), "Basel II, the Revised Framework of June 2004," manuscript.

Cornford, Andrew (2008), "Basel II at a Time of Financial Peril," *TWN Global Economy Series*, March.

Cox, Adrian and Garnham, Peter (2009), "Moody's Warns of Eastern Europe Risk," *Financial Times*, February 17.

Daly, J. H. (1990), "Sustainable Growth: An Impossibility Theorem," *Development*, no. 3–4, pp. 45–47.

Dam, Kenneth W. (1982), *The Rules of the Game, Reform and Evolution in the International Monetary System*, The University of Chicago Press, Chicago.

Danthine, Jean-Pierre and John B. Donaldson, (2005), *Intermediate Financial Theory*, 2nd Edition, Elsevier Academic Press, Amsterdam.

Daub, C. H. and Ergenzinger, R. (2005), "Enabling Sustainable Management Through a New Multi-disciplinary Concept of Customer Satisfaction," *European Journal of Marketing*, vol. 39, no. 9/10, pp. 998–1015.

Davis, Stephen, Lukomnik Jon and Pitt-Watson, David (2006), *The New Capitalists. How Citizen Investors are Reshaping the Corporate Agenda*, Harvard Business School Press, Boston.

Dembinski, Paul H. (2008), *Finance Servante Ou Finance Trompeuse?* Parole et Silence, Desclée de Brouwer.

Diamond and Rajan (2005), "Liquidity Shortage and Financial Crisis," *The Journal of Finance*, 60, pp. 615–46.

Dooley, Michael P. and Folkerts-Landau, David, and Garber, Peter M. (2009), "Bretton Woods II Still Defines the International Monetary System," NBER Working Paper Series 14731. http://www.nber.org/papers/w14731.

Dür, Andreas (2000), *Theorizing the Contagious Effects of Regionalism : European Integration and Transatlantic Trade Relations, 1957–1963*, Dissertation, European University Institute, San Domenico di Fiesole.

Drezner, Daniel (2008), *Bric by Bric: The Emergent Regime for Sovereign Wealth Funds*, Fletcher School of Law and Diplomacy, Tufts University, August.

Ebenstein, Alan (2003), *Friedrich Hayek, A Biography*, The University of Chicago Press, Chicago.

ECB (2008), Financial Stability Report, December.

Economist, the (2008a), "A Magyar Mess," March 27.

Economist, the, (2008b), "When Fortune Frowned, A Special Report on the World Economy," October 11, p. 4.

Economist, the (2008c), "Kreppanomics. How a Banking Crisis Brought Down a Small Economy," October 9.

Economist, the (2008d), "Who is Next?" October 23.

Eichengreen, Barry (2004), *Capital Flows and Crises*, The MIT Press, Cambridge, Mass.

Eichengreen, Barry and Richard Baldwin (Editors) (2008), *What G20 Leaders Must Do to Stabilise Our Economy and Fix the Financial System*, Center for Economic Policy Research, A VoxEU.org publication, November.

Elise, Luci (2008), "The Housing Meltdown: Why Did It Happen in the US," BIS Working Papers no 259, September.

Erhard, Ludwig (1962), *Deutsche Wirtschaftspolitik. Der Weg der Sozialen Marktwirtschaft*, ECON Verlag, Düsseldorf.

Eschweiler, Bernhard and Fernandez, David (2008), *Sovereign Wealth Funds: A Bottom-up Primer*, J P Morgan Research N.A., Singapore Branch, May.

Ethan Kaplan and Doni Rodrik (2001), *Did the Malaysian Capital Controls Work?* Harvard University, J. F. school of Government, February.

European Bank for Reconstruction and Development (2008), Transition Report. London.

EU calls for code of conduct for sovereign wealth funds, Feb 27, 2008, BRUSSELS (AFP).

European Commission (2008), "Sovereign Wealth Funds and Financial Stability— Guide," European Commission, Brussels, 27 February.

European Union (1997), "EU Resolution of the European Council on the Stability and Growth Pact Amsterdam," June 17. Official Journal C 236, 02/08/1997 P. 0001—0002.

Financial Stability Forum (2008), Report on Enhancing Market and Institutional Resilience, April 7.

Fisher, Éva (2008), "Challenges of Financial Integration in the Central and East European Region," MNB Bulletin, no. 12.

Fischer, Stanley (1999), "On the need for an international lender of last resort", *The Journal of Economic Perspective*, 13 (4), pp. 85–104.

Fleckenstein, William A. with Frederick Sheehan (2008), *Greenspan's Bubbles. The Age of Ignorance at the Federal Reserve*, McGraw Hill, New York.

Fock et al. (2002), "Influenza Pandemic: Preparedness Planning in Germany," *Euro Surveillance*, 7, pp. 1–5.

Fontela Montes, Emilio and Joaquin Guzman Cuevas, (Editors) (2005), *Brasil y la economia social de mercado*, Cuadernos del Grupo de Alcàntara, Universidad de Extremadura, Caceres.

Frentrop, Paul (2003), *A History of Corporate Governance, 1602–2002*, Deminor, Brussels.

Friedman, Milton (1953), "The Case for Flexible Exchange Rates," in Milton Friedman, *Essays in Positive Economics*, University of Chicago Press, Chicago, pp. 157–203.

Friedman, Milton and Anna Jacobson Schwartz (1963), *A Monetary History of the United States, 1967–1960*, (A Study by the National Bureau of Economic Research), New York, Princeton University Press, Princeton.

Galbraith, John Kenneth (1990), *A Short History of Financial Euphoria*, Penguin Books, New York.

Galbraith, John Kenneth (1997) *The Great Crash 1929*, Mariner Books, Houghton Mifflin Company, Boston.

Gandolfo, Giancarlo (2002), *International Finance and Open-Economy Macro-economics*, Springer, Berlin and Heidelberg.

Gardner, Richard (1956), *Sterling-Dollar Diplomacy, Anglo-American Collaboration in the Reconstruction of Multilateral Trade*, Clarendon Press, Oxford.

Gaved, Matthew (1996), "Euro-Baladi and the International Corporate Governance Network," *The Corporate Governance Newsletter*, London, August.

Giscard D'estaing, Valéry (2009), "L'échéance politique de la crise, ce sera le printemps 2009," Interview, *Le Monde*, Paris, 13 January.

Global Finance, *Journal of International Affairs*, Columbia University, School of International and Public Affairs, New York, Fall/Winter 2008.

Goldstein, Andrea (2007) *International Investment of Sovereign Wealth Funds*, OECD, Directorate for Financial and Enterprise Affairs, Investment Committee, Paris, October.

Gordon, Gary, B. (2008), "The Subprime Panic," NBER Working Paper Series, w14398.

Green, Russell and Tom Torgerson (2007), *Are High Foreign Exchange Reserves in Emerging Markets a Blessing or a Burden?* Occasional Paper no. 6, US Department of the Treasury, Office of International Affairs, Washington, D.C.

Greenspan, Alan (2007), *The Age of Turbulence. Adventures in a New World*, The Penguin Press, New York.

Greenspan, Alan (2005), "Remarks on the *Current Account*," at Advancing Enterprise 2005 Conference, London, February 4, Federal Reserve Board.

Group of 20 (2009), *Declaration on Delivering Resources Through the International Financial Institutions*, London, 2 April.

Group of 20 (2009), *Declaration on Strengthening the Financial System*, London, 2 April.

Group of 20 (2009), *The Global Plan for Recovery and Reform*, London, 2 April.

Group of 20, Working Group 3 (2009), *Reform of the IMF, Final Report*, London, 4 March.

Group of 20, Working Group 2 (WG2) (2009), *G20 Working Group on Reinforcing International Cooperation and Promoting Integrity in Financial Markets*, London, 2 April.

Group of 20 (2009), *G20 Finance Ministers' and Central Bank Governors' Communiqué and Annex to Communiqué, March 14*, London, UK Government G20 Website.

Group of Twenty Summit (2008), *Declaration of the Summit on Financial Markets and the World Economy* November 16, The White House.

Group of Thirty (2009), *Financial Reform. A Framework for Financial Stability*, Group of Thirty, Washington, D.C., 2009.

Hankel, Wilhelm, Wilhelm, Noelling, Karl Albrecht Schactschneider, and Joachim Starbatty (2009), "Die Europäische Währungsunion vor einer Zerreissprobe. Kritik an der Rolle der Schwachwährungsländer im Euro-Einzugsgebiet," *Neue Zürcher Zeitung*, 14–15 February, Zürich.

Hansard (1993), *Commons Sitting, Dr. Jeremy Bray*, 6.41 PM, 2 December.

Harbulot, Christian (1992), La Machine de Guerre Economique, Economica, Paris, pp. 23–33.

Harris, Ethan S. (2008), *Ben Bernanke's Fed. The Federal Reserve After Greenspan*, Harvard Business Press, Boston, Mass.

Harris, Seymour E. (Editor) (1965), *The New Economics, Keynes' Influence on Theory and Public Policy*, Augustus M. Kelley, Reprints of Economic Classics, New York (first edition 1947).

Hayek, F. A. (1990), *Denationalisation of Money*, Institute of Economic Affairs, London.

Hayek, Friedrich, A. (1937, 1964), *Monetary Nationalism and International Stability*, Augustus M. Kelley, Reprints of Economic Classics, New York.

Helleiner, Eric (1994), *States and the Reemergence of Global Finance, From Bretton Woods to the 1990s*, Cornell University Press, Ithaca.

Helleiner, Eric and Andreas Pickel (2005), *Economic Nationalism in a Globalizing World*, Cornell University Press, Ithaca.

Heilperin, Michael A., (1968), *Aspects of the Pathology of Money*, Michael Joseph, London.

Hieronymi, Otto (1990), *Economic Policies for the New Hungary: Proposals for a Coherent Approach*, Battelle Press, Columbus—Richland.

Hieronymi, Otto (forthcoming), "Rebuilding the International Monetary Order: The Responsibility of Europe, Japan and the United States," in *Revista de Economia Mundial*.

Hieronymi, Otto (2008), "Les responsabilités des gouvernements et les enterprises à l'époque de la finance globale," unpublished manuscript presented at Modena Office of Confindustria, 14 March.

Hieronymi, Otto (2007), "The Spirit of Geneva and Globalization," in Hieronymi, Otto and Kathleen Intag, (Editors), *The Spirit of Geneva in a Globalized World*, Refugee Survey Quarterly, Oxford University Press, vol. 26, no. 4, pp. 274–305.

Hieronymi, Otto (2005), "The 'Social Market Economy' and Globalisation: The Lessons from the European Model for Latin America," in Emilio Fontela Montes and Joaquin Guzmàn Cueva (Eds): *Brasil y la Economia Social de Mercado*, Cuadernos del Grupo de Alcantara, pp. 247–300.

Hieronymi, Otto (2004), "The Outlook for International Economic and Political Order: the Role of Japan and Europe," in *Kudan Square*, Institute For International Economic Studies, Tokyo, no. 17, March, pp. 8–11.

Hieronymi, Otto (2004) "A Turning Point for the Better or the Worse? The Current Outlook for International Order," *Foresight, Journal of Future Studies and Strategic Thinking and Policy*, vol. 6, no. 4, pp. 204–07, Emerald Group Publishing Ltd, Bradford.

Hieronymi, Otto (2002), "Wilhelm Röpke, the Social Market Economy and Today's Domestic and International Order," in Otto Hieronymi, Chiara Jasson, and Alexandra Roversi (editors), *Colloque Wilhelm Röpke (1899–1966), The Relevance of His Teaching Today: Globalization and the Social Market Economy*, HEI-Webster University, Cahiers HEI, Geneva.

Hieronymi, Otto (2002), "Political Order and Universal Values in the 21st Century," in *Humanitarian Values for the 21st Century, Proceedings of the 7th Annual Humanitarian Conference of Webster University, Refugee Survey Quarterly*, vol. 21, no. 3, pp. 126–34, UNHCR, Oxford University Press.

Hieronymi, Otto (1998), "Agenda for a New Monetary Reform," in *Futures*, vol. 30, no. 8, pp. 769–81, Pergamon, Elsevier Science Ltd.

Hieronymi, Otto (1996), "The International Financial Institutions and the Challenge of Transition and Reconstruction in the Former Communist Countries of Central and Eastern Europe," in Szabo-Pelsoeczy, Miklos (Editor), *Fifty Years After Bretton Woods*, (Sixth Conference of the Robert Triffin-Sziràk Foundation, Brussels 1994), Averbury, Aldershot, pp. 129–40.

Hieronymi, Otto (1995), "The Case for an 'Extended EMS': A New International Monetary Order to be Built by Europe, Japan and the United States," in Szabo-Pelsoeczy, Miklos (Editor), *The Global Monetary System After the Fall of the Soviet Empire*, (In Memoriam Robert Triffin – 1911–1993, Sixth Conference of the Robert Triffin-Sziràk Foundation, Sziràk, 1993), Averbury, Aldershot, pp. 57–67.

Hieronymi, Otto (1990), *Economic Policies for the New Hungary: Proposals for a Coherent Approach*, Battelle Press, Columbus.

Hieronymi, Otto (1990), "Monetary Policy, Competition and the International Division of Labour," in Szabo-Pelsoeczy, Miklos (Editor), *The Future of the Global Economic and Monetary Systems*, (2nd Sziràk Conference, 1988), Budapest, pp. 157–69.

Hieronymi, Otto (1985), "Que Valor Tiene el Dolar? Los Tipos de Cambio Flotantes y la Permanente Crisis de la Economia Mundial," *Argus*, Boletin de Informacion Economica del Banco Garriga Nogues, Barcelona, April, pp. 3–15.

Hieronymi, Otto (1982), "In Search of a New Economics for the 1980s: The Need for a Return to Fixed Exchange Rates," in Hieronymi, Otto, *International Order – A View From Geneva, Annals of International Studies* Institut Universitaire de Hautes Etudes Internationales, vol. 12, pp. 107–26, Geneva.

Hieronymi, Otto (1980), "Wilhelm Röpke et la Crise de Notre Temps," CADMOS, Cahiers trimestriels publies par la Centre Europeen de la Culture et l'Institut Universitaire d'Etudes Europeennes de Geneve, no. 10, pp. 33–46, Geneva.

Hieronymi, Otto (1978), "Growth and Economic Order: The Long-Term Outlook," in Braillard, Philippe (Editor): *Quel nouvel ordre économique international? Essais sur les futures possibles, Annals of International Studies*, Geneva, vol. 9, pp. 51–9.

Hieronymi, Otto (1976), "The New International Economic Order: the Need for Increased Growth in the Developed Countries," in Etienne, Gilbert (Editor), *North-South Relations: An Uncertain Future, Annals of International Relations*, vol. 7, Geneva, pp. 91–101.

Hieronymi, Otto (1973), *Economic Discrimination Against the United States in Western Europe, 1945–1958. Dollar Shortage and the Rise of Regionalism*, Librarie Droz, Genève.

Hieronymi, Otto (Editor) (1980), *The New Economic Nationalism*, Macmillan, London.

Hieronymi, Otto and Catherine Currat (2004), "The Complexity and the Organizing Principles of International Order," *Foresight, Journal of Future Studies and Strategic Thinking and Policy*, vol. 6, no. 4, pp. 198–203, Emerald Group Publishing Ltd.

Hieronymi, Otto, Chiara Jasson (2004), "The Foundations of the Atlantic Community," *Foresight, Journal of Future Studies and Strategic Thinking and Policy*, vol. 6, no. 4, pp. 232–6, Emerald Group Publishing Ltd.

Hieronymi, Otto (1996), "The International Financial Institutions and the Challenge of Transition and Reconstruction in the Former Communist Countries of Central and Eastern Europe," in *Fifty Years After Bretton Woods*, Averbury, (Sixth Conference of the Robert Triffin-Sziràk Foundation, Brussels 1994), pp. 129–40.

Hieronymi, Otto and Daniela Bensky (2008), "The Outlook for the Post-War Western Model of International Order and the Prospects for Perpetual Peace," *Paper presented at 8th International CISS Millennium Conference*, Paris, June 13–15.

Hieronymi, Otto, Daniela Bensky, and Teofana Stoyanova (2008), "What Future Domestic and International Political Order for the World?", in *La Politca*, Spirali, Milano, pp. 101–148.

Horsefield, J. Keith (1969), *The International Monetary Fund 1945–1965. Twenty Years of International Monetary Cooperation*, Volume I: Chronicle, International Monetary Fund, Washington, D.C.

Huntley, James (2000), *Pax Democratica, A Strategy for the 21st Century*, Palgrave Macmillan, Basingstoke (second edition).

Hungarian Government (2006), Convergence Programme, Budapest.

IMF (2008a), *Global Financial Stability Report*, Washington DC, April.

IMF (2008b), Hungary: Request for Stand-By Arrangement—Staff Report, November 28.

International Human Dimensions Programme (IHDP), Bonn, UN (Ongoing research program since 1996 respectively since 2007).

International Corporate Governance Network/ICGN (2007a), *ICGN Securities Lending Code of Best Practice*, ICGN, London.

International Corporate Governance Network/ICGN (2007b), *ICGN Statement of Principles on Institutional Shareholder Responsibilities*, ICGN, London.

International Corporate Governance Network/ICGN (2008a), *ICGN Statement and Guidance on Non-Financial Business Reporting*, ICGN, London.

International Corporate Governance Network/ICGN (2008b), *ICGN Yearbook*, ICGN, London.

International Herald Tribune (Editorial) (2008), "Obama's Economic Advisers Need a Tough Boss," IHT, November 26.

International Monetary Fund (2006), "Article IV of the Fund's Articles of Agreement: An Overview of the Legal Framework," prepared by the Legal Department In consultation with the Policy Development and Review Department, June 28.

International Monetary Fund (2007), "Staff Report on the Multilateral Consultation on Global Imbalances with China, the Euro Area, Japan, Saudi Arabia, and the United States," prepared by a Staff Team from PDR, RES and WHD, June 29.

Joanny, Marc (1996), "L'ICGN ou l'internationale du gouvvernement d'entreprise—André Baladi, le globe-trotter de la shareholder value," *L'Agefi-MTF*, Paris, October.

Jobst (2007), "The Treatment of Operational Risk under the New Basel Framework: Critical Issues," *Journal of banking regulation*, 4, pp. 316–52.

Kanas (2005), "Pure Contagion Effects in International Banking: The Case of BCCI's Failure," *Journal of Applied Economics*, 8, pp. 101–23.

Kenen, Peter B. (1995), *Economic and Monetary Union in Europe: Moving Beyond Maastricht*, Cambridge University Press, Cambridge.

Kenen, Peter B. (Editor) (1987), *International Monetary Cooperation: Essays in Honor of Henry C. Wallich*, Essays in International Finance, no. 169, December, International Finance Section, Princeton University, Princeton, N.J.

Kesnar, Janet (2000), "The Art of Shareholder Value," *CFO Europe—The Economist*, London, February.

Kimmitt, Robert (2008), *Public Footprints in Private Markets*, Sovereign Wealth Funds and the World Economy, Foreign Affairs, January/February.

Kindleberger, Charles P. (1984), *A Financial History of Western Europe*, George Allen & Unwin, London.

Kindleberger, Charles P. and Jean-Pierre Laffargue, (Editors) (1982), *Financial Crises. Theory, History and Policy*, Cambridge University Press, Cambridge, (reprinted 2008).

Kindleberger, Charles P. and Robert Z. Aliber (2005), *Manias, Panics and Crashes. A History of Financial Crises*, Fifth Edition, Palgrave Macmillan, Basingstoke.

Krugman, Paul (1999, 2008), *The Return of Depression Economics and the Crisis of 2008*, W.W. Norton & Company, New York.

Krul, Nicolas (1995), "The Enduring Voice of Hayek," manuscript, London.

Kuhn, Thomas S. (1962, 1996), *The Structure of Scientific Revolutions*, The University of Chicago Press, Chicago, third edition.

Lamfalussy, Alexandre (1987), "Current-Account Imbalances in the Industrial World: Why They Matter," in Kenen, Peter B. (Editor), *International Monetary Cooperation: Essays in Honor of Henry C. Wallich*, Essays in International Finance, no. 169, December 1987, International Finance Section, Princeton University, Princeton, N.J., pp. 31–7.

Lamfalussy, Alexandre (2000), *Financial Markets in Emerging Markets. An Essay on Financial Globalisation and Fragility*, Yale University Press, New Haven and London.

Lawson, Nigel (1992), *The View From No. 11, Memoirs of a Tory Radical*, Bantam Press, London.

Leander, Tom (1999), "André Baladi—Portrait of a Founder of the International Corporate Governance Network/ICGN" (*Global Finance*, New York, May).

Lewis, Michael (1990), *Liar's Poker*, Penguin, New York.

Lipson, Charles and Cohen, Benjamin J. (1999), *Theory and Structure in International Political Economy. An International Organization Reader*, The MIT Press, Cambridge, Mass., May 1999.

Luci Elise, The Housing Meltdown: Why Did It Happen in the US, BIS Working Papers no 259, September, 2008.

Luttwak, Edward, "From Geopolitics to Geo-Economics,. Logics of Conflict in the Grammar of Commerce", in The National Interest, Summer, 1990.

Luttwak, Edward, The Logic The Endangered American Dream, New York: Touchstone, 1994; Turbocapitalism. Winners and Losers in the Global Economy London: Weidenfeld & Nicolson, 1998.

Luttwak, Edward (1990), "From Geopolitics to Geo-Economics. Logics of Conflict in the Grammar of Commerce," in *The National Interest*, Summer, pp. 17–24.

Luttwak, Edward N., et al. (1997), "PART 3: New World Order Geopolitics," chapter 16, *From Geopolitics to Geo-Economics: Logic of Conflict, Grammar of Commerce*, Routledge, London, pp. 125–30.

Luttwak, Edward (1994), The Endangered American Dream, Touchstone, New York.

Luttwak, Edward (1998), *Turbocapitalism. Winners and Losers in the Global Economy*, Weidenfeld & Nicolson, London.

Mahbubani, Kishore (2008), *The New Asian Hemisphere, The Irressistable Shift of Global Power to the East*, Public Affairs, New York.

Mccown, Ashby, Patricia Pollard, and John Weeks, (2007), *Equilibrium Exchange Rate Models and Misalignments*, Occasional Paper no.7, US Department of the Treasury, Office of International Affairs, Washington, D.C.

McDonald (1952), "The Analysis of Equilibrium in Malaria," *Tropical Diseases Bulletin*, 49, pp. 813–29.

Meadows, D. (1972), *The Limits to Growth*, Universe Books, New York.

Minsky, Hyman P. (1986, 2008), *Stabilizing an Unstable Economy*, McGraw Hill, New York.

Minsky, Hyman P. (2008), *John Maynard Keynes*, McGraw Hill, New York, (first edition 1975).

Minsky, Hyman P. (1982), *Can "It" Happen Again? Essays On Instability and Finance*, M. E. Sharpe Inc., Armonk, N.Y.

Mishkin, F. S. (2008a), *The Economics of Money, Banking and Financial Markets*, McGraw-Hill, international edition, eighth edition, Ch.16, p. 420.

Mishkin, F. S. (2008b), *The Economics of Money, Banking and Financial Markets*, McGraw-Hill, New York, international edition, eighth edition, Ch.16, p. 420.

Mitchener (2005), "Bank Supervision, Regulation and Instability During the Great Depression," *The Journal of Economic History*, 65, pp. 152–85.

Mol, A. P. J. (2001), *Globalization and Environmental Reform, The Ecological Modernization of the Global Economy*, M.I.T. Press, Cambridge, Mass.

Monetary Control, A Consultation Paper by HM Treasury and the Bank of England (March 1980), Her Majesty's Stationery Office, London, 1978, Cmnd 7858.

Monks, Robert A.G. and Minow, Nell (1991), *Power and Accountability*, Harper Collins, New York.

Monks, Robert A.G. (2008), *Corpocracy*, Wiley & Sons, Hoboken, NJ.

Mundell, Robert A. (1997), "Optimum Currency Areas," extended version of a luncheon speech presented at a *Conference on Optimum Currency Areas*, Tel-Aviv University, December 5.

Mundell, Robert (1993), "Panel Session II: Implications for International Monetary Reform," in Bordo. D. Michael and Barry Eichengreen (Editors), *A Retrospective on the Bretton Woods System. Lessons for International Monetary Reform*, A National Bureau of Economic Research Project Report, University of Chicago Press, pp. 604–12.

Mundell, Robert (1980), "Monetary Nationalism and Floating Exchange Rates," in Hieronymi, Otto (Editor), *The New Economic Nationalism*, Macmillan, London, pp. 34–50.

Mundell, Robert A. and Jacques J. Polak, (Editors) (1977), *The New International Monetary System*, Columbia University Press, New York.

Münchau, Wolfgang (2009), "Eastern Crisis that Could Wreck the Eurozone," *Financial Times*, February 22.

Nicholls, A. J. (1994), *Freedom with Responsibility. The Social Market Economy in Germany, 1918–1963*, Clarendon Press, Oxford.

Nier et al. (2008), "Network Models and Financial Stability," working paper no. 346, *Quarterly Bulletin* Q2. pp. 184–93.

Novotni, Ewald (2009), "Real Implications of the Financial Turmoil—Strategies for Growth and Stability," BIS review no. 19.

Observatoire de la Finance (2008), "For Finance That Serves the Common Good: Manifesto of Observatoire de la Finance," Geneva.

Odell, John S. (1982), *U.S. International Monetary Policy: Markets, Power and Ideas as Sources of Change*, Princeton University Press, Princeton.

OECD (1996), *International Capital Market Statistics, 1950–1995*, OECD, Paris.

OECD (2001), *Environmentally Related Taxes in OECD Countries, Issues and Strategies*, OECD, Paris.

OECD (2006), International Energy Agency, World Energy Outlook, report.

Office of the Comptroller of the Currency (2008), *Quarterly Report on Bank Trading and Derivative Activities*, Third Quarter 2008, OCC, Washington, DC.

Padoa-Schioppa, Tommaso (2000), *The Road to Monetary Union in Europe*, Oxford University Press, Oxford.

Padoa-Schioppa, Tommaso (2004), *The Euro and its Central Bank*, The MIT Press, Cambrdige, Mass.

Padoa-Schioppa, Tommaso (2009), *La Veduta Corta. Conversazione con Beda Romano sul Grande Crollo della Finanza*, Il Mulion, Bologna.

Panitchpakde, Supachai (2008), "Towards a World Financial Organisation," World Economy & Development In Brief, Luxembourg, November 24.

Papadimitriou, Dimitri B., and L. Randall Wray (2008), "Minsky's *Stabilizing An Unstable Economy* Two Decades Later," in Minsky, Hyman P., *Stabilizing An Unstable Economy*, McGraw Hill, New York.

Paulson, Jr., Henry (2008), "Remarks by Secretary Henry M. Paulson, Jr. at The Ronald Reagan Presidential Library," November 20, U.S. Treasury, HP-1285.

Pearl, J. (1985), "Bayesian Networks: A Model of Self-Activated Memory for Evidential Reasoning," Proceedings of the 7th Conference of the Cognitive Science Society, University of California, Irvine, CA, pp. 329–34.

Plickert, Philip (2008), *Wandlungen des Neoliberalismus. Eine Studie zu Entwicklung und Ausstrahlung der "Mont Pélerin" Society*, Marktwirtschaftliche Reformpolitik, Schriftenreihe der Aktiengemeinschaft Soziale Marktwirtschaft, Lucius & Lucius, Stuttgart.

Posner, Michael (Editor) (1986), *Problems of International Money 1972–1985*, Overseas Development Institute, London and International Monetary Fund, Washington, D.C.

Price, Margaret (1989), "Activism on the Rise Overseas," *Pensions & Investments*, Chicago, October 30.

Pulido, Antonio and Emilio Fontela (2004), *Principios des Desarrollo Economico Sostenible*, Fundacion Iberdrola, Alcantara and Madrid.

Putin, Vladimir (2006), "Mineral Natural Resources in the Strategy for Development of the Russian Economy," *Problems of Post-Communism*, vol. 53, no. 1, January/February, pp. 48–54.

Resener, Madeleine (1993), "Shareholders in Europe Unite," *Institutional Investor*, New York, November.

Resico, Marcelo F. (2008), *La Estructura de una Economia Humana, Reflexiones en Cuanto a la Actualidad del Pensamiento de W. Röpke*, EDUCA, Buenos Aires.

Rey, Philippe (1999), "L'ICGN publie la bible du corporate governance," *L'Agefi*, Lausannc, August 3.

Richard M. Weaver (1948), *Ideas Have Consequences*, The University of Chicago Press, Chicago.

Rigby, Bill (2008), "U.S. (Fed) Launches Support Plan as Contraction Takes Hold," *Reuters*, November 25.

Ritter, Gerhard A. (2006), *Der Preis der Deutschen Einheit. Die Wiedervereinigung und die Krise des Sozialstaates*, Verlag C.H. Beck, München.

Rodrik, Doni (1999), "Governing the Global Economy: Does one Architectural Style Fit All?" in *The Brookings Institution Trade Policy Forum, Conference on Governing the Global Economy*, Harvard University, April.

Röpke, Wilhelm (1942), *International Economic Disintegration*, William Hodge, London.

Röpke, Wilhelm (1948), *Civitas Humana. A Humane Order of Society*, William Hodge, London.

Röpke, Wilhelm (1950), *The Social Crisis of Our Time*, William Hodge, London (first German edition, 1942).

Röpke, Wilhelm (1959), *Gegen die Brandung*, Eugen Rentsch Verlag, Zürich.

Roth, Jean-Pierre (2008), "Wir Schweizer sind ein Volk von Uhrenmachern," Interview, *Neue Zürcher Zeitung*, Zürich, 1–2 November.

Ruozi, Roberto (2008), *Viaggio nel mercato finanziario con Dr Jekyll e Mr Hyde*, Spriali, Milano.

Saeki, Yuzo (2008), "Japan Warns of Long Slump," Reuters, November 18.

Sakbani, Michael (2006), "A Re-examination of the Architecture of the International Economic System in a Global Setting: Issues and Proposals," UNCTAD, Discussion Paper, no. 181, Geneva, pp. 5–7.

Sakbani, Michael, (1985), "International Monetary Reform: Issues and Proposals," UNCTAD, *Trade and Development*, no.6, Geneva, pp. 172–94.

Sakbani, Michael (2005) "The Global Economic System: Asymmetries and Inconsistencies", *Foresight, Journal of Future Studies and Strategic Thinking and Policy*, vol. 7, no. 1, pp. 11–25, Emerald Group Publishing Ltd, Bradford.

Sakbani, Michael (2006), *The International Economic System under Globalization: System Problems and Reform Proposals in the Monetary System*, International Development Economic Associates Studies (IDEAs), www.networkideas.org, January, part ii, Governance of International Flows, Geneva.

Sen, A. (1980), "Equality of What?" Tanner Lectures on Human Values, Cambridge University Press, Cambridge, UK.

Senarclens, Pierre de and Kazancigil, Ali (2007), *Regulating Globalization—Critical Approaches to Global Governance*, United Nations University Press, Tokyo, New York, Paris.

Sharma, Shalendra D. (2003), *The Asian Financial Crisis. Crisis, Reform and Recovery*, Manchester University Press, Manchester.

Skidelsky, Robert (2000), *John Maynard Keynes, Volume 3: Fighting for Britain, 1937–1946*, Macmillan, London.

Slaughter, Anne-Marie (2004), *A New World Order*, Princeton University Press, Princeton and Oxford.

Solomon, Robert (1982), *The International Monetary System 1945–1981*, Harper and Row, New York.

Soros, George (1997), "Avoiding a Breakdown," Financial Times, London, 31 December.

Soros, George (1998), *The Crisis of Global Capitalism: Open Society Endangered*, The Public Affairs Press, New York.

Soros, George (2003), *The Alchemy of Finance*, John Wiley and Sons, New York.

Soros, George (2008), *The New Paradigm for Financial Markets. The Credit Crisis of 2008 and What it Means*, Public Affairs, Perseus Group, New York.

Sovereign Wealth Fund Institute, (January 2009), http://www.swfinstitute.org

Sovereign wealth funds and financial stability – guide, European Commission, Brussels, 27 February 2008.

Statement of Ben Bernanke before the New York Bank Association, NY. October 14, 2008.

Stern, N. H. (2007), *The Economics of Climate Change: The Stern Review*, Cambridge University Press, Cambridge, UK.

Stewart III, Bennett (1991), *The Quest for Value*, Harper Collins, New York.

Stiglitz, Joseph (2002), *Globalization and its Discontents*, Penguin Books, London.

Stiglitz, Joseph E. and Bruce Greenwald (2003), *Towards A New Paradigm in Monetary Economics*, Cambridge University Press, Cambridge.

Stiglitz, J. E. (2004), "The Way Ahead", in *Essential Reading in World Politics*, 2nd Edition, Norton, New York.

Studer, Margaret (1990), "Nestlé Faces Legal Battle Over Shareholders' Rights," *The Wall Street Journal*, New York, November 22.

Studer, Margaret (1995), "Shareholders Must Work to Maximize Investments in European Companies," *The Wall Street Journal*, New York, August 21.

Summers, Lawrence (2000), "International Financial Crisis, Causes, Prevention and Cures," *Papers and Proceedings*, American Economic Association, New Orleans, May.

Szabó-Pelsőczy, Miklós (Editor) (1990), *The Future of the Global Economic and Monetary Systems*, (2nd Sziràk Conference, 1988), Budapest, Institute for World Economics of the Hungarian Academy of Sciences.

Szabó-Pelsőczy, Miklós (Editor) (1993), *The Future of the Global Economic and Monetary System With Particular Emphasis on Eastern European Developments* (*Foreword* by Otto Hieronymi) Robert Triffin-Szirak Foundation, Budapest.

Szabó-Pelsőczy, Miklós (Editor) (1995), *The Global Monetary System After the Fall of the Soviet Empire*, (In Memoriam Robert Triffin – 1911–1993, Sixth Conference of the Robert Triffin-Sziràk Foundation, Sziràk, 1993), Averbury, Aldershot.

Szabó-Pelsőczy, Miklós (Editor) (1996), *Fifty Years After Bretton Woods*, (Sixth Conference of the Robert Triffin-Sziràk Foundation, Brussels 1994), Averbury, Aldershot.

Szabó-Pelsőczy, Miklós and Gusztáv Báger (Editors) (1998), *Global Monetary and Economic Convergence. On the Occasion of the Fiftieth Anniversary of the Marshall Plan*, Ashgate, Aldershot.

Taleb, Nassim Nicholas (2007), *The Black Swan—The Impact of the Highly Improbable*, Random House, New York.

Tarullo, Daniel K. (2008), *Banking on Basel. The Future of International Financial Regulation*, Peterson Institute for International Economics, Washington, D.C., August.

The Group of Lisbon (1995), *Limits to Competition*, The MIT Press, Cambridge.

Thomas Jr., W. L. et al. (1956), *Man's Role In Changing the Face of the Earth*, Chicago University Press, Chicago.

Treaster, Joseph B. (2004), *Paul Volcker. The Making of a Financial Legend*, John Wiles & Sons, Inc., New York.

Triffin, Robert (1957), *Europe and the Money Muddle, From Bilateralism to Near Convertibility, 1947–1956*, Yale University Press, New Haven.

Triffin, Robert (1961), *Gold and the Dollar Crisis*, Revised Edition, Yale University Press, New Haven, Conn.

Trigueiros and Taffler (1996), "Neural Networks and Empirical Research in Accounting," *Accounting and Business Research*, 26, pp. 347–356.

Truman, Edwin (2008), *A Blueprint for Sovereign Fund Best Practices*, Peterson Institute for International Economics, Washington, April, p. 3.

Tumpel-Gugerell, Gertrude (2009), "The Financial Crisis —Looking Back and the Way Forward," BIS Review, January 22.

UNCTAD (2008), *World Investment Report, Transnational Corporations and the Infrastructure Challenge*, United Nations, New York and Geneva.

Unger, Roberto Mangabeira (2007), *Free Trade Reimagined. The World Division of Labor and the Method of Economics*, Princeton University Press, Princeton.

Ungerer, Horst (1995), "Political Aspects of European Monetary Integration After World War II," Paper Presented at ECSA Conference, Charleston, S.C. May 13.

Ungerer, Horst (1997), *A Concise History of European Monetary Integration: From EPU to EMU*, Quorum Books, Westport, Connecticut.

United Nations (2004), *Disclosure of the Impact of Corporations on Society*, UNCTAD/ITE/TEB/2003/7, Geneva.

United Nations (2006), *Guidance on Good Practices in Corporate Governance Disclosure*, UNCTAD/ITE/TEB/2006/3, New York and Geneva.

United Nations (2008a), *Guidance on Corporate Responsibility Indicators in Annual Reports*, UNCTAD/ITE/TEB/2007/6, New York and Geneva.

United Nations (2008b), *Terms of Reference of the Commission of Experts of the President of the UN General Assembly on Reforms of the International Monetary and Financial System* ("Stiglitz Commission").

United Nations (2009), *Promoting Transparency in Corporate Reporting: A Quarter Century of UNISAR*, UNCTAD/DIAE/ED/2009, New York and Geneva.

United Nations Environment Programme (UNEP) (1972), Summary Report of the International Conference on Human Development in Stockholm, UNEP, Nairobi.

United Nations Environment Programme (UNEP) (2008), *Sustainable Reporting Guidelines and Financial Services Sector Supplement*, GRI, Amsterdam.

United Nations General Assembly, Commission of Experts on Reforms of the International Monetary and Financial System (2009) Recommendations, United Nations, New York, 19 March.

US Economic Statistics Administration (2008), *Economic Indicators*, 2 October.

Van Houtyen, Leo (2002), "Governance of the IMF; Decision Making, Institutional Oversight, Transparency, and Accountability" IMF Pamphlet Series No. 53.

Volcker, Paul (1997), "Global Markets and the Emerging Economies," Lecture in honor of Fritz Leutwiler at The University of Zurich, December 15.

Volcker, Paul (1999), "The Implication of Globalism is Globalism," The Joseph I. Lubin Memorial, Stern School of Business, New York, New York, April 20.

Volcker, Paul (2000), "Globalization and the International Financial System," A speech at a dinner honoring the 72nd birthday of His Majesty King Bhumibol Adulyadej, Bangkok, Thailand, January 27.

Volcker, Paul (2001), "Globalization and the World of Finance," The 2001 Hutchinson Lecture, University of Delaware, April 30.

Volcker, Paul and Toyoo Gyothen (1992), *Changing Fortunes: The World's Money and the Threat to American Leadership*, Times Books, New York.

Wagstyl, Stefan (2009), "Banks Ask for Crisis Funds for Eastern Europe," *The Economist*, January 21.

WCED (United Nations World Commission on Environment and Development) (1987), *Our Common Future* (Brundtland Report), UN, New York.

Weber & Menoud (2007), "Systemic Risk as a Topic of Financial Conglomerates' Financial Supervision," *Banking and Financial Law Review*, 22, pp. 377–403.

Wellink, Nout (2008), "The Importance of Banking Supervision in Financial Stability," Keynote Address by the President of the Netherlands Bank and Chairman of the Basel Committee on Banking Supervision, at the High Level Meeting "The Role of Banking and Banking Supervision in Financial Stability," Beijing, 17 November, BIS, Basel.

Wiener, Jarrod (1999), *Globalization and the Harmonization of Law*, Pinter, London and New York.

Wikipedia (2008), "The United States Housing Bubble," http://en.wikipedia.org/wiki/United_States_housing_bubble, September.

Williamson, John, (1979), *Failure of International Monetary Reform*, Nelson, Sunbury-on-Thames.

Winters, Alan (2004), "Trade Liberalisation and Economic Performance: An Overview," *The Economic Journal*, Volume 114, Issue 493, London, pp. F4–F21.

Wolf, Martin (2004), *Why Globalization Works. The Case for the Global Market Economy*, Yale University Press, New Haven and London.

Wolf, Martin (2008), *Fixing Global Finance*, The Johns Hopkins University Press, Baltimore.

World Bank (2006), *Global Development Finance. The Development Potential of Surging Capital Flows*, World Bank, Washington, D.C.

World Bank, *Poverty and the WTO: Impacts of the Doha Development Agenda*, 2006 Washington, D.C.

World Trade Organization, *The Integrated Framework explained*, Geneva.

World Trade Organization (2001), *The Policy Relevance of Mainstreaming Trade into Country Development Strategies: Perspectives of Least Developed Countries*, Geneva, April.

World Trade Organization (2004), *Understanding the WTO*, May, Geneva.

World Trade Organization (2008), Information viewed at: http://www.wto.org/, December 22.

Zaki, Myret (2001), "Le blocage des voix nuit à l'image de la Suisse," *Le Temps*, Geneva, November 22.

Zhou Xiaochuan (2009), "Reform the International Monetary System," People's Bank of China, 23 March. http://www.pbc.gov.cn/english/detail.asp?col=6500&id=178

Index